PIONEERING IN SOUTH BRAZIL.

"É SALTO! É SALTO!"—SCENE ON THE TIBAGY.

PIONEERING

IN

SOUTH BRAZIL.

THREE YEARS OF FOREST AND PRAIRIE LIFE
IN THE PROVINCE OF PARANÁ.

By THOMAS P. BIGG-WITHER,

ASSOC. INST. C.E. ; F.R.G.S.

IN TWO VOLUMES.—VOL. II.

WITH MAP AND ILLUSTRATIONS.

GREENWOOD PRESS, PUBLISHERS
NEW YORK

Originally published in 1878 by John Murray, Albermarle Street
London

First Greenwood Reprinting, 1968

Library of Congress Catalog Card Number: 68-55177

CONTENTS.

PART II.

(Continued.)

PART III.

CHAPTER I.

CHAPTER II.

CHAPTER III.

CHAPTER IV.

PART IV.

CHAPTER I.

CHAPTER II.

CHAPTER III.

CHAPTER IV.

CHAPTER V.

CHAPTER VI.

CHAPTER VII.

CHAPTER VIII.

CHAPTER IX.

APPENDIX.

Note A.

Note B.

Note C.

Note D.

LIST OF ILLUSTRATIONS.

PIONEERING IN SOUTH BRAZIL.

PART II.

(Continued.)

———◆———

CHAPTER IX.

End of the summer.—Flora and Fauna.—Ferns.—Brazilian botanical
knowledge.—The 9th of March.—Sad news.—Curling goes to
Curitiba.—My first tapir.—Remarks on tapirs and other animals.
—A moonlight journey.

THE insect world had had its day : the summer was
nearly past. Mosquitoes, *Botucas, Polvoras,* and all
the other abominations of a hot season in a tropical
forest were bidding a last farewell to their long-suffer-
ing and much-enduring victims.

An observant eye could discern here and there,
amidst the yet luxuriant green of the forest, a tinge of
yellow or brown betokening a summer departing. The
shrill whistle of the *cigarra* or *cicada* was no longer
heard either in camp or forest by day; and at night
the wail of the summer goat sucker, the booming flight
of the great fire beetle, the irritating buzz of the
hungry mosquito, and the many other mysterious bird

and insect sounds had given place to a deep unbroken
silence.

The great forces of nature which year by year, in
these Brazilian forests, exert themselves in thunder,
lightning, and ceaseless rain, through the months of
December, January, and February, were now once
more spent or tired out. The grand scouring process
which had been, almost continuously, going on during
these same months amongst the great hills and mountains around, carving out new features or deepening the
impression of old ones, had also for the time ceased
to operate. The Ivahy, though still flooded and turbid
from the result of these operations, was yet falling inch
by inch towards its normal winter level.

On this day—the 8th of March—for the first time
for a long series of weeks, no venomous snake had
crossed our path in the forest.

Delightful it was now in our little palm-built camps
by the river side, in the cool evenings, after the day's
work was over.

Freed from the stern necessity of unceasingly
battling with one's insect foes, I had taken up again,
with some enjoyment and pleasure to myself, the
study and work of collecting *flora* and *fauna.**

* In the forests of this part of Brazil, the great difficulty is in preserving the specimens of *fauna*, in our case rendered still greater by
the necessity we laboured under of dragging them about with us by
land and water for a great length of time. Special precautions had to
be taken. For all the smaller skins, such as those of birds, snakes,
&c., alum was a sufficient preservative if applied liberally at the time
of skinning. The larger skins of deer, ocelot, puma, jaguar, &c., we

The magnificence of the flora of a Brazilian tropical forest has been described over and over again in works both of fiction and travel.   But all description that I have ever read is poor compared to the reality, and I am not going to attempt to give another.   One family alone I will say a few words about, because the various species of it generally enter largely into the backwoodsman's medicine craft.   These are the ferns, which from the gigantic individual which, rivalling in height the tall palm-trees by its side, spreads out its fronds like great branches, under whose shade a dozen men may recline, down to the lowly *adiantum* which we daily trod under foot, form, with their countless diverse brethren, almost a forest in themselves.

The most remarkable, as well as perhaps the most beautiful of all the multiform varieties of this great family, was a certain climbing fern whose name I have not been able to obtain, but of which the subjoined woodcut, taken from a dried specimen of a single frond, will give some idea.

This fern generally chooses as its support some young tree or sapling with a rough bark, round which it climbs to a height, sometimes, of seven or eight feet. The long dropping fronds hanging round the trunk make a very pretty effect, and the whole might serve as a rare model for designers in the precious metals.

were obliged to submit to a process of tanning—a decoction of the bark of a kind of laburnum-tree called *Anjica* being employed for the purpose. Butterflies and insects generally were merely dried in the sun. It was also necessary to submit one's entire collection to a monthly drying operation of four or five hours in the hottest sun.

PORTION OF FROND OF CLIMB-
ING FERN. ⅔ NATURAL SIZE.

The Brazilians of these remoter regions, who, like all
semi-savage people, have little
or no appreciation for the
beautiful, employ the root of
this fern as a *remedio* for a
particular disease. This root
has an extraordinary effect
upon the secretion glands,
and if a piece of it is chewed
in the mouth for a few seconds,
the person so doing will be
forced to expectorate continuously for the next hour or more
afterwards. The Brazilians,
as well as the Indians, make
use of the mashed leaves of
other species of ferns as poul-
tices for application to wounds.

I have now to record an
event, (the news of which
reached us first on the 9th day
of March) which not only inflicted the expedition, upon
which we had long been labouring, with a loss, the greatest it could have sustained,
but at the same time filled each
individual member of it with
the most lively sorrow.

Our chief, Captain Palm, had died in Rio de Janeiro of that terrible scourge, Yellow Fever, on the 4th of February.

The details of events since he had left us on the 8th of September, full of life and spirit, were very simple as well as very sad. He had followed his intention of first returning to where the first Staff were working, and paying them a flying visit in their camp. After this he had gone round to Miranda, viâ Antonina, Monte Video and the River Plate. From this point, having made all final arrangements with the 3rd and 4th Staffs, and started them on their respective sections, he had returned to Rio, arriving there about the end of January. Almost immediately, he was attacked by yellow fever, which we now learnt had been raging in that pestilential city during the past summer with terrific severity, and after a brief illness, died.* This, briefly told, was the whole sad story.

Misfortunes never come singly. The same messenger who brought us the intelligence of the death of our chief, was the bearer of a summons to Curling to repair at once to Curitiba, there to consult with an agent from Rio.

Weakened as our staff already was, by the desertion

---

* It is no mere form of speech to say that Captain Palm was beloved by us all. In addition to being a man of wonderful energy and capabilities (without which, indeed, he would never have succeeded singlehanded as he did in thus planning and bringing to maturity this great scheme of a trans-Brazilian railway), he was also an open, generoushearted friend and delightful companion to all who knew him.

of one of its members, and from the almost constant illness of another, the loss of yet a third, even though but for a few weeks, would almost amount to a disaster.

Curling went, though not without first carefully weighing the *pros* and *cons*. On the 9th we heard of Captain Palm's death. That night Curling and I sat up for many hours over our camp fire deliberating and making arrangements. By ten o'clock the following morning he was on his way to Curitiba, and I found myself left alone with one sick companion to carry on the expedition.*

About a week after Curling's departure, an event that I had longed for for weeks and months past happened—I bagged my first tapir !

On the particular morning when this momentous event occurred I had occasion to go some distance down the river to fix the site for, and build a new camp, and had taken with me Miguel and Hypolito, whom I had lately installed as my canoe-men in chief. Besides my own canoe, which was generally known as the "Piroba hunting canoe," another large dug-out accompanied us, with seven men whom I had detached from *picada*-work for the occasion.

Not, however, intending to hunt, I had taken nothing with me but a little pea-rifle belonging to Curling and but six cartridges. One of the hunting dogs, by name Sybadelle, was in my canoe, having slipped in unperceived when we started. These dogs of ours were always immensely keen after sport. The

---

* See Appendix, note D.

sight of a gun, and the well-known sound of the word
"*embarca*" would usually cause a regular *stampedo* of
them down to the canoes, into which they would jump
helter-skelter, whinnying with excitement. The breed,
or rather breeds, must, I think, be peculiar to the
country; certainly I have never seen similar dogs at
home or in any part of the world, but Brazil.

Having chosen a suitable spot for the camp, we dis-
embarked, and the axes were soon at work clearing the
ground, when, all of a sudden, the sharp, clear yap yap
of the dog was heard about a quarter of a mile off upon
the slope of a *Serra*. I speedily got into my canoe
again with Miguel and Hypolito, and we paddled
across to the other side of the river which was, at this
point, about 120 yards wide, and very deep, and
waited. The sound of the dog hunting grew fainter
and fainter, till at last it became inaudible.

Ten minutes we waited in perfect silence, then, in
the far distance, up the wooded side of the *Serra* the
faint sound of the dog in full cry became again audible.
Louder and louder it grew, till at last it seemed close
to the opposite bank. Every second I expected to
see the splash of the hunted animal as it dropped into
the water. The two men were standing up, one at the
bow, the other at the stern, paddle in hand, ready to
put their whole strength into the race, the moment
the game should drop into the river. Presently,
splash! went a big animal into the water, close under
the bank, nearly opposite to us. The men needed no
telling what to do. In another moment the foam was

flying from our bows as we rushed through the water towards the opposite bank. Another splash, and Sybadelle was in the water too, turning his head rapidly from side to side, looking for the game which was nowhere to be seen. We had got about half way across, when a cry of : " There he is !" from one of the men, and a sudden change in the direction of the canoe caused me to look up stream. There, about sixty yards distant, was a huge head appearing above the water. At the same moment, the dog too caught sight of it, and immediately recommenced his " yap ! yap ! "

The tapir, for tapir it was, thought only of the dog, and did not, at first, take any notice of us, so while the men were frantically paddling towards it, I had a good look at the brute. He looked very savage, with his bristly mane erect, and his elongated proboscis thrown well up in the air, snorting with rage and terror.

We were within thirty yards of him, and I was just going to pull the trigger, when he dived. The dog stopped crying, and the men stopped paddling, and all was again still and calm. For half a minute or more we waited, one man looking up stream, the other down. "There, there!" and off we went again, stern foremost down stream, where the huge ungainly head was once more appearing. The eager cry of the dog began again, and all was once more excitement. "Agora, Agora ! " (now, now !) and as the tapir gave his head a half turn round to look at us, a bullet out of the little pea-rifle went in near his ear and passed out again at his lower jaw. He shook his head savagely, and plunged madly down as though he would burrow through the earth, leaving a red stain upon the water above.

Again we waited, and I rapidly slipped a fresh cartridge into the little rifle. Very soon the tapir rose, appearing to be badly wounded ; the canoe was so unsteady that the next bullet missed, striking the water, beyond the animal, and ricochetting off far away down stream. The report made the tapir dive again.

Another short lull—then, up again. This time the bullet struck too low, going in at the cheek. I began to fear that we should lose him after all, as I had only three more cartridges left. Another dive, and another bullet—and then he came up within fifteen yards of the' canoe, evidently much exhausted. His broad open ear offered a tempting mark at this short distance—another scarcely audible crack from the little pea-rifle, and the huge animal slowly sank dead beneath the waters of the Ivahy.

Thus ended my first tapir hunt. The excitement, while it lasted, was intense, but the feeling of satisfaction at the successful result, was marred by our not being able at once to " bag " the game. We tried with long *varajões* to find him, but the river, in the part where he had sunk, was too deep for the poles to find the bottom at all ; so there was nothing for it but to wait patiently till the body should rise to the surface, which, in the case of a tapir, generally takes place about two and a half hours after death.

Herbivorous animals, such as tapir, deer, and pig,

we found to "buoy" in from two to four hours, much depending upon the temperature of the water, and upon the length of time the animal had been hunted. I have known a well-hunted tapir "buoy" in an hour and a quarter, but that is an exceptional case.

Carnivorous animals, such as jaguar, puma, and otter, on the contrary, do not "buoy" sometimes for days. Many have been the otter skins that I have lost, on account of these animals not "buoying" till after putrefaction has set in. Of the numerous otters that I have from time to time killed in the river, not one could I ever recover. Though the river swarms with these animals, and no day passed without several being seen by us, yet a good otter skin could not be got at the colony under 5$000 (11*s*.); whereas, a tapir's skin would not fetch more than 2$000 (4*s*. 6*d*.), and yet this animal itself is much more rarely seen, and the skin considerably more useful. Indeed, the leather made from tapir hide is far more durable than the common bullock leathers of the country; a pair of boots, for example, made of tapir leather is almost everlasting. The reason for this superiority appears to be that a tapir's hide, besides being much thicker, is of a more oily nature than a bullock's, and this oily matter is not entirely extracted by the tanning process; consequently, the leather is but little affected by water, and rots but with difficulty.

Two long hours we waited for the tapir to "buoy," and then the big round carcase suddenly appeared, floating upon the water; nobody seeing it rise, though several pairs of eyes had been looking at the very spot for the last quarter of an hour.

It is a curious fact that I have only known one man who professed to have seen a tapir in the act of "buoying;" and this was our hunter Hypolito. He says that they rise with such an impetus as to be carried more than half out of the water at the first appearance, and only find their position of equilibrium after several rebounds. This, if correct, makes it all the more curious that the act should be so seldom observed.

Our tapir was soon towed to the bank, and the united efforts of some half dozen men could scarcely pull the body sufficiently out of the water to enable the beak of the canoe to be got underneath it. The weight of these animals is enormous in proportion to their height. The biggest tapir stands but little over three feet high, and such a tapir would weigh nearly 800 pounds. It is marvellous how such animals can successfully keep ahead of the dogs when hunted. That they do so is proved by the fact that the longer the hunt before the animal takes to the water, the greater is the distance which it puts between itself and its pursuers. This is no doubt partly due to its far greater power in proportion to its size, of forcing a way through the tangled forest growth.

Anyone who has ever seen a tapir, cannot but be struck, first by the peculiar wedge-like shape of its head and neck, and secondly by the enormous development of muscle in the neck, shoulders, and limbs

generally—the two together fitting it most admirably
for the life it leads in these mountainous, tropical-
forest lands.

One of the uses to which it occasionally has to
apply its great strength, is to tear its way through
the thickest jungle at full speed with a jaguar upon
its back, in order to scrape its powerful enemy off,
before this latter has time to inflict any deadly wound.

The hunt somewhat delayed my plans on this day,
and it was late before I was able to start away for
the big camp, where it was necessary that I should
be on this evening, and which was distant full five
miles up the river. Even the vigorous arms of my
two canoe-men, Miguel and Hypolito, could not make
us cover more than three miles before it became quite
dark. As there were two rather difficult corredeiras
yet to be overcome, we were obliged to halt at the
foot of the first till the moon had risen, when we again
started on.

Accustomed as I was by this time to rapids, the
scene in them never grew stale; and now as we
struggled up each little cascade and fall with the
spray sparkling about our bows and upon the long
varajões of the men, under the moonlight, the scene
was simply enchanting, and one not easily to be forgotten.

We arrived at the big camp about 9 P.M., letting
off, on our approach, a volley from the pistols of the
men, according to the invariable and time-honoured
custom amongst the Brazilians when returning from

any successful expedition, or after a longer absence than usual.

We had brought the tapir up with us, as I intended to have it skinned. It was too late, however, to get it up out of the canoe this night, so we fastened one of its legs securely to the stern rope of the canoe, and then tipped the carcase overboard into the river, where it would be safe from the dogs till morning.

CHAPTER X.

Another tapir hunt.—A successful ruse.—Guns and rifles.—A noble river.—The Brazilian *Pato*.—The *Corvo d'Agua*.—Wild life.—A hunting ground.—Tapir again.—The trail of a jaguar.—A big gridiron.

A FEW days after the tapir hunt related in the last chapter, I chanced to come in for another, equally unexpectedly.

I was travelling up the river from one party of *picada*-cutters to another with my usual attendants, Miguel and Hypolito, when the sharp eye of the former discerned a black spot upon the water nearly half a mile away up the river, which he at once recognised as the head of a tapir.

Again I was armed only with the little pea-rifle, though fortunately on this occasion I had got a pouch full of cartridges.

Seeing that the animal was rapidly coming down stream towards us, we drew close in under the bank, and waited motionless and silent, half concealed by some thick overhanging branches that came down almost to the water's edge.

The tapir kept well out in the middle of the river, as though suspicious of lurking danger.

In a few minutes from the time when it was discovered, it had arrived abreast of our place of concealment, though at a distance from it of about one hundred
yards. It was swimming at a very rapid rate, being
aided by a powerful current.

In a few seconds more it would have passed beyond the
range of the little pea-rifle, when suddenly a tiny "crack"
from the neighbourhood of our concealed canoe told it
that its enemies were upon it. The little bullet struck
the long flexible proboscis, piercing it like a piece of
cardboard, and ricochetted away into the opposite bank.

The tapir reared its great bulk half out of the water
with rage and surprise at receiving such a salute, and,
waiting only to see us dart out of our hiding-place
under the bank, and to hear the shout with which
we opened the chase, immediately dived. Now once
more began the exciting game of hide-and-seek, where,
on the one side, the prize is a fresh rump-steak for
dinner, and on the other, dear life itself.

Four times already since the chase had commenced
had the tapir appeared upon the surface of the water,
and as many times had the little rifle sent it down
again in dire astonishment and fear. Miguel and
Hypolito were panting and blowing with the tremendous spurts which they had been making, and still the
hunted animal showed no diminution of strength or of
power to remain under water. Its dives were so long
that it never rose within 200 yards of the spot at which
it had last disappeared; and it dodged about under
water, so that we could never guess whether it would

reappear up stream or down. For the fifth time we were waiting with paddles in the water in eager impatience for the reappearance of the animal, hoping that the next bullet might end the chase, when, to my disgust, it suddenly rose close in under the bank, beyond the effective range of the pea-rifle. Before we could make more than half a dozen strokes with the paddles it was already leaving the water and climbing up the steep bank to the forest. Our rump-steak was vanishing hopelessly, and in another second the hunt would have terminated in favour of the *Anta*, and he would have disappeared into the forest to die of his wounds in solitude, or to fall an easy prey to the prowling jaguar, when all at once Miguel from the bow of the boat began to bark like a dog. The effect was like magic. The tapir wheeled sharply round, turning his tail to the forest, and came rushing back into the river as though a veritable pack of hounds was at his heels, and, diving beneath the water, did not show his head again till he was once more out in the middle of the river. Brought back once again to within our reach, the hunt recommenced, and for another quarter of an hour continued in the same mode as before. It was not until I had fired nine times, and put no less than five bullets into different parts of the animal's head, that he at last succumbed. The whole chase must have lasted fully half an hour, and it terminated more than a mile below the point at which it had originally commenced.

It is very difficult, during the excitement of a tapir hunt, such as that I have just described, to estimate time with even tolerable accuracy, and therefore it was only after I had killed so many tapirs that the excitement of the hunts had begun to pall upon me, that I was really able to decide how long a time it was that the animal usually remained under water during its dives. I came to the conclusion that this time, which often used to seem immensely long, never in any instance exceeded two minutes, and more generally the limit was but little over one minute. The nostrils of a tapir, through which, like the horse, it alone takes breath, are capable of being closed at pleasure; thus, when the animal is about to dive it always first closes the nostrils and curves the flexible proboscis downwards beneath the under lip. Before firing at a tapir in the river at a long distance, I used to wait till I saw the proboscis begin to curl down, and then I knew I must either fire at once or wait till after the next dive. When ammunition is not very plentiful, a knowledge of this little habit of the tapir is often useful, as saving perhaps a good many unnecessarily hurried shots. I generally found that a tapir would allow itself to be approached to within thirty or forty yards by a canoe before attempting to dive, and therefore, unless the canoe was a very slow one, it was seldom necessary to fire at long ranges, an ordinary double-barrelled smooth-bore, throwing a ball from eighty to a hundred yards, answering all purposes.

Next to this kind of weapon, the most generally useful to a sportsman, leading a life such as ours, would certainly be some kind of pea-rifle, light and

easy to carry in the forest, and yet capable, on an
emergency, of giving a good account of the largest
game, such as the tapir, as well as of birds, like the
Jacu, parrots, and others, which have to form so constant an item in one's daily bill of fare.   A heavy rifle
throwing a ball long ranges, is, on rare occasions, a
very useful weapon to have at hand.   In the forest
itself there is, of course, no room for the play of such
a weapon, but on the river banks long range shots at
pigs or jaguars are sometimes offered.

Each staff of the expedition was originally provided
with twelve short Snider rifles, sighted up to 800
yards, to serve as defensive weapons against Indians.
This class of rifle we found well suited to the rough
work required of it both on the river and in the forest,
while at the same time its shooting up to 800 yards
was very accurate indeed.

Notwithstanding the absence of Curling, which had
already lasted a fortnight, the progress of the surveys
had now become much more rapid than it had hitherto
been, owing partly to the improved nature of the
country through which we were now passing, but
chiefly to the fact that we were now able to adhere
closely to the banks of the main river, thus allowing
all locomotion and all transport of stores to be done
by canoe at an enormous saving of time and labour.
The weather, too, was now settled fine, and no rains or
floods occurred to temporarily disorganise the transport
service.

On the 24th of March it became necessary to move

our big depôt camp another step of ten miles or so onwards.

This had now become a weighty undertaking, owing, firstly, to the greatly increased size of the staff,* and, secondly, to the fact that all our tents having by this time rotted away, a number of large huts had to be built at each new camp for the accommodation of men and stores.

The old depôt which we were about to desert, was situated on a part of the river enclosed by high wooded mountains, where the channel in consequence was abnormally compressed. For a distance of nine miles above this point the river was compressed in a similar manner, its course on this length being full of small but awkward rapids and cataracts, which in time of floods could not be ascended by canoes, so powerful was the rush of water down them.

Below this same depôt we were acquainted with the river for a distance of some six miles only; beyond this nothing was as yet known of it.

Now, however, we were going to explore away down it for several miles.

I took with me on this occasion three big canoes, sixteen men and a large supply of stores, for I intended while the camp was building to make an expedition myself for another twenty miles or so down the river.

As we descended, the Ivahy gradually widened out

* See Appendix, note D.

till it attained in parts a width of nearly a quarter of a mile. For long reaches its surface presented an aspect smooth as glass, without a ripple, a strange contrast to its broken and torrent-like course a few miles above.

Instead of lofty mountains crushing it in on both sides, only a low undulating country, thickly covered with forest, appeared on either bank, except in the far distance, where the dim blue outlines of mountains could still be seen.

For the first time, since coming upon this river, I saw the great Brazilian " Pato," or wild goose. A small family of five of these beautiful birds were floating unwarily and unsuspectingly within the mouth of a little stream flowing into the river on the right bank. As my canoe, which was in front of the others, arrived opposite this little stream, the birds all got up simultaneously with a tremendous noise, offering a splendid mark for a shot as they wheeled round past our bows at thirty yards. I fired and brought down the biggest bird of the lot, which was probably the " paterfamilias ; " the remaining four meanwhile continuing their flight down stream, when, at a distance of a mile, I marked them again drop into the water.

The plumage of the Pato is superb. At a short distance it appears to be coal black with snow white markings. On close inspection, however, the black turns out to be dark purple of the richest hue. The head of the bird is surmounted by a topknot of black curly feathers, very similar to those worn by the "Curassow." The individual which I shot on this occasion proved delicious eating. Its skin I preserved and afterwards brought home with me to England.

Besides the "Pato" another most delicately flavoured bird, whose presence we had long missed on the river, now reappeared. This was the dark green Ibis, or, as the Brazilians called it, *Corvo d'agua.* This bird delights in the muddy banks of smoothly flowing rivers, fleeing from the sight and sound of *Corredeiras* and *Cachoeiras,* which always betoken rocky margins. Notwithstanding its delicious flavour, which is very like that of woodcock, the Brazilians refuse to eat it, calling it a *Corvo,* an unkind name which it is far from deserving. Its food consists really of nothing more objectionable than earth-worms, which it extracts from the soft mud of the river banks by means of its long slender curved bill. Sometimes, though rarely, I have come across this Ibis deep in the forest, a mile or more from the main river, but in these cases there is always sure to be some muddy stream close at hand, of whose near neighbourhood the harsh and sudden cry of "kurruck, kurruck, kurruck," from the bird as it rises from the ground is perhaps one's first warning. The *Corvo d'agua* is generally found singly, though sometimes in pairs. When suddenly flushed from its feeding ground on the river bank, it does not follow the course of the river either up or down stream, like the *Pato,* the *Marreca* (wild duck), the *Biguá,* the

Cigonia (heron), or even the kingfisher, but rises straight up and turns sharply into the forest, where it generally perches on some tree not twenty yards inland, there to wait till the supposed danger has passed by.

We arrived at the proposed site of the new camp before midday, and at once set to work with axes and *fouces* to clear it of forest. I had brought five of the best hunting dogs with us, for I intended after having completed the laying out of the plan of the camp, to hunt for fresh meat in order that our other stores might be economised as much as possible.

Before dark we had already cleared a large space for the camp, and, as the night was fine we did not waste time in building temporary cover for ourselves, but slung our hammocks in the open air between palm-trees left for the purpose, in a circle round the fire.

Throughout the night the dogs were very restless, constantly giving alarms, and making frantic rushes for short distances into the forest. Most probably the cause of their uneasiness was the presence of a *Jacuterica* or Ocelot, for on the following day one of the Brazilians discovered the fresh tracks of an animal of this species on the muddy banks of a little stream which flowed past at the back of the camp.

In the morning I started down the river in my hunting canoe with Miguel and Hypolito, taking with me three of the dogs. I had the double object before me of fixing new points for the line of exploration, and of hunting for fresh meat.

When we set off, the river was still enveloped in the

dense fog, which had now, since the cessation of the summer rains, become one of the most regular of all the meteorological phenomena of the country and climate. Before long, however, the sun's rays, penetrating here and there, split up the dense, dripping, white pall into detached masses, which in their turn were presently operated upon in like manner, resulting finally at about 9 A.M. in the complete dissipation of every particle of the fog. The effect produced by this final breaking and dissipating of the fog is very fine when witnessed upon the broad open river. On this occasion we were already some miles below the camp when the occurrence took place. We found that the country on each side of the river had become more mountainous than that through which we had passed on the previous day. The curious amphitheatre- or crescent-shaped Serra ranges which I have once before noticed, were now again prominent features. The river itself still maintained the stately proportions of the day before, and we came to no obstruction of sufficient importance to be dignified by the name of Rapid.

We discovered many fresh tracks of tapirs on the banks, but it was some time before we found one that exactly suited the particular notions of the hunters, whose choice in these matters is greatly influenced by the chance positions of the surrounding Serras, the great object always being to enclose the hunting ground in such a manner, by high hills or mountains, that the hunted game must either cross these latter (which it is generally loath to do), or drop into the river at some

point, which can, in common with the other likely
spots, be commanded by the hunting canoe. When
two or three canoes are employed in the hunt, there is
no need to be thus particular in the choice of a hunting
ground, for the animal can scarcely escape from being
seen by one or other of them—each canoe, of course,
being so stationed as to command different reaches of
the river.

At length we came upon a tapir track in a position
altogether satisfactory for our purpose. The scent
upon it was so fresh and strong, that the dogs caught
it, while we were yet some yards from the bank, and
began to whinny with excitement and eagerness to land.
We softly ran the bow of the canoe on to the bank and
examined the track. It was so fresh that the water
which had fallen from the tapir's body when leaving
the river, was still trickling down between the deeply
impressed hoof marks. Miguel whispered his opinion
that the tapir had not been out of the water ten
minutes! At a sign the three dogs were slipped, and
with the usual sharp yelp of delight, disappeared in
the pursuit. We immediately pushed off for the
purpose of crossing the river and gaining the opposite
bank whence we should obtain a better view. Scarcely,
however, had we got half way across, when a terrific
chorus of dogs burst forth in the forest behind us, apparently not fifty yards inland. We stopped paddling
at once, and I seized my big double-barrelled gun,
which, in company with a Snider and a pea-rifle, was
lying already loaded at the bottom of the canoe, and

waited with pulse beating at high pressure for the appearance of the tapir, which I knew would almost immediately come into view.

We heard the crashing of the big brute and the sound of his heavy cart-horse-like galloping, as he came thundering along towards the river, and one second later he burst into view and rushed headlong down the steep bank, with the dogs literally upon his back, into the water, under which he disappeared, leaving the latter swimming about upon the surface, turning their heads this way and that in bewildered astonishment, looking for their game.

With eyes keenly watching the smooth surface of the water in all directions for the reappearance of the great brown head with which I was now already becoming so familiar, we kept our station motionlessly in the middle of the river, the two men at bow and stern standing with paddles firmly grasped ready to dash away in pursuit at a moment's notice. "*Alli ! Alli ! por cima, por cima,*" " There, there ! above, above ! "

The tapir had reappeared not fifty yards above us. I steadied myself for a second, standing up in the canoe and then fired. The big round ball struck the tapir on the jaw, crashing through it as though it were glass. He did not give me time for a second shot, but, with a furious snort, dived. After a comparatively short interval he again reappeared a little farther up stream— we raced up to within forty yards of him, and then I gave him the contents of the second barrel, which pierced the hump of his neck, sending him down again immediately. Before I could reload the gun he came up again, being evidently too hard hit to remain long beneath the water. I fired a shot with the pea-rifle, which, however, missed the mark. The tapir did not dive at the report, but began to make for the bank, doubtless hoping yet to escape from us into the forest. The Snider rifle was still loaded, and I now took it up in order to give him the *coup de grace.* A careful aim, followed by a touch on the trigger, sent the animal to the bottom with a bullet through his brain. The river was fortunately neither deep nor swift where the tapir had sunk. Marking the spot carefully with the eye we paddled up, and soon succeeded, by means of sounding with the *varajões*, in discovering the exact position of the body. Hypolito then stripped, and diving in soon brought it to the surface. This was not such a difficult operation as might be imagined, for though the weight of a tapir may be from 700 to 800 pounds, its bulk is in proportion, and its specific gravity is but little greater than that of the water around it. We speedily secured it to the stern rope of the canoe, and after some rather severe paddling, brought it to the bank in tow, and there made it fast to a branch of a tree with a piece of the useful *cipó.* Let me here remark that the proper way by which to secure a tapir to a canoe for the purpose of towing it any distance through the water, is by the proboscis. If secured by any other part, such as by a leg or a hoof, the resistance which the great bulk of the animal offers to

the motion through the water is so enormous that
only a very heavy and powerfully manned canoe can
overcome it.   Even if the tapir is killed, say, but half
a mile below camp, it will generally pay better to take
the trouble of towing it to the nearest bank and
there take it on board, rather than to tow it over
that half mile, especially when the water happens to
be too deep for the *varajões* to be used instead of the
paddles.

We re-embarked the dogs; and, continuing our
journey down stream, soon came to another fresh track
of a deer on the bank.   The dogs were still game for
hunting, and bounded off eagerly on the new track.
After waiting for a short time, we heard the quarry
started, and the voices of the dogs began again to
ring merrily in the forest.   Suddenly, however, a most
remarkable change took place in the tone of their
voices.   The rich mellow note with which they usually
hunted, became short, sharp and abrupt, now and then
ceasing entirely, and then repeated in single " yaps "
given at long intervals.   After listening to it for a
minute or two, the hunters said that the dogs had
probably crossed the scent of a tiger, meaning a
jaguar, and this latter they had now taken up and
were following, instead of that of the deer.   I was
very anxious to land with one of the men and follow
the dogs up, in hopes of getting a shot at the royal
beast.   We had already put the canoe's head towards the bank, with this intention, when the sound
of the dogs' voices altogether ceased, and presently,

first one, then another, and then the third appeared upon the bank, and began to bark to be taken on board.

Both the men were agreed in saying that it would be no use our attempting to find the jaguar now, as the dogs would certainly not go into the forest again. They were unfortunately not " tiger-dogs," and from fear they had deserted the track of the deer, and then that of the jaguar, and had now returned to us. The hunters said they would hunt no more that day; and so it proved, for we tried them on another tapir track about a mile distant from this spot, and they followed it up for about twenty yards, and then immediately returned to the canoe with their caudal appendages well tucked in between their legs.

Our day's hunting being thus summarily put a stop to, we returned to where we had left the first tapir, whose carcáse we could only get on board by sinking the canoe beneath it and then baling out the water afterwards.

Arriving at the site of the new camp where the cutters were at work, our prize was speedily hauled up the bank by ropes and a dozen pair of strong arms. A large gridiron was constructed of green wood; and upon it the massive ribs and four quarters of the animal were laid ; a fire literally big enough to roast an ox being piled beneath.

When the sunset and the labours of the day were terminated, the Brazilians all assembled round the great gridiron, and with their *facões* helped themselves to whatever they fancied off the limbs or ribs of the tapir.

Neither were the dogs forgotten, liberal junks of the meat, which they had helped to obtain, being awarded to them also. Butchers' bills do not grow in the backwoods of Brazil.

CHAPTER XI.

AMONGST the multitudinous details necessary to the
existence and successful progress of an exploration
party, through the heart of a wild and unknown
country, very many can find no place at all in a work
intended for general readers. In our particular case
the details of the commissariat alone, dependent as
this service was upon the vagaries of "merchants,"
the vagaries of half-wild *camaradas,* and the vagaries
of floods, would, if written, fill a good many chapters
to the profit of no one but the printer.

There is, however, one class of detail which is less
uninteresting, and which, therefore, need not be so
rigorously kept in the background ; namely, that by
which an exploration party, such as ours, endeavours
to secure itself from the dangers of human enemies.

We had now penetrated well within the borders of
an Indian country, and signs were not wanting in the
forests around, of the more or less recent presence of
wild Indians themselves. Such being the case, we

had for the past few weeks been employing picked men
as scouts to warn and guard us against surprise.
Before any great step in advance was taken by our
main body, these scouts were sent on before, to scour
the forest on either bank of the river for Indian signs,
and to bring back a report thereon.

When I returned to the new camp from the morning's tapir hunting, described in the last chapter, I
found that the scouts, who had been out for three
days, had just returned, information having been
previously given them where to find us.

Their report I had been looking for with more
than usual interest, for there were many quaking
spirits amongst the *camaradas* now with me, who
openly avowed their intention of fleeing up the river,
at the first information of *Bugrés* having actually been
seen. Fortunately for my peace of mind, it did not
prove to be of so disquieting a nature as I had more
than half expected. No Indians had been seen, though
the scouts had announced the discovery of several of
their paths, one of which, indeed, passed down the
right bank of the river, within a mile of our present
camp. None of the paths, however, showed signs of
any very recent usage.

I had been waiting but to receive this report, to
start myself on an expedition down the river to see
and explore a certain famous fall, called the *Salto do
Ubá*, which was reported to be so great an obstruction,
as to entirely prohibit the passage of canoes either
up it or down it. The prospect of exploring this

Salto was rendered somewhat more than usually
exciting, by the fact of its having been hitherto always
spoken of by the *camaradas,* as though it was the very
end of the earth, beyond which some strange unknown
kind of country existed, into which no man in his
senses would dream of attempting to penetrate. Thus
its very name had come to be surrounded by a halo of
dread and undefinable fear, such as more than anything else works demoralisation upon the Caboclo
mind. One man alone of those now with me had
ever been so far down the river as this Salto. This
was the hunter Hypolito ; but even he had not been
so far for many years, and now showed no particular
desire to renew his acquaintance with the spot. On
sounding his recollections of his previous journeys, I
found, as I thought, that the inevitable *Bugré brabo*
was at the bottom of everything. I firmly believe that
from having told so many yarns about his former expeditions to the Salto, and repeated the same so many
times, which yarns had originated primarily in his own
fertile imagination, he now really believed that there
was great danger and risk to be encountered there.

This night when we were all squatting round the
great gridiron, upon which portions of the tapir were
still roasting, many were the yarns which Hypolito
spun, perhaps for the hundredth time, to an enrapt
audience, about his former adventures on the very
part of the river on which we now were. I must
confess that both the yarns themselves and his mode
of telling them were very impressive, related as they

were in the darkness and stillness of the night, amidst the mystic surroundings of the wild forest, and upon the very site of their supposed occurrence.

We were to start an hour before sunrise on our expedition; I therefore did not remain to listen to the end of Hypolito's tales, but early retired to my hammock to sleep comfortably beneath the feathery palms and starlit sky.

Long before daylight, Hypolito, Miguel, and myself had turned out of our hammocks. A dense fog, as usual, had formed in the small hours of the morning, and my hammock and blankets were soaked with moisture, my hair and beard being also dank and dripping from the same cause. A cup of hot coffee into which was poured a *pinga* of *cachaça*, soon drove out the chill from our lungs. Then, by the light of a glowing brand from the fire, we filed down the steep path that led from the camp to the water's edge, bearing our breakfast of beans and farinha tied up in a bag, a large junk of tapir-meat, a blanket apiece, and, last but not least, guns, rifles and pistols. No dogs were allowed to come with us, for they might have hampered our movements, seeing that we had other objects in view this day than hunting. Thus equipped, we embarked in a light though rather slow-going cedar canoe, which, however, had the advantage over my usual hunting canoe, of being more commodious and better fitted, by reason of the greater height of its prow and gunwales, for navigating rapids or cataracts.

For the first hour we paddled steadily along in the darkness, making, however, good way. By seven o'clock, we had arrived at the farthest point reached by us on the previous day, which I calculated to be about half-way to the Salto. Here we halted for breakfast, going a little distance up a *Barra,* whose banks were radiant with large sweet-smelling pink and purple flowers growing on shrubs. We discovered a fig-tree crowded with little figs that were just getting ripe, of which we ate a great number as a relish to our beans and tapir-meat. This was the only wild fig-tree that I ever saw bearing fruit. Probably, if we had re-visited it a week later, we should have found it already stripped by the many fruit-eating birds and animals of these forests.

Proceeding another mile, we heard the first roar of a *corredeira.* Simultaneously with its coming into view, the river widened out to nearly four hundred yards from bank to bank, at the same time becoming shallower and swifter. The roar of this rapid was greater than that of any that I had yet heard, though its fall was insignificant, being less than three feet in a distance of perhaps one hundred and twenty yards. On account of the comparative dryness of the river at this time, the *corredeira* had been split up into hundreds of tiny cascades, which from above were invisible, but which, when seen from below, formed a most lovely spectacle. It was the number rather than the size of these cascades, which produced the great volume of sound which we had noticed. We had no difficulty in running down by one of the several channels, with which this, as well as the generality of rapids, was liberally provided.

After descending a similar rapid, a short distance farther on, we came within hearing of another roar, sounding like the mutterings of distant thunder. This was the first indication that we were approaching the great Salto itself. After a time it ceased. Owing to a sharp bend in the river, a lofty hill had intervened and cut off the sound. Another sharp turn, and a quarter of an hour's steady paddling brought us in sight of another rapid, which I at first mistook for the Salto itself. Hypolito, however, now told me that he remembered that this rapid was situated just above the real Salto, an intervening bay of still, deep water separating the two. Breaking through the noisy uproar of the rapid before us, the deep throbbing of the Ubá itself was now again audible.

It was some time before the two canoemen could make up their minds as to the best course to take down this new rapid; which, from above, appeared both long and wild, white water ominously predominating in it. At length, they came to a decision, and, backing the canoe off the rock on which we had temporarily brought up, steered for a funnel-shaped opening in the line of broken water which guarded the entrance to the *corredeira*. In another minute, we were in the midst of the boiling waters, slipping past the banks at a rate of twelve or fifteen miles an hour.

We bumped once or twice on hidden rocks, and now
and then the crest of a breaker came on board; but
on the whole we got down the two hundred yards or
so of rapid very satisfactorily, though I should have
considered twice before attempting the "run" with
any less skilful canoemen. Arriving at the bottom, we
found ourselves in the bay of which Hypolito had
spoken. At first, no visible outlet for the river was
apparent; neither was there any perceptible current
to show in which direction the water was running.

On paddling more towards the middle of the bay,
we found that the river made first a sharp turn to the
right, and then again bent back abruptly to the left,
so that in reality the Falls were straight in front of us,
though concealed from view by an intervening pro-
montory of land, jutting sharply out from the left
bank. Several large flat rocks stood up in the middle
of the bay, which, when I first caught sight of them,
were occupied by several pairs of otters, engaged in
sunning themselves, or in devouring fish. These
rocks were strewn with the remains of fish of various
kinds, amongst which I especially recognised fragments
of *dourados* and *cascudos*. I would not fire at the
otters, though I was greatly tempted to do so, because
I wished not to give notice of our presence prematurely
to any Indians that might chance to be within hearing.

We now steered for the right bank, and, keeping
close to it, continued our course till we came, in about
three hundred yards, to the head of a long inclined
plane, of perhaps a quarter of a mile or more in length,

studded with rocks and gaunt tree-trunks, down which
a great body of water was rushing tumultuously.
Here we landed upon some rocks, which, standing
some height above the surface of the water, gave us a
better view. The cataract which was roaring in front
of us was evidently the outlet of but a portion of the
pent-up waters above. On the left, the real Salto
thundered; and it was by this latter that, probably,
more than one-third of the river found its way down
to the smooth plane below. The fall itself was invisible from where we stood, being concealed by an
island which intervened: a thin cloud of vapour
rising up above it pointed out accurately enough its
actual position. By rough calculation, and by the
aid of a pocket "clinometer," I estimated the total
fall of the cataract or "Salto" to be about sixteen
feet—a pigmy to many that I have since had to ascend
and descend, but a giant compared with any we had
yet encountered.

Having secured our canoe to the bank, we landed
and prepared to cut our way through the forest down
to the bottom of the falls. We had, however, no
sooner reached the top of the bank, which was here,
as is very generally the case on the borders of a
corredeira or *cachoeira*, very low, than we found ourselves in a path already made for us. My companions
at once pronounced it to be a *Bugré* path or *picada;*
pointing out to me twigs and little branches that had
been bent back and broken at a height above the reach
of any wild animal. Neither was there a single sign

of a knife having been used upon it, which would have been the case, had it been the work of some Brazilian hunter.

We followed the path with some caution till we arrived at the banks of a large *barra* about thirty yards wide, named on the maps "Rio Peixe" or "Fish River," which flowed into the Ivahy, at the foot of the Ubá Cataract. Crossing this river by wading and jumping from one rock to another, we picked up the path on the other bank, and again followed it for a long distance, perhaps a mile and a half, carefully keeping our eyes open to discover any signs of recent usage. My two companions, who were both adepts in forest lore, came to the conclusion, that it had not been used for some weeks at least; for, in the first place, there were no recent breakages of twigs visible, and, in the second place, young shoots of bamboo and other plants were so obstructing it in places, as to make it certain that no human being had passed since their growth, for we ourselves had to cut or break a passage through them. These were the signs by which my companions judged that the path had not been trodden very recently, though there were abundant proofs to show that it had not been out of use for more than three months.

Retracing our steps, we arrived once more at the head of the falls, where we had left the canoe, and sat down upon the rocks to refresh ourselves with beans and tapir-meat, washed down with water and a *pinga* of *cachaça*.

The work that I had planned out for us was by no means yet concluded. I wished, when we returned to the camp up the river, to be able to tell our men two things—that there were no Indians now at the Ubá, and that we had actually navigated the Salto from the top to the bottom. This would give them fresh encouragement, and perhaps be the means of keeping many of those with us, who had now given notice to leave at the end of the month, solely, as I believed, from a certain undefinable dread of danger ahead.

Miguel and Hypolito were quite willing to make the descent of the cataract at once. We allowed ourselves half an hour, in which to eat our lunch and smoke our cigarettes, and then prepared for action. First, everything was taken out of the canoe and deposited upon the bank, with the sole exception of the *rarajões*. The men then stripped themselves of all clothing from the waist upwards, and the knees downwards. I followed their example, with the exception of keeping my boots on; for unaccustomed feet cannot tread the sharp rocks of a rapid with impunity. Thus prepared, we embarked, Miguel and myself taking up our station in the bows, while Hypolito stood in the stern to steer.

The total fall of the cataract into which we were about to venture, was, as already given, about sixteen feet in a distance of a quarter of a mile. On paper, this does not look very alarming. Neither perhaps is it so, when, as in the present case, the water of the river is low, and the volume, therefore, forming the cataract, comparatively small. To those, however, who are a little familiar with rivers encumbered with rapids, such a fall in such a distance would not, at the best of times, recommend itself as an every day pleasure-trip. The long incline of wild broken waters is apt to look still longer and wilder, and the black rocks over which the white foam is tumultuously dashing, seem to lose somewhat of their picturesque appearance when viewed from on board a canoe that is on the point of entering amongst them. I have often seen, on these occasions, brave men's faces blanch, and their legs tremble beneath them with fear.

Somewhat different tactics had to be pursued in this case to those which we had hitherto adopted in the descent of smaller rapids. We did not dream now of rushing at the obstacle like a bull at a gate, in the hopes of steering clear of the rocks till we arrived at the bottom. Shipwreck, with, probably, not a few broken limbs and ribs in addition, would have been the certain result. There was, indeed, one big channel that seemed to run right through the cataract from the top to the bottom; but there were great waves in it of five feet in height, which would have swamped the biggest canoe; besides which, the rush of water through it was so tremendously powerful, and the channel itself so tortuous, that no canoeman, however skilful, could have guided a canoe safely down it.

With our long poles, or *varajões*, thrown out well to the front, and with our bodies straining upon them to keep the canoe from getting beyond control in the swift rush of water, we slowly entered the top of the cataract, scaring many otters from their sunning places on the rocks, and causing the *Biguás* or "divers" to expand their wings for flight, and look askance at the unaccustomed intruder on their wild domain.

In this cautious manner we descended some rather rough water, always keeping the canoe well in hand. Now we entered a channel, straight and free from rocks for some fifty yards or more, along which a powerful current was rushing, throwing up in its course ridges of white water from two to three feet in height.

"*Larga!*" shouted Hypolito from the stern, and, for the first time, we gave the canoe her head, while she, for a few seconds, flew along unimpeded down the open channel at race-horse speed.

"*Segura!*" shouted or rather yelled Miguel from the bows, his voice heard above the roar of waters— "*Segura!*" and down upon the rocky bottom went the long *varajões*, thrown well to the front. Our headlong course was instantly checked, while the stout poles bent like willow wands under the sudden strain put upon them. We were but just in time, for in another second we should have gone over a vertical fall of some four feet in height, at the bottom of which a big foam-crested wave and various ugly looking rocks were in readiness to have received us.

This is always the great danger of running an unknown rapid or cataract; namely, the suddenly and unexpectedly coming upon a vertical Fall or "Saltinho" in the midst of it, when in full career. These falls can rarely be detected from above until the canoe is close upon them, and when, perhaps, it is too late to stay its course.

While the two men strained on their poles to keep the canoe back, I jumped out on to some rocks and secured the stern rope of the canoe round one of them. The men then got out into the water, and, by our combined exertions the canoe was safely lowered over the fall, and brought to rest for the present upon some rocks in shallow water.

We now had time to look around us. We were nearly in the middle of the cataract, and the roar was so great that we could only hear ourselves speak by shouting loudly. The great Salto on the left was now in full view, and the vibration caused by the immense body of water falling some ten feet vertically, reached us where we stood, a hundred yards distant.

Below the Fall, the river again suddenly widened, and many islands covered with the tall and graceful reed, the *Ubá*, which gave its name to the Falls, rose in its midst.

Above us the scene was wild and desolate in the extreme. There was nothing but a chaotic expanse of rock, foam, and gaunt, black skeletons of trees, which, in some former floods, had been brought down, and stranded in the shallow waters of the cataract. These gaunt skeletons, which had long since been stripped of all their beauties of foliage, twig and bark, were thronged with *Biguás*, which stood in rows upon each blackened trunk and bare arm, sunning themselves with wings outstretched, after the manner of the carrion birds of the prairies.

While we were resting thus for a few minutes from our labours, a pair of otters swam up to the very verge of the Saltinho down which we had just come, and, poising themselves vertically in the midst of the powerfully rushing waters, indulged in a prolonged stare at us, at the same time indicating their disapproval of our presence by loud snorts, which were audible even above the noise of the waters. Suddenly they dived, and I expected to see them re-appear below the fall. But no, in about half a minute they reappeared about twenty yards higher up the channel, again raising their bodies half out of the water to gaze at us, and remaining perfectly stationary, notwithstanding that the current in the channel was rushing with such force that a mill-race would have been a joke to it. Twice more they repeated the same performance, after which they disappeared from view altogether.

The second part of our course was longer though less risky than the first, and in about three quarters of an hour from the time of entering the cataract, we found ourselves safely at the bottom. The spell was broken. The name of the *Salto do Ubá* was fast being shorn of its terrors. It but remained now to examine the forest on the left bank of the river to satisfy ourselves completely on the question of the Indians, and then I should have completed the chief objects for which this little expedition had been undertaken.

My companions returned by land to the head of the cataract whence we had started, to fetch the various articles which we had there left. After their return, the remainder of the day was spent in making a short exploration by water down the river, and in an examination of the forest on the left bank. Though many tracks of wild animals, chiefly of tapir, deer, and pig, were found upon the banks and in the forest, no further signs whatever of *Bugrés*, whether past or recent, were discovered. Thus, then, as far as our necessarily brief explorations enabled us to judge, the only evidence relating to the existence of Indians in the neighbourhood was the *picada* first discovered.

Night fell, and we camped at the foot of the Falls, on a rocky island covered with drift-wood, and partially sheltered from the heavy dew by the flowery tops of the *Ubá* reed, which was here growing to a height of fifteen or sixteen feet. We kept watch in turn for three hours each, for none of us relished the idea of being pounced upon while asleep by some prowling jaguar or sneaking puma.

By two o'clock the following day we were again in camp, and Miguel and Hypolito were engaged in recounting what I hoped was now a true version of their adventures at the *Salto do Ubá*. Certainly no man after this came to me with yarns of the terrible dangers which were there to be encountered.

CHAPTER XII.

- THERE are probably but few readers of travels or of explorations in uncivilized countries, such as those of Livingstone and Cameron in South and Central Africa, and others of many less-known pioneers of civilization in the wild regions which are yet to be found in both North and South America, that have not been made familiar, *usque ad nauseam*, with the all too wearisome trials, vexations, and disappointments which travellers in such countries have to endure from the capricious vagaries of their hired followers.

From compassion to the reader, I have hitherto refrained to a great extent from disburdening my mind of the troubles and difficulties with which we too had to contend from this same wearisome cause. Neither do I now intend to do more than very briefly draw attention to them.

It will be remembered that at the very outset of the work of the 2nd Staff, it had been foreseen that

Colonia Thereza by itself would not be able to supply our full wants in respect of men, except for the first few weeks after the commencement of the explorations, while the requirements were yet small; and that plans, more or less dependent for their execution upon the return of Captain Palm by a fixed date, had been made, whereby supplies could be drawn from more distant centres, when the necessity for so doing should arise.

It was not many weeks after the commencement of the work, that the colonial men began to give the first indications of refractoriness, and of a disposition to combine together for the purposes of coercion in some form or other.

Although, in those early days, we generally succeeded without much difficulty in enforcing our will against their resistance, the warning was one not to be overlooked, as being a symptom of a danger which might, unless early precautions were taken against it, crop up suddenly in the not distant future, and create an overwhelming disaster.

This danger lay in the power that the men had of deserting us *en masse*, at any moment, without appreciable injury to themselves, though to the enormous detriment of the work of the explorations.

The precautions which we early began to take against it were, *first*, the introduction of a system of written contracts, whereby each man, as he joined the expedition, bound himself, subject to the penalties of a law relating to employer and employed, known as

the law of September 13th, 1830, to remain for a
certain fixed period with the expedition; *secondly,* in
the case of those who could not be induced to sign
long contracts, but who were nevertheless men whom
it was desirable to retain on the work, the having a
clear understanding between ourselves and them, that
that they would not be allowed to leave without a
month's previous notice, under the penalty of forfeiture
of whatever pay might be due to them; and *thirdly,*
the physical obstacle of separating them into two or
more distinct bodies, so as to prevent, on all ordinary
occasions, any disagreeable combination on their part
for the purposes of bullying us, their employers.

There always existed, besides, two moral causes
which, in all our many and wearisome disputes and
negotiations with our Brazilian *camaradas,* seldom
failed to turn the scale in our favour, as long as right
was on our side. The first of these causes was their
strong sense of the first principles of justice, which led
them to say in practice: "If I break my side of my
agreement with you, I won't say a word if you break
yours, and we'll cry quits." Thus, if a man broke his
contract, whether written or verbal, he never dreamt
of demanding any balance of pay which might be owing
him; for, by our side of the contract, he knew he had
fairly forfeited it.

The second cause had more of the character of a
superstitious ignorance, by virtue of which the average
caboclo accords an almost blind respect to a *written*
contract. In no other way than this, can I account

for the universal respect of contracts, made between the *patrão* or employer, and *camarada* or employed, which exists amongst the *caboclo* or labouring class, even in the most remote parts of the province of Paraná, where it would be almost impossible for the arm of the law to reach either party.

Could we have induced every man who engaged himself with us, to have signed a contract binding himself to remain with us till the end of the expedition, I have no doubt whatever but that the great majority would have done so, as long as we broke no part of our side of the contract, and as long as the men themselves were not affected by an Indian panic. As it was, however, many would sign no contract at all, and a still greater number would only sign for short periods of two or at most three months, while not more than half a dozen contracted for longer periods than this.

It was not till, in despair, we finally adopted the plan of offering a somewhat large extra monetary inducement to such as would bind themselves for longer periods, that we ultimately succeeded in obtaining men willing to contract for the comparatively long period of six or eight months. None would agree on any terms to bind themselves for more than eight months.

At the present time, however, none of these long-service contracts were in force; and, consequently, as each month came round, a large number of men became free, many of whom, before re-engaging, wanted to take perhaps a fortnight's holiday at Colonia Theréza, thereby throwing into disturbance all the plans and arrangements of the work; or, more often still, wasted precious days of our time in haggling for increased pay, or in dallying between their desire to earn more money by stopping on another month, and their equally strong inclination to squander away in riotous pleasures that which they, had already earned.

Generally the time-expired men endeavoured to strengthen their position by inducing their companions, whose contracts had perhaps yet another month or two to run, to join with them in trying, by means of persuasive promises or ingenious lies, to obtain leave of absence without detriment to the terms of their contracts or verbal agreements.

So marvellously fecund and withal so persistent were they in their lying, that it was with difficulty that their arguments could be resisted; and I have many times been forced to take refuge in the unanswerable "*não entendo*," "I don't understand," in order to avoid inconvenient controversy.

They attacked somewhat in the following fashion, each man having a different story to tell.

"Will the *patrão* give me leave to go up to the Colony?"

"What for?"

"I want to see how my affairs (*negocios*) are going on!"

"Can't possibly spare you till your time is up."

"But, *patrão, minha familia* is starving because there is no one to gather in the Roça."

"You have got money, hire a *camarada* to gather it in for you."

"*Não posso*; besides, my mother is just dead, and I must go and bury her !"

When the conversation reached this mournful stage, it was generally convenient to fall back upon one's ignorance, real or assumed, of what the man was talking about.

In most cases, if not very strongly urged on by his companions, the fellow would, after one or two mild rebuffs of this nature, give up the attempt as hopeless, and settle quietly down to his work again. A rough impatient refusal, by stirring up his pride, would send him up the river like a shot out of a gun, willing to endure any forfeiture of money, rather than be spoken to or treated like an *escravo*.

The general character of our Brazilian *camaradas* was that of high-spirited children, hence the *suaviter in modo etc.* policy of management was generally by far the best to pursue.

Above all it was necessary to treat them with the strictest justice; for, as with all semi-barbarous people, this was the virtue that appealed to their understanding with the greatest force.

As I have already indicated, they had two, what may be called, pet prejudices;—No. 1 being an absurd pride of free birth, which, in a land where slavery is still an institution, renders them abnormally sensitive as to their mode of treatment by the *patrão*; and No. 2, an insane fear of the *Bugré Brabo* or Wild Indian.

A good illustration of the ridiculous extent to which a Brazilian belonging to what we at home should call the labouring class carries his pride of free birth, is to be found in the very name *camarada* or " companion," with which he dubs himself.

He is not too proud to *do* certain kinds of labour for hire, but he strongly objects to the logical sequence of being *called* a *trabalhador* or " labourer," which he considers as almost synonymous with *escravo* or " slave."

In the large towns, where labour is abundant and living hard, this silly pride is soon knocked out of him; though, I must confess, he loses in the process much of the charm of manner which is natural to him in his more free and independent country life.

During the first few months of the exploration we lost several men by reason of pet prejudice No. 1.

On the occasion of Messeno's swamping me in a cataract, as already related, I removed him from river to *picada* work. Taking this as a punishment, and his pride rebelling at the fancied indignity, the following day he left the expedition, drawing away two of his relations who sympathised and made common cause with him.

Before he went away, I reminded him that, by so doing, he was liable to the forfeiture of the whole of his arrears of pay, amounting altogether to nearly eight pounds of English money. His answer, given with the lofty air of a perfect independence, was, "The doctor may of course do as he pleases, he may pay me or not, but in any case I go away (*vou m'embora*)."

A month later he applied to be taken on again, and was quite surprised when he was told, that having left at his own pleasure, he must now wait for ours, before being re-admitted to our service.

Cases such as these were harmless, so long as they were confined to single individuals, and ordinary tact could always prevent their spreading too far.

As regards the extraordinary dread of the Brazilians for the Wild Indian, it is but doing bare justice to their courage, to say that the *Bugré* is far more terrible to their imagination than to their actual senses.

It must be, I think, a peculiarity of ignorant semi-wild people, like the Brazilian back-settler, to be more afraid of prospective and imaginative danger, than danger real and present. The Salto do Ubá, for example, lost its terrors, immediately it was approached and looked in the face ; though, till then, its influence had been so potent, as to have been within an ace of driving a number of strong and otherwise brave men to desertion.

As will be seen in the sequel, the Cataracts proper of the Ivahy, which commenced some 140 miles below Colonia Theréza, continuing almost uninterruptedly for fifty miles, were so dreaded in prospective, that at one time it seemed very doubtful whether ten men would be found to accompany us down them. Yet, when we ultimately came to close quarters with these Cataracts, the very same men, who had before spoken only of their existence with 'bated breath, now daily and hourly risked their lives in them with the greatest possible pluck and bravery.

As ill luck would have it, no less than two thirds of our men would be free at the end of the present month of March, and they made no secret of their intention of combining to force me to raise their pay ~ely, as the price of re-engag; but   Our agent at   Theréza had failed of Nero,   n were to be   had but one neck,   dreds of miles   e upon the whole   ect of fighting

ur Staff not been   ng of the plot   the present stage   re the end of   would have been   ies of the men   country for new   part as difficult   released from   réza.   ery hard times of   which I h   ys' wearisome and   s subject   o a sufficiently satis-   barous   which I gained their   sible   retatively small cost of a   is   ent. in the pay of the   skill e others exactly where   they   Peop en accustomed to employ   labour es, where it is abundant,

may perhaps find it difficult to understand why more
decided measures, such as they are in the habit of employing towards their troublesome workmen, were not
employed by us in our dealings with our refractory *em-
ployés*.   Others, however, who have had to deal with
those national nuisances, " Trades Unions," will understand the impossibility of always carrying out justice
with a high hand.   They will sympathise with us in
the long series of petty annoyances, struggles and even
defeats, which we had to endure at the hands of our
hired labourers, often with a smiling countenance
sometimes, I fear, with a heart like that
fiercely longing that all *camaradas*
that we might wreak our vengeanc
class at one single blow.

Had the official *personnel* of o
so reduced in numbers, long before
of annoyance had been reached, one
told off to scour the surrounding
sources of supply that we might be
oppressive thraldom of Colonia The

Reader, I have exceeded the limit
posed to myself when commencing th
so sore a one with travellers in bar
but it would have been almost impos
veyed anything like a just idea of th
dition of our life and work in fewer
insect world in summer, it was an e
in our side, and probably had more
influence upon the fortunes of the

anyone of the numerous other difficulties with which we had to contend.

On the 4th of April, the somewhat severe responsibility that, since the 10th of March, had rested upon my unaided shoulders was at length to be removed or shared.

It was within half an hour of sunset on this day, when, from one of my little camps on the river bank, I observed the usual signs announcing the approach of a canoe from up the river. First, a pair of broad winged *Patos* came flying by, sheering widely off the bank on which our camp stood as they caught sight of the moored canoes. Next followed sundry couples of wild duck (*marrecinhas*) all in full flight down stream, quacking methodically at regular intervals. After a few minutes, one or two *Biguás* appeared skimming along just above the surface of the water, silently, like black ghosts or evil spirits. No prophets of evil were they, however, on this occasion. They were the *avant-coureurs* of a canoe that was bringing Curling back to the expedition. Presently the canoe itself appeared in sight, and with shouts and firing of pistols came racing down a rapid that stood just above my camp, and in another minute not only Curling but also my old friend Edwards landed on the bank.

For a few moments I indulged in the blissful hopes that the latter had come to fill the place left vacant by S—. Alas! these fond expectations were speedily dissipated. He had come merely to pay us a flying visit of two days' duration, and we were still doomed for an indefinite period to suffer from the want of another assistant.*

Now that our friend Edwards had come so far to see us—for his Staff were still some four or five days' journey on the other side of Colonia Theréza—it was incumbent upon us to do our best to render his visit both amusing and profitable to him. -

He had already seen something of the beauties of the Ivahy on the journey down from Colonia Theréza to our camp, and he was sufficiently enthusiastic on what he had seen thus far, to encourage us to show him something more. He had done deer-stalking on the prairies, in addition to the milder sport of snipe, quail, and prairie-hen shooting, but there his experience of *la chasse* in Brazil ended.

The first object that met his eye on arriving at my little camp, was a dead tapir lying in a canoe at the landing-place, and our dinner on the same night consisted of fish (*Dourado*), and palm tops, followed by tapir steak and black beans, all more or less unaccustomed food to him. Thus hopefully his education into forest and river life had commenced, and early the following morning we started down the river in two canoes with dogs and guns, with the intention of actually showing our guest how we killed our tapirs.

Unhappily the dogs had been hunting almost every

* To a man whose lot is cast in the Empire of the Southern Cross the one virtue most abundantly needful, for his own peace of mind's sake, is Patience. We lost our assistant in October, his place was not re-filled till the following July.

day for the last week or more, and were thoroughly sick of it, and not even Cachorronha could be got to follow up the tapir tracks on to which she was put. At length we got her to run a very fresh deer track, and the exciting music of her voice in full cry in the forest, cheered us up when we were almost in despair. The deer was brought down to the river after a smart chase by the canoes, captured by the tail, and killed with a knife.

More than ever on this occasion did I become convinced that the real pleasure of a deer or tapir hunt is not when the game is in the water and the canoes are in chase, but while the music of the dogs is still heard hither and thither in the forest, and up and down the wooded slopes of the Serras, and while it is still uncertain whether the game is tapir, deer, or some small fry like the *cutia* or *paca*, or whether it will take to the river in sight or out of sight of the expectant hunters. I must candidly admit that when the game is in the water, the remainder of the hunt is mere butchery, more or less exciting of course, but still mere butchery. The animal, if it is a deer or a tapir, has but the barest chance of escape, about as much, perhaps, as a rat from a terrier in the open field. Certainly, I myself killed every one of the first fourteen tapirs that I saw alive, and the fifteenth only escaped because I could not get within 400 yards of it before it had got out of the river and dived into the forest. I remember that I used frequently to say to myself, after perhaps a more exciting tapir hunt than usual, " Well,

I should much prefer a day's rabbit shooting with beagles in a small English covert, to all the tapir hunting in the world." *Now* I would give something substantial for the chance of another shot at a tapir !

After the hunt, we continued our course down the river till we reached the foremost of the working parties, which was now not more than seven miles from the Salto do Ubá. Here we spent the remainder of the day, and, when night came, slept altogether in one large palm-shed, whose eaves touched the ground on two sides, the two ends being open. With me the novelty of these rude wild camps had long since worn off, but to our visitor, who was accustomed to sleeping every night in a well-ordered tent, with the luxuries of a comfortable bed and more or less elaborate toilette arrangements, all was new and strange.

On the next day, we again endeavoured to show Edwards a live tapir, but without success. This night we passed at an old camp, eighteen miles higher up the river, the same from which I had formerly been expelled by the plague of fleas, and which I had not since visited. The last two or three *corredeiras* we ascended by moonlight, and the river was consequently seen in its utmost perfection of beauty and loveliness.

The *pulgas* had not departed from the camp, and I, therefore, passed a night of sleepless torment, my companions, however, sleeping peacefully as though there were not at least ten score fleas jumping about in each of their hammocks.

On the following morning, to our great regret, our

guest departed. We gave him our best available canoe and three good men, with a stock of provisions, to take him up to Colonia Theréza, and with three hearty cheers from our two selves and Miles the cook, the only other European in the camp, started him on his somewhat long return journey.

The very day after his departure, I came across a tapir in the forest, with which I had an exciting little piece of sport. As it was different from the common everyday river hunting or butchery, of which perhaps I have already almost wearied the reader, I will relate it.

We, that is myself and a party of men, were sitting down to lunch in the middle of the *picada.* I had been working with two instruments—the theodolite and the level—both of which were standing up in the *picada*, at the points at which I had last been using them, the theodolite being about ten yards in front of where we were sitting, and the level about a hundred yards behind. All at once, Estudante—one of the hunting dogs which happened to be with us on this occasion—was heard to break out in full cry, scarcely more than a gunshot distant; and immediately a magnificent tapir, with the dog close at his heels, burst out into the *picada* in front, and came galloping blindly along the clean cut avenue, straight towards us.

" Pedro, Pedro, the instrument, quick!" I shouted. The man rushed forward, and, snatching the theodolite from its perilous position, established himself and it

in safety behind a gigantic, buttress-shaped Monjôlo-
tree, which just at this point partly jutted out into the
picada.   The tapir, mad with fear of the dog, saw
nothing besides, but thundered past, scattering the
contents of our luncheon-bags in every direction, and
utterly ignoring us, who had opened our ranks to right
and left of his course to allow him to pass.

I had got my gun with me, one barrel of which was
loaded with ball cartridge, and the men had drawn
their pistols with the intention of opening fire on the
animal's rear the moment he had passed.   Their
intention, however, was frustrated by the dog, which
at times was almost on the tapir's back as it ran.
Straight before them was the level, which in another
few seconds would receive the impact of the tapir's
big, hulking body upon its delicate organization, with
a result that need not be described.

There was nothing for it but to risk a shot, though
with the two-fold chance of hitting the instrument
and killing the dog.   Seizing the first opportunity the
dog gave of sighting the animal's stern, I took a
hurried aim, and pulled the trigger at sixty yards.
At the report, the tapir dropped like a stone—this
much I saw before the smoke from the barrel obscured
the view.   Rushing forward to get clear of the smoke,
I looked again, and lo! both tapir and dog had disappeared from the *picada*.

One of the Brazilians now shouted out that the shot
had broken one of the animal's legs, and, just at that
moment, I heard Estudante begin to " bay " in the

forest on the right of the *picada*. Regardless of thorns and thick jungle I dashed into the forest, making the best of my way towards the sound, and presently came upon the scene of action.

The tapir was standing in a little rocky stream scarcely knee-deep in water, keeping the dog at bay by the threatening action of its head and fore-feet. One hind leg was broken just above the knee, and this prevented it from charging the dog, though just as I arrived on the scene, it made a vigorous but futile attempt to do so. Some of the Brazilians had already come up before me, but, knowing that I liked to finish off work of this kind that I had myself commenced, were not attempting to interfere with the two animals.

The tapir was elevating his proboscis, showing his red gums and big front teeth, while the dog was perfectly mad with excitement, darting forward to within a foot of the game, and scarcely retreating before the savage blows with which, by means of its fore feet, the tapir was endeavouring to defend himself. A bullet through the brain delivered at close quarters ended the combat.

This was the first tapir that I had killed on land, though it made the sixth that had now fallen to my gun. In the whole time—more than eighteen months altogether—during which I lived in the forests of this valley, I only shot one other tapir on land, though I bagged no less than twenty-eight of these animals to my own gun during that period. The second occasion was a very simple one. I was coming up the river in

a canoe just at sunset, when one of the canoemen
pointed out to me a tapir standing upon the bank,
which was at that spot nearly flat and covered with
long grass, apparently watching us. As I turned to
take up my rifle which was lying behind me in the
canoe, the animal wheeled round and galloped up the
muddy grass-grown slope towards the forest, offering
a splendid mark for a bullet as he ran. Before he
could get into cover I fired, and tumbled him over like
a hare in a fallow, at seventy yards.

Chances such as these are, however, rarely given in
these regions of universal forest, and when, therefore,
they do by chance occur, they are, as a natural consequence, all the more highly esteemed; not the least
part of the pleasure imparted on such occasions being
the wonder and amazement with which such, to us,
simple feats of sportsmanship are regarded by the
Brazilians, who never dream of shooting at a bird
flying or an animal running.

CHAPTER XIII.

THE Ivahy, for a distance of about nine miles above the Salto do Ubá, is remarkable for its greater depth and for the general sluggishness of its current.

In consequence of this changed character of the river in this part, a new genus of reptile here makes its appearance, namely, the *jacaré*, a species of alligator that grows to the length of seven or eight feet.

My first acquaintance with this repulsive-looking beast, immense numbers of which we afterwards met with on the lower Ivahy, was made at one of the working camps situated on the bank of the river about eight miles above the Salto do Ubá. A full-grown individual had taken up its quar s a little below our camp, and was daily to be seen lying asleep upon the muddy bank, nearly at the same spot.

On two occasions I went stealthily out in a canoe, in the hope of shooting it, but each time the brute slipped into the water and disappeared, before my eye had

caught sight of it upon its resting-place. On the
sec nd of these occasions, however, I did not return
altogether bagless, for I discovered four baby *jacarés,*
each about eight inches long, lying close to the spot
which the old one had just vacated. Notwithstanding
that even at their tender age they showed no little
amount of vice, snapping at my fingers whenever I
brought them near, I took them all prisoners without
difficulty, and brought them into camp.

We dug a little basin in the ground, which we lined
with wet grass from the river bank, and here we kept
them for some days, feeding them on little bits of
fresh meat, whenever such could be obtained.

They had a very curious mode of taking their food,
never condescending to take it tamely, but whipping it
into their mouths with their tails by a quick concerted
movement of the whole body, which was suddenly bent
into the form of a semi-circle, and then again, after
the object had been seized, as suddenly straightened.
The sharp decisive way in which this double movement was executed gave one the idea rather of a piece
of mechanism than of a living animal. One snap of
the jaw was all the visible eating process. There
was no biting, chewing, or gnawing.

If a stone or a piece of stick was offered, it made no
difference; the tail whipped it into the mouth, the
jaws snapped upon it, the body again sprang back to
its stiff straightness, and the ugly-looking green eye,
with its vertical black slit, stared evilly and un-
blinkingly as before. I became weary of the unin-

teresting brutes after the first few days, and we therefore slaughtered them.

One of the men of my party, by name Joaquim Soeiva, who afterwards became the hero of more than one daring adventure, conceived an intense longing to slay the old *jacaré*, for he had once lost a valuable dog through one of these reptiles, and his revenge had not yet been fully satisfied.

Accordingly, when Sunday came, and he was free for the day, he gave out that he intended to do the deed.

He took his double-barrelled pistol, loaded it with several bullets, after the approved Brazilian custom when real business is meant, and embarked alone in a little cedar canoe—the same in which I had been swamped by Messino in a cataract some months before —with the intention of putting his project into execution.

The *jacaré* was asleep on its favourite mud bank, about one hundred yards below the camp. So cautiously did Joaquim approach, that the animal, usually so wary, was not disturbed, but remained snoozing comfortably in the hot sun, little recking what a murderous assault was about to be made upon it. Laying down his paddle softly and gently, Joaquim drew his well-loaded pistol from his belt, and, taking careful aim at the reptile's head from a distance of not more than ten feet, fired. The *jacaré* gave a slight start and then lay quite still, while blood began to slowly issue from the wounds made by the bullets in its head.

Joaquim, highly delighted with his success, beaked the canoe upon the bank, and leaning over the bows got hold of the reptile by its tail and by one of its hind claws, and commenced hauling it on board. He had got the animal partly into the canoe, when to his surprise it began to show very disagreeable symptoms of restored vitality, dashing its tail about in such a manner that he could no longer keep his hold upon it. He still, however, retained possession of the claw, which, by bending it round over the gunwale of the canoe, he was enabled to secure beyond the utmost power of the animal to draw away.

Meantime the canoe had drifted off from the bank into deep water, and now came the tug of war. The *jacaré* was again in its element, and its strength and fury increased every moment, as though its naturally cold and sluggish blood was becoming warmed and quickened by the struggle.

Two men from the camp, seeing the turn of affairs, pushed off to the rescue in another canoe. Before, however, they had time to arrive near enough to render aid, the *jacaré*, finding a direct struggle to escape was useless (for Joaquim was both a plucky and a strong little fellow), changed its tactics, and, suddenly rearing up its head, seized the gunwale of the canoe between its powerful jaws, threatening to tear a great gap in the side. This sudden movement on the part of the *jacaré* caused the frail craft to capsize, and in a moment, as I saw from my station on the bank, both man and reptile disappeared beneath the water.

The former almost immediately reappeared upon the surface, and was hauled into the second canoe, which had now reached the scene of the struggle. The *jacaré*, however, was seen no more, and poor Joaquim, besides the aggrieved sense of defeat, had to bear both the loss of his pistol, which had sunk to the bottom of the river beyond recovery, and also the jeers and jokes of his companions.

The *jacaré* never reappeared in its old haunts. Either it died, or else, astonished and disgusted at the rough and unprovoked treatment which it had received, it had deserted the place.

If cats have nine lives, *jacarés* certainly have twenty. It is almost impossible to kill them by any ordinary means. I once sent a bullet from a big Snider rifle into the back of the head of one of them, at close quarters, and the only apparent effect of this pretty strong treatment was to stir the brute's slow blood up to a frantic pitch of excitement, to which it gave vent by rushing about hither and thither on the surface of the water at a tremendous speed, till a blow from a *varajão* caused it to dive down and disappear beneath the waters. On another occasion I caught a half-grown *jacaré* asleep upon a sandy island, and put no less than three big revolver-bullets into its head before I could quiet it. In spite even of this strong dose, it gave signs of vitality for four hours afterwards.

It was very shortly after his fight with the *jacaré* that Joaquim distinguished himself in an act of skilful daring which won my heart completely.

He was out hunting with me on the river, and a
tapir had been brought down from the forest by the
dogs in the usual manner, at which, after wounding it
rather badly, I could no longer fire, on account of a
cartridge having got jambed into the breach of my
gun, rendering it absolutely useless for the time being.
We continued, however, to hunt the animal with the intention of tiring it out in the water and then despatch-
ing it with our *facões*.   The sport was highly exciting,
and we resolutely determined that our game should
not escape us.   The tapir was still swimming and
diving, while our whole efforts were devoted to prevent
it from getting out of the river on to the bank ; for,
once in the forest, it would have been lost to us.
Seeming at length to divine our object, it all at once
made a determined rush for the side, in order to
land ; approaching so near the bank with that intention, that it did not even take the trouble to dive
when the bow of our canoe, coming up from behind,
actually touched its back.   A sudden splash behind,
and the next thing I saw was Joaquim in the water,
clutching the tapir's ear with one hand, and striking
his knife into its neck with the other.   This was
too much for the animal, which straightway dived,
carrying Joaquim with it.   In a few seconds both
reappeared, Joaquim still clinging like a bull-dog to
the tapir's ear.   Blood was thickly tingeing the water
around them, but whether it proceeded from the man
or from the beast I could not tell.   Still retaining
hold of his long *facão*, I saw Joaquim once more strike

it into the thick neck of the tapir, which again immediately dived. Again, after a few seconds, both reappeared upon the surface, but before I could reach
them with the canoe, they had once more disappeared.
Four times was this repeated, Joaquim never relaxing
his hold, and incessantly digging his knife into the
tapir whenever, by coming up to the surface, his arm
was free to strike. At last the animal became too
exhausted from loss of blood to dive any more. The
struggle was over; the tapir had been conquered in
its own favourite element. When I managed to get
close to them again the latter was on the point of
expiring, being but just able to keep itself on the
surface by a last feeble effort. Joaquim kept his hold
upon it till I came up, and then between us we
managed to secure the dying animal to the canoe rope,
and thus prevent it from sinking.

Joaquim then scrambled on board, and we towed
the animal to the bank, by which time it was quite
dead.

A tapir, though never attacking a man wantonly,
is by no means an antagonist to be despised when
it is itself attacked and brought to bay. Not a few
of our dogs were, at different times, maimed and even
killed by them under these circumstances. The most
remarkable point to be noticed in this particular case,
was the manner in which the man still kept his hold
on the tapir when the latter dived, and managed to
bring it again so soon to the surface. He told me
that what he did was this. The moment he felt the

tapir touch the bottom of the river he pricked him under the belly with his knife, which at once caused the animal to rush up to the surface again, thinking that he had got another enemy beneath him. But for this presence of mind displayed by Joaquim, not all his pluck would have sufficed for the accomplishment of such a victory.

Long as it has taken to narrate this occurrence, probably the whole time, from the moment when Joaquim jumped out of the canoe on to the tapir's back, to the time when he was again safely on board, did not amount to more than two minutes, the whole being one of the most exciting as well as the most novel of all the many tapir hunts in which I ever took a part.

I once attempted, by myself, to capture a deer alive in the river, by seizing it by the horns as it was swimming, thinking that if a tapir could be held by the ear, a deer with about a tenth part of the strength of that animal, could certainly be captured in a somewhat similar manner. I never repeated such an experiment, for the animal almost wrenched my hand off by the sudden jerk or twist that it gave with its neck, and my wrist suffered for weeks after.

One night whilst I was still living in the little camp near which Joaquim had met with his adventure with the *jacaré*, we were visited by a countless army of black stinging ants. I was asleep in my hammock, which, in common with those of the men, was suspended within the one big *rancho* that served to accommodate us all, when I was aroused by a pricking sensation on different parts of my body. At first I thought it was my old enemies the *pulgas* come to pay us a visit in our new camp, but I soon found that the pricks were somewhat sharper than could be inflicted by those diminutive creatures, and the moment that I moved, I found also that they were redoubled both in number and in force. Looking round the *rancho* I saw that most of the Brazilians were awake, and many of them squatting round the fire, which was just within the *rancho*, at the farther end. Such expressions as *"formiga damnada"* and *"formiga do diabo"* caught my ear, which at once explained the nature of the disturbers of the peace.

I put my foot to the ground with-the intention of joining the group at the fire, when in a second it was stung and bitten in a score of places. I had placed it down in the very midst of a thick marching column of ants, some hundreds of which had immediately grappled hold and were now swarming up my leg, stinging and biting viciously as they went. With my hands I swept them off by fifties, and then, without leaving my hammock, struck a match and lit an oil lamp, which stood on the canteen close at hand, in order to survey the enemy.

Immediately beneath the hammock there appeared a broad moving line, consisting of tens of thousands of ants, traversing the *rancho* from one end to the other, off which various narrow lines were branching in different directions ; the space between these latter lines being occupied by individual ants which seemed to be running hither and thither with no apparent aim. These latter were, however, as presently appeared, engaged in the most important work of all, namely, in foraging for supplies.

Seeing how matters were on the ground below, I resolved to remain where I was, for as yet only a few scattered individuals had found their way into my hammock. Soon, however, I found that I was between two fires, for the ants were sending their skirmishers up into the palm leaf thatch above, from whence many were dropping in my hammock, and upon my uncovered head and neck, biting and stinging savagely the moment they came in contact with any part of my body. Looking up, I saw that the whole under surface of the thatch was covered with hundreds of thousands of the little animals, all running about in a state of the greatest activity, the noise of their movements amongst the dry palm-leaves sounding like the rustling of autumn leaves when a wind passes over them.

In order to escape this second peril from above, I dived beneath my blanket, covering myself entirely with its ample folds. The ants, falling upon this, got entangled in the wool, and were thus effectually prevented from pursuing their explorations beneath it. Some few, however, found an entrance by running along the cords by which the hammock was slung, so that I was pretty constantly occupied under the blanket in killing these as fast as they made their presence known by bite or sting. The Brazilians, many of whose hammocks had been invaded *en masse*, had surrounded themselves, where they were now sitting, by a circle of hot ashes, which proved effectual in keeping the space within clear of the ants, excepting those that fell from the roof.

In two hours from the time when this vast army first made its appearance in the *rancho*, not a vestige of it remained, either on the ground or in the roof. Every living individual had followed the onward movement of the broad central column, and departed. Only upon our blankets, where some number of individuals had got themselves hopelessly entangled, did any remain. On the following night we had another visitation from these same ants. As on the first occasion they remained two hours, and then entirely disappeared. I never remember observing these ants except at night, and in vast armies such as I have described. I observed, also, that they generally appeared in the same camp on two consecutive nights, and that the time of their stay was invariably limited to about two hours.

Their marches are not mere mobs, but are regularly organised, and seem to be directed by officers, some of which are seen stationed on either side of the main line of march at short intervals apart, while others accompany the main body. Those which I take to be officers are quite double the size of the individuals forming the main bulk of the army. The stationary officers generally stand up on their hind legs, in which position they appear to both give and receive orders, which are communicated by individuals of the smaller

kind, whose duties seem to be something akin to those
of aides-de-camp. If one of these latter be watched,
he will often be seen to run down the column in an
opposite direction to the general line of march, stopping
for a second or more at each of the big stationary
fellows, and evidently telling him something by means
of quick motions of the antennæ, which are seen to
rapidly play with each other for that brief space of
time.   After communicating in this manner with
several of the officers, the little aide-de-camp will
turn back, and be lost in the general throng of ants
pressing forwards in one direction.

I do not know whether any observer has ever given
a complete account of these ants, with especial reference to the mode and means by which the movements
of their great armies are organised and directed. For
my part, I am convinced of the truth of the common
theory that they converse with each other by means
of *touch*, and that this sense answers to them all the
purposes of a language more or less complex and
intellectual.

The skirmishers or foragers which are thrown out
upon each side of the main column do not extend
their explorations to any great distance, the general
limit being from three to four yards on either side.
Within this limit, however, no living animal organism
escapes them. Grubs, caterpillars, spiders, insects of
all kinds, have either to flee for their lives, or be killed
and torn to pieces. As we have seen, they do not
confine their ravages to *terra firma*. They swarm up

any trees or poles, which happen to lie on their track, to a considerable height. When they come to a *rancho*, no nook or corner of its roof is left unexplored, and the many scores of caterpillars, grubs, and spiders, which have been bred or have taken up their abode in the dry thatch, are routed out and utterly destroyed. Even wasps' nests do not escape, for, on one occasion, a small species of black and yellow wasp, having constructed a nest on the ridge-pole of one of our *ranchos*, these ants entered in the night and entirely destroyed it, so that in the morning there was not a vestige of it remaining. Mr. Bates, in his interesting work, " The Naturalist on the Amazons," gives a very graphic account of the destruction wrought by armies of these ants, amongst the lower animal life. My experience of them in many particulars tallies completely with the accounts that he gives. He, however, makes no mention of their being nocturnal in their habits.

Many travellers in Brazil are accustomed to talk and write of the ants in that country as being one of its principal scourges, especially to the farmer and planter. I venture to think this is too sweeping a denunciation. Carnivorous ants, such as the species just described, cannot but be a great boon to the agriculturist in many instances; destroying, as they do, countless multitudes of caterpillars, and other insect larvæ, which, were they allowed to live and multiply, would prove destructive to all vegetation. Everybody knows what a ruinous effect the wholesale destruction of small birds had at one time in certain

countries of Europe, and how speedily the farmers
discovered their mistake, when their crops and their
fruit-trees were devoured by the superabundance of
insect vermin, which rose up in the land. If the
carnivorous ants—and I believe that the great majority
of ants in Brazil are carnivorous—were destroyed,
supposing such destruction were possible, it is safe to
assert that the injury that would accrue to the farmers
and planters would be disastrous. For, in such a
country as Brazil, insect life is marvellously fecund;
and therefore, without the ceaseless war that is for
ever being carried on against it in all its stages by
countless myriads of ants, not a planter but would be
eaten out of his estate in a year. For my part I
always feel deeply grateful to the ant tribe in Brazil.
Without their counteracting influence, the forests, for
at least half the year, would be absolutely uninhabit-
able and even unenterable by any human being.
Even as it is, the plague of insect vermin in the
summer season is terrible enough, as I have sufficiently shown, and any addition to it would be quite
intolerable.

There is, however, one kind of ant, known as the
Saüba ant, which might, I think, with advantage be
improved off the face of the earth. We used frequently
to meet with it in the forest, winding along the ground
in a long narrow line, each individual toiling under
the load of a great piece of leaf, four or five times
bigger than itself, which it had robbed from some
distant tree, and was now bearing away to its colony

in another part of the forest. The funny part is to
see these ants carrying the leaves vertically and not
horizontally. When I first saw them, and noticed
their leaf-carrying propensities, I knew little or nothing
about their economy of life. I used to fancy, from the
fact of their being more frequently seen carrying the
leaves during the rains than during the dry season,
that their idea was to shelter themselves from the rain
by means of these leaves during their marches ; and I
wondered why they so stupidly persisted in carrying
the leaves in the manner which afforded the least protection. Mr. Bates discovered, after long investigation,
the exact use to which these leaves were put. He
says, " the leaves are used to thatch the domes which
cover the entrances to their subterraneous dwellings,
thereby protecting from the deluging rains the young
broods in the nests beneath." His general account of
these ants and their wonderful engineering works is
most interesting. Notwithstanding the havoc they
make in plantations by stripping the young trees of
their leaves, there is no doubt that even these ants
destroy a certain amount of injurious insect vermin,
though it can scarcely be denied that, on the whole,
this particular species is more of a curse than a blessing
upon cultivated lands.

Speaking of ants brings me naturally to the subject
of the great destroyers of these insects, the *Taman-
doás*, or Ant-bears. The chief of these is the *Tamandoá Bandeira*, a specimen of which may now be seen
at the Zoological Gardens in London. I have already

referred to this species of *Tamandoá*, and suggested a possible use to which it might put its wonderful tail. Next to this remarkable appendage, the most curious parts of the animal are (1st) its elongated head and muzzle, containing a tongue nearly a yard in length, by which it is said to lick up the ants from their nests by fifties at a time, and (2nd) the enormous claw or talon with which each of its powerful forelimbs is armed. This claw, when the animal is walking, folds up underneath the pad of the foot or hand, its point fitting into a small sunken orifice which exists, apparently for this very purpose, in the back part of the pad.

I once had a long chase in the forest after a *Tamandoá Bandeira*, which was being hunted by one of our dogs. I had no weapon with me but a revolver, and therefore it was some time before I dared to risk a shot at the animal, on account of the dog incessantly getting in the way. Sometimes it ran on all fours, and at other times on its hind legs alone. Each mode of progression seemed more awkward to it than the other, and I could scarcely believe that it was a terrestial animal. Its powerful and well armed forelimbs are used, it is said, for pulling to pieces the hard dome-shaped structures of the white ant, upon which insect, we are told, it principally feeds. I never, myself, came across any nest of this ant in the forests of the Ivahy, and yet the *Tamandoá Bandeira* was frequently seen and killed by us. In default of white ants, why should not the claws be employed for tearing open a passage into the bees' nests situated in the hollow trunks of trees, the long tongue for inserting itself into the deeper recesses of the nest where the honey lies, and the tail, as before suggested, in warding off the attacks of the bees themselves from without, for which purposes it is most admirably adapted?

The Brazilians say that the Ant-bear is sometimes a match for the Jaguar himself, and that instances have been known of the latter having been found dead in the embrace of the former, from which he had been unable to free himself even after the death of his would-be prey.

On the evening of the 27th of April, being then encamped about five miles above the Salto do Ubá, we had a mysterious visit from some animal, which boldly entered the *rancho*, in which not only I, but all the men of my party were sleeping, and carried off a leg of venison, from which I had but half an hour before been dining. We had on this day no dogs with us, they having gone on to the camp which was now being built at the Salto do Ubá. My hammock and that of Miles were slung at one end of the *rancho*, while at the other end a big camp-fire was burning, around which the remainder of the party were sitting or sleeping.

It was about an hour after sunset. I was dozing in my hammock, and Miles was snoring in his. Between us on the ground stood my canteen, upon which were the remnants of dinner, consisting chiefly of the leg of venison, and two or three iron plates, knives and

forks.   On another box close to my side, my rifle and
an oil lamp were placed.

The dishes all at once clattered.   I looked, but it
was too dark to make anything out, for the fire was
at the other end of the *rancho* several yards off.
Again the dishes clattered.   This time I got up and lit
the lamp, and then discovered that the leg of venison
was gone.   No animal could be seen; but I waited
for perhaps an hour with my rifle on my knees, in the
hope that, whatever it was, it would return.   Nothing,
however, appearing, I put my rifle down and went to
sleep, first letting the men on watch know what had
occurred.   The following day I went out on the *picada,*
and thought no more about the matter, except that I
regretted the loss of a good leg of venison, which, now
that I had no dog with me, was not likely soon to be
replaced.   When evening came, I returned to camp;
and after dinner turned in to my hammock, according to my usual habit, to enjoy a well-earned pipe.
Miles had also turned in, and the lamp was burning
between us.   " Sir, sir, there he is again."   I had
just been talking to Miles about the nocturnal visitor
of the previous evening, and wondering whether it
would appear again this night, so I had no difficulty
in understanding to what the " he " referred.   I looked
and saw an animal which appeared to me to be about
the size of a dog, slowly walking across the field of
view shed by the lamp, about eight yards off.   My
rifle was loaded and lying close beside me.   I took it
up, and, without raising myself from my recumbent

position, cocked it and took aim. At the click of the
spring the animal stopped and looked towards me.
At that moment I fired, and then bounded out of the
hammock to the spot where I had last seen the
animal. It was not there. Only the track of the
bullet in the ground, where it had torn up the loose
soil on the surface, was visible. I was much discom-
fited at not having killed the beast, whatever it was,
and after standing about for two or three minutes with
Miles and some of the Brazilians who had been
turned out by the shot, speculating with them as to
what the visitor could have been, turned into my
hammock again. I did not at once lie down, but
remained in a sitting position in the hammock,
examining the rifle, and regretting that I had not got
my gun, with which it was more easy to take aim at
night. Certainly, not five minutes had elapsed since
the report of the rifle had gone ringing and echoing
away into the forest, when Miles, who again was
sharper-eyed than myself, said "there he is again,
sir," and, to my astonishment, there was the same
animal walking slowly and stealthily towards us, as
though nothing had happened. The movement of my
arm to put the rifle to my shoulder caused it as before
to halt in its tracks. By the dim uncertain light of the
lamp I took the best aim I could, and gently touched
the trigger. This time there had been no mistake;
the big bullet had flown true to its mark, and when I
again reached the spot, there was the animal lying
dead on the ground, the ball having pierced its fore-

head. It was none other than my old friend the
Jacuterica, or "Painted Ocelot," whose barefaced
marauding propensities were now well known to us.

The extreme boldness of this individual was probably
due to the fact of its having a family in the forest close
by, dependent upon its exertions; for it was a female,
lean and gaunt to a skeleton.

The chief food of the Ocelot is the *Jacu* (Penelope),
which, as before stated, is very abundant in these
forests, and as easy of destruction as a barn-door
fowl. The presence of our expedition had the effect
of considerably diminishing the number of these birds
round their favourite resorts on the banks of the river,
and as a necessary consequence the various species of
Ocelots, which preyed upon them, found their sources
of supply grievously diminished. Hence their boldness in entering our camps at night, and robbing us
from under our very noses.

CHAPTER XIV.

Things problematical— A new project. — Lying agents. — The Ubá
Camp.—" Tempora mutantur."—Homeric feasts.—Fishing.—The
Dourado, king of fishes.—The Urú.—Death of the Toucan.—An
acquaintance commenced.

NOTHING had been heard by us of our fellow-workers
of the 3rd and 4th Staffs since their arrival at Miranda,
now more than eight months ago.

When Captain Palm left us early in September of
the preceding year, in order to visit these Staffs, it
had not then been definitely decided how far the
exploration of the 2nd Staff should proceed; whether
it should terminate at a point called the Corredeira de
Ferro, or " Iron Rapid," whichw as supposed to be the
last obstruction to free navigation existing on the
river Ivahy, and, therefore, the extreme point to
which the proposed railway would run, or, whether
it should be carried on by water as far as the Paraná
river itself. This point had probably been decided
when Captain Palm met the 3rd and 4th Staffs at
Miranda, after leaving Colonia Theréza, but owing to
the great misfortune of his sudden death, we were

still in ignorance of what decision had been arrived at between them. In round numbers the Corredeira de Ferro was 300 miles distant from Colonia Theréza; the mouth of the Ivahy, or, in other words, the Paraná river, being no less than 100 miles beyond this, that is to say, 400 miles from Colonia Theréza.

Thus a knowledge of the arrangements that had been made on this point was of some importance to us of the 2nd Staff, seeing that there was involved a difference in the length of our section, of as much as 100 miles.

As time went on, and we progressed farther and farther into the wild unknown country before us, the distance between us and Colonia Theréza ever increasing, we found, as was to be expected, that our troubles with the *camaradas* grew in proportion. It seemed very problematical whether the assistance of which we were so much in need would ever be forthcoming, and therefore it became necessary that we should, while there was yet time, devise some plan by which we might, if necessity demanded it, without any assistance whatever, carry the exploration safely through to the end. It did not require much wisdom on our part to foresee, that before very long a point would be reached when the friction of the ways and means would exactly neutralize the power of progression, unless, before that point was reached, power was added in the shape of assistance from without, or friction was removed by some radical change in the plan of operations hitherto pursued. Despairing of the first from many disappointments, we set ourselves to work upon the second.

Without attempting to lead the reader through the long reasoning process by which at length we arrived at what seemed to be a fair solution of the problem that now beset us, I may in a few words explain what that solution was. Briefly and broadly stated, it was this. The absolute reversal of the direction of the exploration, that, is to say, instead of continuing our present course, by which we were daily moving farther and farther from our base of supplies, we resolved to reverse it by first making a bold dash for the most distant extremity of the line to be explored, namely, to the river Paraná itself, and from thence to work upwards, towards instead of away from our supplies.

The obvious recommendation of this plan would be that the friction, to use the same figure of speech as before, of the ways and means, instead of constantly increasing, would be continually diminishing, in proportion as progress was made. The chief difficulty would evidently lie in the starting of the machine. Once set in motion it was but reasonable to suppose that, no longer being retarded by ever-increasing difficulties, it would gather strength as it progressed onwards, and not stop till its whole course had been fully run.

The preparations for the carrying out of this project would necessarily take some time, for at present our supplies both of men and material were very insuf-

ficient. It was now the beginning of the month of
May, and it was thought that by the end of July or
beginning of August the way might be sufficiently
paved to allow of the first start for the Paraná being
effected. Side by side with the making of the preparations, it was intended to carry on the exploration in
its present direction, till a certain point marked on the
map as the Salto d'Areranha was attained. Here it
was proposed to establish and keep up a large depôt of
provisions and stores, which in fact would form a new
base of operations some 100 miles nearer to us than
the present one at Colonia Theréza. Turning to the
accompanying map, it will be seen that there is a
point, about another 100 miles down the Ivahy, called
Villa Rica. This point marks the termination of a
long and dangerous series of cataracts, which lie
between it and the Salto d'Areranha. Here again
it was decided to establish another depôt. Yet
100 miles farther down the river, at the point marked
as the Corredeira de Ferro, a third and final depôt
was to be established, unless, before that time came,
news should reach us that the 4th Staff, to whom
the river surveys generally had been entrusted, had
been told off to relieve us of the survey of the
Ivahy below the Corr^a de Ferro. I may here, for
the sake of brevity, anticipate a little the course of
events, and say that the 4th Staff did so relieve us
of that portion of the work, and thus the necessity
for the establishment of the third depôt was done
away with.

In addition to these depôts it was proposed to keep up a constant transport service by means of canoes along the whole line from Colonia Theréza, to the extreme point at which the surveying party might be working at any given moment. This arrangement, if sufficient means or, in other words, a sufficient number of men and canoes could be obtained to carry it on, would be theoretically perfect; for, by starting, in the first place, with a full three months' supply of provisions at each depôt, irregularities in the canoe service, such as would at times be unavoidably brought about by floods in the river, accidents in the rapids, or other possible or probable causes, would have no immediate effect upon the working staff, which would still be able to continue drawing supplies from the nearest depôt.   At the same time, the reserve supplies at the depôts would be more or less constantly kept up by the transport service, which, like a stream flowing into a tank, would be continually, though perhaps irregularly, from the causes just mentioned, pouring in fresh supplies to them from above, to counteract the constant drain which would ever be going on from below.

It was not to be expected that the men who had already once compelled us to raise their rate of pay, on account of the increasing distance, and consequently increasing dangers and hardships of the exploration, would tamely submit to accompany us another 200 or 300 miles deeper into the wilds, without making a hard struggle to obtain a still further advance.   I may

again anticipate events by saying that in the end we
obtained their adhesion to the new project, by giving
in to another small rise of twelve and a half per cent. in
their wages, making therefore twenty-five per cent. as
the total increase upon the original pay of the canoe
men. This under the circumstances must be considered a very moderate imposition. It is certain that,
had we not given ourselves plenty of time, from May
to August, in which to arrange with the men, they
would have compelled us to have about doubled their
pay. This, in fact, was what they stood out for at first,
till Curling went himself a month's journey into other
parts of the province, and collecting a large number of
men, chiefly from the towns of Guarapuava and
Tibagy, returned with them to the Staff. Curling
took advantage of this opportunity to establish an
agency at the town of Tibagy, for the supply both of
men and stores to the expedition. Though successful as regards the latter requirement, this agency
failed entirely in regard to the former. In a country
like Brazil, where lying is a recognised commercial
institution, without the aid of which no native dreams
of transacting any important business, it is very difficult
to ascertain the true reason of the non-fulfilment of
any engagement. Our agent declared that in this
instance, the priests had worked against him, and
prevented the men, whom he had engaged for us, from
coming. I should think, of all Roman Catholic
countries in the world, Brazil is the least under the
influence of the priesthood. Indeed, in the province

of Paraná, of which I more especially speak, the
Padres have absolutely no influence at all with the
masses of the people, whilst by the more educated
classes they are held in the greatest contempt.* It
is the landed proprietors, or large fazendeiros, who
alone have influence with the Caboclo class from
which our camaradas were drawn; and it was unfortunately the case that our agent was closely connected with this landed class, which, as a rule,
has the greatest objection to labour being drafted
away from its neighbourhood. This, I have no
doubt, was the true explanation of the failure of our
agency at Tibagy to obtain men. The *will* was
absent.

The relations which exist between the two classes,
the large landed proprietor or *fazendeiro,* and the
caboclo or labourer (I use this term in default of a
better) will be more fully explained in the sequel.
At this time, however, we were ourselves ignorant in
these matters, and fully believed our agent's plea of
the priestly influence having been exerted against us.

To return, however, from these digressions.

On the 1st of May I found myself once more at the
Salto d'Ubá. The axe had been at work on the right

* If it is true of Europeans generally, as has been affirmed, that on
going out to Brazil, they pitch their consciences overboard at the
"line," more particularly is it true with the Italian priests, who
come like hirelings to the country, and lead such lives, in very many
cases, as to make their name a bye-word of contempt. Perhaps, however, the province of Paraná may be unusually unfortunate in its
experiences in this respect.

bank at the head of the falls, and a large clearing had been made, where before the only sign of man's presence had been the solitary Indian path winding through the dark, still forest. *Ranchos* also had been built, and, in short, another little colony had sprung up in the wilds.

Curling and I inhabited a hut which closely fronted the river, so that, when sitting at the table within it, working or at meals, we could see all that was going on in the wide bay which, as before described, stood at the head of the falls.

One of our favourite amusements consisted in practising with our rifles at the otters frequently to be seen sunning themselves on the rocks about 250 yards distant. If we ever hit them, we certainly never had a chance of bagging them, for they slipped off the rocks at the flash of the rifle, and were generally under water before the bullet could have had time to traverse the long intervening distance.

The early mornings were cold and generally foggy, the thermometer going down to perhaps 45° Fahr. We invariably turned out at sunrise, and, wrapped in our ample blankets, sat by the camp-fire, warming ourselves and sipping hot coffee, till all lingering drowsiness had departed, after which the day's work would commence.

We did not breakfast till about 11 o'clock, when a repast, which would have won the hearts of even Homer's lordly revellers, was usually served up. Fish of many kinds, from the delicate sprat-like *Alambari* to the kingly *Dourado,* or Brazilian salmon, first appeared. Huge ribs of tapir, or haunches of venison followed; for game was at this time so abundant in the neighbourhood of the Salto, that it was only necessary to take the dogs across the river to the opposite side of the bay, and land them there on the bank, to make sure of a tapir, or deer, being brought to the water within an hour. On two or three occasions we were able to shoot our dinner without leaving the camp, or at most were but obliged to get into a canoe, and paddle a few hundred yards to obtain it. The bay proved a regular trap to the tapirs, for, with a long rapid immediately above it, and a roaring cataract below, there was very little chance of escape, except by returning to the forest, and there were always enough guns and dogs at hand to prevent this.

Fish were equally abundant, and were to be caught in great variety. In the still deep pools of the bay, the fat and sleek *Surubims* crowded the bottoms. *Cascudos* in great numbers were captured nightly in our nets; and close to the landing-place, the delicious little *Alambaris** could at certain times be pulled out of the water as fast as hook could be baited and thrown in.

The grandest fish of all, and the only one that afforded real sport, was the *Dourado.* Curling was an

---

* These fish are about the size of whitebait, and of even superior flavour. The most taking bait was plain dough, a tiny ball of which put on the point of the hook, was usually all-sufficient.

enthusiastic fisherman, and we used daily to go together to the foot of the falls, where the water was
swift and broken, provided with large steel hooks,
several sizes bigger than a butcher's meat hook, attached to stout fishing lines and baited with junks
of fresh deer and tapir meat, and there fish for our
breakfast.

The *dourados* were not too plentiful or too easily
caught to cause the pleasure of this sport to grow stale,
as that of tapir hunting had now to a certain extent
become.   One fish per hour on ordinary occasions was
good work, and an unskilful fisherman could seldom
land more than this.

Owing to the fact of the *dourado* being essentially
a carnivorous, not to say bloodthirsty monster, we
were, on occasions, enabled to land more than 100
pounds weight of the fish in the course of a short morning's work.   When, for example, a tapir or deer had
been killed below the falls, we had nothing to do but
to bring the body up to the middle of the fishing
ground, and there disembowel it.   The *dourados* tast-
ing the blood as it was disseminating far and wide
down stream, would rush up by the score to the scene
of operations, eager to get a taste of the fresh-killed
meat.   Plenty of hooks and lines were, on such occasions, in readiness for them, and they got themselves
caught with the most astonishing rapidity, for as long
a time as the blood continued to taint the water and
excite their appetites.

Now and then in the midst of the scene of excitement thus caused, an otter would boldly come up and share in the sport; seizing perhaps a fish, which was already caught upon a hook, and making away with the best part of its body, leaving the head only hanging upon the line.

The colour of the *dourado* is black and gold, and it is by far the handsomest, as well as the gamest fish in the river. Its favourite localities are at the immediate foot of the larger cataracts and falls, where the water is swift and turbulent. It grows to an enormous size, one having been killed by a member of the expedition that weighed eighty-four pounds. An epicure would certainly go into ecstacies over a *dourado's* head, the substance upon which very much resembles the flesh of turtle.

The romantic beauty of the scenery in whose midst the fishing-ground lay, added much pleasure to the sport. The river in this part was split up by islands into numerous little channels, down which, between walls of sweet smelling flowers, and overhung by the feathery tops of the graceful *Ubá* reed, the water, still white with the foam from the Salto above, rippled and sparkled like a thing of life, over its clear bed of rock or gravel. The absolute perfection of climate, which now, at this time, ruled, and the complete sense of wild freedom in all the surroundings, gave also a charm that cannot be described.

Besides fish and big game, there was another very delicate dish that occasionally appeared upon our table. This was a bird, something like a small partridge in appearance, called *Urú*, an Indian word of the meaning of which I am ignorant.

This bird we had not before encountered. Indeed, it is never to be found except in the immediate proximity of the bigger falls and cataracts. It runs about upon the ground in coveys of from eight to a dozen individuals. When disturbed, the birds generally fly up from the ground, one after the other, with loud twitterings, and settle for a minute or two upon the low bushes and shrubs around, after which they fly a few yards and again drop down upon the ground. Their habits are insectivorous. They never leave the shelter of the forest, and, as far as I know, never go farther inland from the bank of their especial cataract, than from fifty to a hundred yards. Of what nature the peculiar attraction of a cataract is to the *Urú* I cannot guess, unless it is that the food upon which it lives is found only in such neighbourhoods, and not in any other localities.

It would not be difficult to kill a whole covey of them off in a day, for they never fly more than half a dozen yards, trusting for safety more to concealment by crouching on the ground, than to any powers of leg or wing. Like children playing hide and seek, one bird is sure, before many minutes, to betray its presence by a nervous twitter, which is then taken up by all the others ; and then they lose their presence of mind, and fly up on to the small bushes again, presumedly to see who or what their disturber is.

I remained at the Salto d'Ubá ten days, and this

was the most enjoyable time of the whole three years that I spent in Brazil.

I had almost forgotten to make mention of a sad event which occurred on the first day of my arrival. This was the death of the toucan. The poor bird had been a faithful and amusing companion to me for a long time, and I felt real sorrow when it died. A coroner's jury, sitting upon it, would have been justified in bringing in a verdict of *felo de se*, for the cause of death was apoplexy brought about by persistent over-eating. It habitually devoured more than its own weight of food every day.

On the 2nd of June, Curling once again left the Staff on an expedition up country to obtain men and supplies. On the 7th, I left our beautiful camp at the Ubá for another spot twenty miles lower down the river, where a new depôt-camp was building at the head of the great falls of the Areranha.*

Having been delayed *en route* by a tapir hunt, we did not reach our new destination till an hour or more after sunset, when it was already quite dark. In reply to our signals made while we were groping our way close in under one bank, ignorant of the exact position of the camp, men with flaming bundles of dry bamboo stems appeared above us to guide us to the landing place.

---

* The *Salto de Areranha* is the largest single obstruction that exists on the Ivahy. It has a total fall, at low water, of about thirty-three feet in a distance of 800 yards. In time of floods the height of the fall is much reduced, owing to the tendency such obstructions have to "level up," when the flow of water over them is from any cause increased.

By the lurid light of these torches and with the din
of the great *Salto* sounding preternaturally loud in
the stillness of the evening, I commenced my acquaintance with a sport destined to be the scene of the most
startling, as well as of some of the most painful events
in the history of the expedition.

CHAPTER XV.

DAY of the year, August the 16th. Time, 8 P.M. Scene, a palm-*rancho* at the Areranha Camp. Dramatis personæ,—Luco a Caioá Indian, and self.

"The doctor does not know what these expeditions are," Luco was saying.

"Never mind, I shall soon learn; and besides I want to see for myself what sort of fellows these are who are making cowards of us all."

"The doctor will be very tired—we shall be two, three, perhaps four days in the woods."

"*Naò e nada*—we will take provisions with us to keep our strength up for that time. How many men shall we want?"

"Six or seven *Camaradas boms* will be enough."

"Very well, choose your own men and send them in to me at daybreak for 'powder, and we will start to-morrow morning."

Luco having finished his cigarette and *pinga* of

cachaça, rose up to go.   "*Então até amanhãa, Sr. doutor.*"

"*Até amanhãa Luco,* remember it is settled!"

"*Está bom,*" and in another minute I was left alone in the *rancho* to my solitary cogitations.

It will be necessary to go back a little way in order to find the key to this conversation.

Several weeks had elapsed since the event spoken of at the conclusion of the last chapter. Many things had happened since then. A new assistant had at length been sent to us from Rio de Janeiro. The first jaguar had been killed, having been caught prowling round one of the *ranchos* late one evening and shot dead by Armstrong, the storekeeper.

The survey had been completed up to the Salto d'Areranha, and the first start, in accordance with our new scheme of work, for Villa Rica and the Corredeira de Ferro, had been made. Curling and Vander Meulen (our new companion) had both gone down the river *en route* for these points, taking with them half-a-dozen or more canoes and about five and twenty men. A *roça* was being prepared opposite the camp, as an additional safeguard against future shortness of supplies, which would, at the same time, afford employment for the men who were ultimately to be left in charge of the depôt.

I remained at the Areranha which had now become the key position of our whole long line of communications.

All would have been well but for one cause of

anxiety, and this, unfortunately, a grave one. Within the last few days the old bugbear of the *Bugré brabo* had been suddenly, though not altogether unexpectedly, resuscitated. A wild Indian had been seen by one of the *camaradas* who had gone into the forest at the rear of the camp to bring in fire-wood. He had raised an alarm, and the other Brazilians in the camp at the time had turned out in a body, with pistols cocked and knives drawn, and rushed into the forest in pursuit. Of course the poor *Bugré* had fled, and after a time the men returned, having seen nothing. Whether true or false this incident was the commencement of a panic, which from that day grew and developed at an alarming rate.

But two days before the conversation with which this chapter opened took place, two men had applied for permission to return up the river to their houses, on the plea of sickness. Their request, however, having been refused,—the sham being palpable,— on the following morning it was discovered that a canoe was missing, and with it, these same two men. The several watches, which since the supposed appearance of the Indian spy had been doubled, when interrogated, declared that they had heard nothing and knew nothing. It was very evident, then, that the two men had fled, and, what was more important still, that the remainder could not be depended upon, but might, and probably would, themselves desert before long under the influence of example and fear.

To allow the present state of uncertainty as to

the Indians to continue, to know nothing of their
number, their intentions, or even as to what tribe
they belonged to,—for there was no doubt from the
reports brought in from time to time by our scouts,
that we were well within the borders of an Indian
country,—was clearly playing into the hands of the
timid and discontented, till in the end the whole lot
would turn tail and flee up the river.

Such were the circumstances, then, under which
it was decided to make a bold effort to stop the growing panic, once and for all; or, at least, to prove that
it was justifiable, and not to permit the expedition to
be ruined by the mere shadow of danger.

Luco* was the one man with us who was thoroughly
acquainted with all the ways and habits of wild
Indians; for his whole previous life had been one
long series of adventures with them. He, too, stood
almost alone in not giving way to the general tone of
panic which was now existing in camp. Upon him,
therefore, my choice had fallen to carry out a plan
that should cut at the very root of the panic, which
seemed to me to be the offspring of sheer ignorance
as to the nature and possible intentions of the Indians
around us.

This plan was a very simple one. It was to make
an expedition into the forest for the purpose of
finding out all we could about these wild Indians,
and, if possible, to establish some friendly relations.

* See Appendix, note H., "*Luco the Caió.*"

with them. This was the expedition which Luco
had implied would be no child's play for those who
undertook it, and upon which I was resolved to go.
Apart from the important results which I did not
doubt it would yield, there was a smack of "Cooperian"
adventure about it quite different from that of our
everyday hunting or exploring expeditions, which to
me was very enticing.

In the morning, at the appointed time, six men,
whom Luco, according to instructions, had picked
out to form the party, entered my *rancho* all ready
girt for the start; and fine fellows they looked with
their legs bared up to the knee, and feet broad and
spreading, each toe standing out straight and sturdy,
undeformed by boot or sandal.

Luco himself soon after came in. He looked the
perfect model of a backwoodsman. Like the others
he was free from all clothing that might in any way
impede freedom of motion. His sole garments were
a thin cotton shirt, a pair of *ceroulas,* or cotton
drawers, turned up above the knee, and a short apron
of untanned otter skin, secured round the waist by a
broad leathern belt, into which were stuck the usual
short double-barrelled pistol, and the long broad-
bladed *facão,* useful alike for picking out a thorn,
cutting down a tree, or giving the *coup de grâce* to a
wild beast. His remaining equipments were a striped
fawn-skin pouch in which were carried flint and steel
and tobacco, suspended from the belt, and a strip of
red cloth or baize flung over one shoulder and tied

loosely beneath the opposite arm, to serve as a blanket. at night.

My own equipments were necessarily more elaborate,. and included a strong pair of English shooting boots, surmounted by short deer skin gaiters for protection against thorns. Instead, too, of the double-barrelled pistol of the Brazilian, one of Daw's big-bore, central-fire six-shooters hung from my belt, side by side with a long steel-bladed hunting knife. A short Snider rifle with a pouch-full of cartridges completed my defensive outfit.

All being ready and the last instructions having been given to those who remained in camp, our little party of eight men started on its wild expedi-tion.

Immediately behind the camp there was a lofty mountain ridge, covered with open forest, which rose to perhaps 800 feet above the level of the river, at the point at which we intended to cross it. Through this forest there were many paths, some made by ourselves, and others by the wild Indians whom we were on our way to seek. The two men, whom we had before employed as scouts, were both with us, and one of them now acted as guide.

Slowly we filed up the long slope of the mountain, winding in and out amongst giant *pirobas*, stately cedars and huge ungainly looking *figueiros*. The silence of the forest was broken only by the sweet melancholy note of the *pomba*, which was heard now near, and now far, seeming never to come twice in succession from the same place, but always on the move, like the note of our own cuckoo. Presently, as the sun began to dispel the morning fog, the hoarse croak of the toucan also began to make itself heard, hailing in its own fashion the source of life from some tall tree top.

We wasted no words on these or on any other of the familiar sights and sounds of the forest, which, as the day advanced, successively greeted us. We marched steadily on, following an old Indian *picada*, which our guide said would bring us a little before midday to a small deserted Indian *schosse* or hunting *rancho*, which he and his companion had discovered on one of their earlier scouting expeditions.

Hour after hour the march continued, seldom a word being spoken by anyone of the party. Only now and then when some particularly inviting streamlet crossed our path was a momentary halt made, when each man, after first rinsing out his mouth, would lap up a little water with his hand, swallow it, and pass on. Once and only once did anything worthy of notice cause us to halt for more than a minute. A stream that we crossed was observed to be charged with thick yellow mud, whereas all the others had been perfectly clear. A slight consultation was held, the result of which was that most of the men agreed that the mud was caused by nothing more important than pigs, which had crossed the stream at some point higher up, and by so doing, stirred up the clayey bottom and rendered the water dirty for a certain distance below. Soon after this we actually came across fresh tracks of pigs, showing that the opinion of the Brazilians was in all probability correct.

About midday we arrived at the *schosse*, which was a tiny bamboo hut, situated close to a small *barreiro*. It had evidently been intended as a place of concealment from whence the *Bugrés* might shoot their arrows at the animals and birds that came to eat the *barreiro* earth. No signs of recent use however appeared, and we therefore sat down to rest for a short time and to refresh ourselves with beans and farinha, which, with a little deer meat already cooked and chopped up, was the only kind of food we carried with us.

It was now that we expected our real work to commence. Up to the present the march, though long and tedious, had not been hindered or hampered by the necessity of any great caution. The ground we had been traversing had already been trodden more than once by our scouts and we were tolerably sure that no Indians would be found in this part of the forest. We did not make a long halt at the *schosse*, but as soon as the cravings of nature had been satisfied, belts were tightened and once more the march continued.

Luco himself now led; for the scout, who had hitherto guided us, knew nothing of the country into which we were entering. Neither indeed did Luco, but his knowledge of forest lore was superior to that

of any of the other men of the party, and this was
what was now chiefly needed. We were winding
through a thick cane covert by a path which seemed
well used; though being very low and narrow, it
obliged us continually to go in a stooping position,
most fatiguing to the body. Every now and then
Luco would stop for a moment and examine some
twig or leaf, then go forward again, apparently with
renewed zest. I was walking immediately behind
him, the other six men following in close order.

Perhaps two hours had passed in this manner since
we had started from the *schosse*. We had left the
cane brake and were now moving along a path
through more open forest. Luco had once or twice
pointed out to me freshly broken twigs, showing that
Bugrés had lately passed along it. As we proceeded,
his eagerness seemed to increase, and I found it
difficult, heavily equipped as I was, to keep up with
him. All at once he turned round and said : " There
are *Bugrés* close in front, running before us."

He had suspected this for the last half hour, which
accounted for the eagerness that I had noticed. Some
sign, to me utterly imperceptible, had now it seemed
convinced him beyond a doubt that such really was
the case.

We all increased our pace to a sort of slouching
run—the quickest motion which the peculiar nature
of the *picada* would permit of—for we had once more
come into a thick cane brake which would not allow
us to run upright in it. In other respects the *picada*

had been carefully laid out by the *Bugrés* in order to avoid as much as possible all steep and rough ground.

For a quarter of an hour or perhaps rather more, we continued running. We had again left the cane-jungle and were now passing through a bamboo under-growth, which was rapidly becoming more and more open as we advanced. Great pines also, here and there, appeared, towering up above the other trees, a sure token that we were approaching some more open part of the forest.

Luco all at once stopped short.

" What is it, Luco ? "

" Don't you smell, *patrão* ? "

" No, what ? "

" *Fogo*—Fire. We are near some encampment."

Luco again went forward though now at a slower and more cautious pace. Presently he stopped once more.

" *Estamos pertinhos.* We are very close now ; I go on alone."

Without waiting for a reply, he loosed the red cloth which he had hitherto worn round his shoulders, and letting it drop off on to the ground so as to be perfectly unencumbered, advanced silently and stealthily, and was almost immediately concealed from our view by a bend in the *picada*.

We all stood still in our tracks waiting silently for his return. The smell of fire was now perceptible enough to us all. We waited for long minutes that seemed hours, and still Luco did not return. In-

action was becoming painful. I strained both eyes
and ears to catch the slightest sign of anything, and
my heart was pumping to such an extent with the
excitement of suspense, as to render breathing difficult. We were now to all intents and purposes,
hunting wild men, and what excitement can be
greater than this ? A tapir or even a jaguar hunt
is tame in comparison. Still no sign of either *Bugré*
or Luco. The only sound was the buzz of an
occasional mosquito in one's ear.

At length Luco reappeared, returning as suddenly
and silently as he had gone.

"Well, Luco, speak! what have you discovered?"

"A small clearing with a *rancho* and a fire in the
middle of it."

"Any *Bugrés* ?"

"*Não sei, não vi.* I don't know, I saw none."

"What are we to do, Luco ?"

"There may possibly be *Bugrés* in the *rancho,*
though I do not think we shall find any. The tribe
is 'Botocudo.' They will run if they can, but if
not, they will fight. The *rancho* is very small; it
cannot contain more than six or seven *Bugrés;* we
can capture them without fighting."

"How?"

"By making a rush all together at the *rancho.* If
any *Bugrés* are there they will be taken by surprise,
and we shall capture them easily."

Our plans were soon made, and, led by Luco, we
once more advanced, each man, however, now leaving

his blanket and the provisions he was carrying on the *picada*, so as to allow more freedom of action.

I could not help observing that the men who in camp had shown themselves so susceptible to vague fears of these very Indians upon whom we were on the point of ourselves initiating an attack—though, of course, we intended to inflict no harm upon them —were now absolutely free from fear, as far as could be judged by their words and manner.

After a cautious advance of about five minutes Luco again stopped. "We are quite close: the *rancho* is not five *braças* (ten yards) off in that direction," pointing as he spoke between two great pines which rose up tall and straight just before us. "The edge of the clearing is here." We closed up our files and, at a given signal, rushed forward in a body.

There was the little *rancho*, as Luco had described it, with smoke rising up through its dome-shaped roof. In a moment we had reached and surrounded it, bursting our way into the interior through the yielding bamboo sides, for doorway or opening there was none to be seen.

Alas! our hopes were disappointed—the *rancho* was perfectly empty. A stone axe was lying upon the hard beaten floor, and a few gourds were suspended from the blackened roof. The fire appeared as though it had been replenished perhaps not more than an hour before our arrival. Luco was right when he said *Bugrés* were running before us. We had evidently been discovered while on the trail, and the inhabitants of the *rancho*, being warned of our approach, had hurriedly fled.

I had opportunity now of examining the whole place carefully.

The clearing was very small—less than twenty yards in diameter. The *rancho* was placed nearly in the centre. It was dome-shaped, thus differing from the Coroado *ranchos*, and was constructed entirely of bamboo. The apex of it was only seven feet high inside, and the diameter at the bottom not more than nine feet. There had, apparently, originally been two small openings close to the ground for the *Bugrés* to crawl in and out at; our rush had however increased their dimensions perhaps four fold. The *rancho* appeared to be about two years old and, from the continual fires inside it, the whole inner surface of the dome was covered with a shiny black glaze, which gave an almost metallic appearance to the bamboo ribs or framework.

At one end of the clearing was a large white-looking heap, which, on closer inspection, proved to be composed entirely of bones. This heap I somewhat carefully examined, being anxious to find out what animals the wild *Bugrés* managed to kill for food, and also whether they were anthropophagous, as, it is said, many of the wild Indians of Brazil still are. I found bones of many familiar animals, such as deer, pig, *cutia*, and even tapir, and at length came to a lower jaw-bone, having the teeth still in it, which bore a most suspicious resemblance to a human jaw. I

showed it to one of the Brazilians, and he said it was
the jaw, not of a man, but of a kind of monkey, called
Bugio. I afterwards shot several specimens of this
monkey, which is a "howler," possessing a curious
cup-shaped cavity in the windpipe, by the aid of which
the loud roar, for which these monkeys are so named,
is produced.

Near this bone-heap were a bed of gourds and
another of tobacco. This latter I was very much
astonished to see, as I knew that the wild Indians of
this part of Brazil were ignorant of the common use of
tobacco. Luco, however, explained that the Botocudos
used the leaf of the plant for rubbing over their bodies,
as a protection against mosquitos, from whose attacks
even they are not exempt.

One of the Brazilians just now discovered a bow
with a bundle of arrows, lying, as though concealed,
just within the edge of the jungle. While some of us
were engaged in handling the bow which was already
strung for use, and examining the cruel looking
arrows, which were most of them full seven feet long,
having long jagged heads of hard wood, Luco, whom
the first sight of the weapons had recalled to his former
cautious bearing, and who had left us for a minute,
returned, and surprised me by the abrupt question,
"*O Doutor quer ver Bugré ?*" (Does the Doctor want
to see a *Bugré ?*)

Those who heard him stared open-mouthed, wondering what he meant.

"The owner of that bow is now watching us, and you

can see him if you like." At the same moment Luco pointed up to the top of one of the tall pine trees which grew just outside the clearing.

The tree was full a hundred feet high, the trunk rising up straight and branchless to within ten feet of the summit. At this point, crouching, as it seemed, close to the trunk, and resting on one of the branches which shot out at right angles to the tree, a dark mass could plainly be seen; but that it was a man, or had even any resemblance to a man I failed to perceive. The Brazilians round began to mutter "*E Bugré mesmo*," though, if it was a *Bugré*, how he could have got up there I could not guess.

In the meantime Luco himself took the bow and carefully fitted an arrow to the string. Having done this he walked nearly to the foot of the tree and began to make signs for the *Bugré*, if *Bugré* it really was, to descend. Not a movement, however, answered to his signals.

"That's no *Bugré*, Luco: that's a bees'-nest!" for we had often seen the nests of a certain kind of biting bee perched on the very topmost branches of trees, and I was therefore familiar enough with such a sight.

"*Espera um pouco, Sr. Doutor.* Wait a moment and you will see." So saying Luco pulled the bow several times as though to try its power, and then suddenly let fly the long slender arrow up into the dark mass of mingled branch and foliage above our heads, in which the supposed *Bugré* was ensconced.

There was a movement. There was no doubt now that it was an animal of some sort that I had supposed to be only a bees'-nest. Luco no sooner saw the effect of his shot than he threw down the bow and made renewed signs for the creature to descend.

I could now make out that it was either a man or a monkey, though, from the height of the tree, I could not distinguish which of these two it was. Presently, as it moved into another position, I could see that it had long shaggy hair covering the face and neck, imparting to it a wild, fearful appearance. It was evidently making preparations to descend, and I, for my part, watched for the operation with great curiosity, for there was nothing but the rough bark to cling to, and the trunk of the great pine for at least sixty or seventy feet of its height was far too big to be " swarmed."

The *Bugré*, for there was now no room to doubt but that it was a *Bugré*, was not long in showing how he intended to come down.

Round his ancles was tied a withy of what proved to be split bamboos, leaving about two feet or thirty inches " play " for the feet. Under the arms was passed a similar withy, encircling both the man and the tree. With no other aid than these simple contrivances, the *Bugré* appeared rapidly descending from his giddy height, looking more like some hideous ourang-outang than the human being he really was.

In a few minutes he reached the ground. He did not attempt to escape, but stood facing us with a miserable, downcast look.

Though to some extent prepared for the sight which now met our eyes, I could not repress an exclamation of astonishment and disgust. Could Darwin have introduced an accurate picture of the being now before

THE WILD BOTOCUDO OF BRAZIL.

us in his work on the "Descent of Man," he would have done more to convince the mind of the general public of the closeness of the connection existing between man and monkey than any amount of written argument.

Imagine a being about five feet four inches high, bow-legged, naked and filthy beyond description. From the head of this being soot-black locks of tangled matted hair hung to below the shoulders. On each side of the head, secured to the hair with lumps of bees'-wax, were the skins and feathers of several toucans' breasts. Over the forehead alone the hair was cut short, after the fashion so much in vogue in England a few years ago with little boys and girls, allowing the use of a pair of black bleared eyes, which had neither brows nor lashes like ordinary human beings, every hair having been pulled out of them. Still more hideous and repulsive was the lower part of the face. A huge appendage, in size and shape like a big fir cone, formed of hard and polished wood, hung suspended from the under lip, which was dragged down by the weight of the ornament (?) to some distance below the chin, disclosing the gum of the toothless lower jaw—toothless, that is as regards the front incisors—flanked by abnormally big and white eye-teeth. Saliva dribbled from the mouth thus hideously distorted.

The redeeming feature, if such a face could be said to be redeemable by anything, was the nose, which, contrary to the usual style of *Bugré* noses, was distinctly Roman, being thin and slightly hooked. The whole face, and more especially the forehead, was furrowed with deeply marked wrinkles, such as one sees in the countenances of certain kinds of monkeys. Round the neck was suspended a necklace of teeth, bearing a suspicious resemblance to human eye-teeth, which proved, however, to be those of the *Bugio*, or howling monkey, before mentioned. Round the wrists, waist, and ancles were twined thick coils of string, which were made from the fibres of a big stinging-nettle called *Ortigu*.

The skin on parts of the body, more especially on the back, was mottled, black and brown, as though it had been burnt, feeling to the touch rough and coarse, like undressed leather. On other parts, more particularly about the knees and thighs it hung down in folds, as one sees in the hide of a rhinoceros. The feet were broad though not large, and turned inwards. They were clothed with thick folds or wrinkles of tough skin, seemingly impenetrable by thorns or even by the sharp fangs of the *Jararaca* itself.

Such was the general appearance of the being before us. Luco had already put the tribe down as belonging to the Botocudos, the most brutish of all South American Indians, and now his opinion was confirmed. We were at last face to face with the wild Botocudo of Brazil.

CHAPTER XVI.

WHAT was to be done with our unexpected prize? To what good use could he be turned? These were the questions now to be decided. There were still nearly three hours of daylight before us, and, notwithstanding the laborious march we had already made, we were not yet disposed to rest upon our oars.

Luco addressed the Botocudo in both the Caioá and Coroado languages, but he did not appear to comprehend either. No ray of intelligence or understanding crossed his dull and brutish countenance. We tried by signs to make him understand, first, that we were not enemies, and secondly, that we wanted him to guide us to his people.

The Botocudo at length seemed to understand what was required of him. Choosing one of the many paths that radiated from the clearing, he began to follow it at a good pace, closely followed by a tall, strapping young Brazilian, by name Pedro Baptista d'Araujo, who had been told off for this especial duty. The *Bugré*, however, seemed to have no idea of attempting to escape, the rapid pace at which he moved along the *picada* being no doubt natural to him at all times.

Signs of the *Bugrés*, as we proceeded, were numerous. Rotten timber, split into small pieces by their stone axes, for the purpose of extracting the maggots of which all wild Indians are so fond; hollow roots and stems of trees blackened by fire—for Indians on the march always carry fire with them, propagating and replenishing it at short intervals; trunks stripped of their bark; bands of *cipós* curiously twisted and tied upon them; miniature copies of bows, sometimes with one, sometimes with many twigs, representing arrows, stuck in the ground beside them, whose signification was known only to our guide, all told of the frequent and recent presence of the *Bugré brabo*.

The sun was getting low, we had been following the guidance of the Botocudo for nearly two hours without a halt; Luco had several times dropped behind, re-appearing again in our rear, after a more or less prolonged absence. On the last of these occasions, he passed the word up our files to halt. The strong hand of Pedro Baptista descended upon the naked shoulder of our guide, causing him to pull up short in his tracks. Luco, in a few brief words, explained that he believed we had over-shot the mark, for that he had heard the *buzinas* * of the *Bugrés* signalling to each other in our rear.

We stood still and listened attentively. Presently the melancholy wail of a pomba came up, clear and distinct, from the forest behind us, and almost immediately, an answering note went back from a point on one side of our line of march.

Without doubt the sounds were deceptive. They were a very clever imitation of the cry of the pomba, produced by the wild *Bugrés* who were thus signalling to each other. I glanced at the countenance of our Botocudo guide, but it betrayed no unusual intelligence; the same dead expression marked it, as heretofore.

It was exceedingly doubtful, however, whether he did not, in spite of his apparent dullness, intend to play us some trick. Certainly, from the fact that, for the last half hour, he had been guiding us in a direction away from these sounds, which he must have recognised all along as proceeding from his own people, he did not intend to lead us to them.

It was now within half an hour of sunset. We therefore camped, choosing for the spot one of the many little clearings of *Bugré* origin, which abounded by the side of the *picada*. Here we rested our weary

---

* The *buzina* is a kind of bamboo trumpet by which sounds may be produced by skilful lips, resembling the plaintive and far-sounding notes of a certain *pomba*, or dove, which is one of the most characteristic sounds of the forest in the early summer months, namely, from August to October.

limbs, reclining upon the ground, waiting for darkness to come on, that we might, with safety, light a fire, listening meanwhile to the occasional "calls" of the *Bugrés*, who, to judge from the gradual converging of the sounds, seemed to be collecting their scattered numbers at a point about half a mile behind us. Luco gave it as his opinion, that this point was at the very same *rancho* which we had quitted some three hours before, and that we had, all this time, been following paths which had been leading us more or less in a circle round one and the same spot, namely, that on which the dome shaped *rancho* stood. Whatever may have been the object of our guide, he had over-reached himself, for we should now, with our present knowledge, be able to surprise and capture the whole party of *Bugrés*.

Night came ; we lit a fire, and arranged watches. One of the Brazilians had thoughtfully brought some *mate* and a *bomba* or *mate*-cup, with him, and with this aid the night could be passed pleasantly enough. We had brought nothing in which to boil water, but this did not matter, for bamboos grew around us, and their green hollow stems had many times before served in the stead of kettles.

The night was beautifully clear and still, and through the dark foliage of the trees above now and then a bright star came and looked down upon us sleeping or watching, and passed on its way. The luxury of reclining full stretch upon the ground at ease, beneath the grand silent forest, breathing the soft and pure tropical air, after a long, toilsome, and exciting day, was indescribably pleasant and soothing.

The watch that had fallen to my share did not commence till midnight, but for the long hours before this I could not sleep, knowing that wild Indians were so near to us in the forest—perhaps even themselves watching us.

It was curious to note the instantaneous effect which the sound of a twig snapping, had upon the watchers by the fire. I had frequently observed this same thing before, even in our earlier and safer forest days. Men talking and laughing round the camp fire, with all the freedom of supposed security from danger, at that one little sound, instantly pause in their mirth or in the story they are telling, and listen in dead silence for its recurrence. A bough may break, or a tree may fall, and yet produce no stoppage of the flow of conversation. The instinct is a true one, which attaches importance only to the lesser sound. The snapping of a twig always betokens the footstep either of man or beast, and in these forests, unlike to civilised countries, all moving life must be presumed to be hostile till proved to be the contrary.

At length my watch came on—Luco was to be my companion. We drew up to the fire, and, squatting on logs with our blankets over our shoulders, proceeded to make ourselves comfortable with cigarettes and hot *mate*. The Botocudo was lying naked, close to the fire, apparently asleep. To keep himself warm he had taken a few brands out of the big fire, and with them made another little fire on the other side of him, so that both back and front might be warmed at the same time. As a precaution against sudden flight, we had secured his ankles together with a piece of *cipó*. With this exception he was entirely free.

Luco now unfolded the plan by which he proposed to capture the remainder of the *Bugrés*, who were, as he believed, collected together in the old *rancho*, not half a mile from us.

He proposed that we should start away from our camp an hour before daybreak, so as to arrive at the edge of the clearing in which the *Bugrés* were, before dawn, that we should then lie in wait till there was sufficient light to enable us to distinguish objects readily at a few yards' distance, when we should once again repeat our former rush upon the *rancho*, and capture all who might be within, while still the greater part were asleep.

The only difficulty would be in finding and following the path which led to the *rancho*, for we should have to traverse it in the darkness. This, however, was a difficulty upon which Luco expressed no anxiety. He knew the exact direction in which the *rancho* lay from us, and when once the *picada* leading to it, had been discovered, he could follow it, as indeed could any one of our party but myself, through the thickest darkness, merely by feeling his way with his bare feet.

To find this path in the first place, that is, the point whence it branched off from the *picada*, we had been

following the day before, we could use torches, for
there would be little risk of our presence being discovered, while yet at such a distance from the *rancho*.

After these and all other details had been fully
explained, we still sat by the fire sucking *mate* and
smoking cigarettes, Luco telling yarns about fights
that his tribe, in alliance with the Brazilians, had had
in former days with the Coroados Indians.

In speaking of the Botocudos, Luco showed clearly
enough that his opinion of them was of the lowest
description.   He said that their custom was to live in
small families, such as the one we were now engaged
with, because of the difficulty they experienced in
finding sufficient food for their existence in large
communities.   Occasionally these scattered families
combined together to resist some common enemy,
such, for example, as the aggressive Coroado, but
they were, as a rule, the most peace-loving and harmless of all the Indian tribes.

When, however, my companion began to talk about
the Coroados Indians, it was easy to detect a tone of
respect, if not of absolute fear in his voice.   He told
me of one fight, in which he, with some Brazilians and
other members of his own tribe, had been engaged
against the Coroados, in which even the women of the
latter had taken a part.

On this occasion the Caioás and Brazilians, who
were then at war with the Coroados, were encamped
in a little clearing, that they had made in the forest,
when, just before daybreak, the watch gave the alarm

of the stealthy approach of the enemy, which their keen ears had detected by the snapping of a twig or the rustle of a leaf in the forest. Immediately upon the alarm being given, a loud yelling and shouting burst forth from the forest in their rear. Most of the party, thinking the attack was coming from that quarter, faced round, and prepared to resist the expected onslaught in that direction. Some of the more experienced men, however, suspecting a *ruse,*—the nature of the Coroado Indian being to give no sign of his approach till he is right upon his enemy—kept their ears and eyes directed to the side from whence the first suspicious sounds had proceeded. Slowly and cautiously, creeping nearer and nearer, their movements almost covered by the tumult going on upon the opposite side, and, as they doubtless thought, unsuspected by their intended victims, the Coroado *cacique* and his fighting men were actually approaching on this side to fall upon the rear of their enemies deceived by the shouting. Having thus succeeded in coming up to the verge of the open clearing, with a wild yell they rushed forward, to find themselves met by a well-delivered volley of arrows and buck-shot, from the bows and pistols of their expected victims, who had fathomed the *ruse* attempted upon them. The first shouting had been made by women who are thus trained to aid their lords and masters in battle. Throughout the fight, which lasted but till broad daylight appeared, the women, themselves remaining well concealed in the forest, continued to harass and perplex the Brazilians by their shouts and feigned attacks.

Luco had a way of telling his exciting stories which though he scarcely ever raised his voice above a low murmur was most impressive. While he was relating the above story, which he did far more circumstantially than I have given it, I found my own ears instinctively growing keener and more watchful to detect the slightest sound in the forest around us. The Botocudo had not stirred once since our watch had commenced, but, notwithstanding this quietude on his part, I felt impelled to go to where he was lying, and examine carefully the bonds of his ancles. My suspicions, however, proved groundless. The *cipó* had not been tampered with, and the *Bugré* himself was soundly sleeping.

Our watch was now to be relieved. When the next two men came to take our place by the fire, I laid myself down upon the ground, wrapped in my rug, with my revolver for a pillow, and slept.

It seemed scarcely a minute that I had been thus asleep, when I felt a hand upon me, and heard a voice whispering, " *Doutor, doutor, ja imos s'embora.*" I was wide awake at once, and found all the party standing up by the fire, girt for the trail, the *Bugré* also standing silently by.

We rapidly fell into our places, Luco leading the van, carrying a torch in his hand, and without a word being spoken, the final act of the drama was commenced.

A dense fog had fallen over the forest since I had

first fallen asleep, and now I shivered with the cold damp vapour penetrating my bones.   After a quarter of an hour's torch travelling, we struck a *picada* which Luco said would lead direct to the *rancho*.   It was no longer safe to continue to employ the torch; it was therefore extinguished, and we now groped our way along in pitchy darkness, each man touching the man before him.   The Botocudo was left behind when the torch was extinguished, in charge of one man, it not being thought advisable to incur the risk of his giving an alarm at perhaps the critical moment.

Our march was now so slow, on account of the greater caution necessary to prevent our approach being discovered, that the first dim coming of dawn was already visible, when we at length found ourselves at the edge of the well remembered clearing.   The dark outline of the dome-shaped *rancho* loomed big through the white fog, as we waited silently not ten yards from it, watching the light grow.   That the *Bugrés* were inside it, was soon evident, for we heard sounds of breathing or murmuring, and smelt the odour of burning wood.   Presently a movement in the side of the *rancho*, was dimly perceived, and a moment later, a *Bugré* crept out and stood upright in the open, looking around him.   At this moment we rushed forward.

*   *   *   *   *   *

Twelve miserable looking beings were squatted upon the ground sunk in the apathy of deep dejection.   We had made our capture without much difficulty.   The

inmates of the *rancho* were taken completely by surprise, and had offered hardly any resistance. There
were two men, four women, and five children, besides
our first captive, making twelve in all. It was difficult
to believe that in them we were really looking at specimens of our own kind. The men were simply terrible
in their repulsiveness. The women, in consequence
of their not wearing the lip appendage before described,
were one degree less dreadful to look at. The children
were pitiable objects, having enormously swollen
bellies, with arms and legs as thin as sticks. All were
entirely naked, though in the rancho was found a
coarse garment, something of the texture of cocoa-nut
matting, apparently designed less for ordinary wear
than as a coat of mail to resist the claws of wild beasts
or the arrows of an enemy. Men, women, and children
all wore their hair alike, that is, cut short over the
eyes, but hanging in tangled masses down the sides and
back of the head. All were adorned with toucans'
feathers, stuck to the hair with wax. Most of them wore
bead necklaces, the beads being little black seeds
through which a hole had been pierced for the reception of the string. Amongst other curious things such
as tooth necklaces, string amulets, and the like, we
found two articles which Luco said were deer " calls."
One was a collection of dried deer and pig trotters,
perhaps five-and-twenty in number, each secured to
separated pieces of string, the free ends of which were
tied altogether, so as to leave about six inches play for
each trotter, thus forming a kind of rattle.

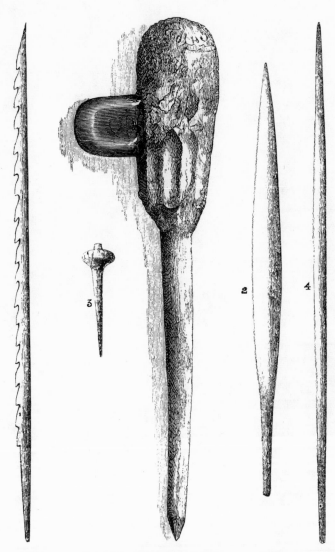

STONE AXE AND WOODEN ARROW HEADS, USED BY BOTOCUDO
WILD INDIANS.

No. 1.—For jaguar shooting from ambuscades.
Nos. 2 and 4.—For tapir, deer, pig, and the larger monkeys.
No. 3.—For birds and the smaller kinds of monkeys.

The second was like a baby's toy, being merely a dry gourd attached to a short handle. This gourd contained seeds, which had been put in through a small hole, which had afterwards been closed with bees'-wax. Thus another kind of rattle was obtained which served a similar purpose as the first.

A lasso made of the bark of the black *cipó* was also found in the *rancho*. Before this, we had seen a similar lasso set in a tapir track, and no doubt the Botocudos obtain their food as much in this way, as by shooting with arrows.

There were four kinds of arrow heads amongst the bundle of arrows which we also found. They were all made of the wood known as the *pao d'arco* which is perhaps one of the hardest and strongest kinds of wood that grows in the forest. The bows were made of *Cabriuba preta*, another very strong and tough wood, which, however, is not remarkable for elasticity. In fact none of the bows, though they were full seven feet in length could be drawn more than eight or nine inches, and this only by a great exertion of strength.

One of the three men now captured was very remarkably different from the other two. In the first place, he had both beard and whiskers, of which his companions were entirely destitute ; in the next place, his skin was a shade lighter than that of the others, his features generally having more of the Brazilian, than of the pure Indian cast in them. So remarkable was his resemblance to a Brazilian, notwithstanding the hideous distortion of the lip and the long growth of matted hair, that it was noticed by us all, and one suggested that he might actually be a Brazilian who had been kidnapped in his youth by the Botocudos, and brought up by them. We spoke to him in Portuguese, in the faint hope that he might understand us, but no ; his countenance remained dull and dead like those of all his companions.

It struck me as being very curious that these Indians, who belong to a tribe the most brutal and degraded of all the South American aborigines, should, in so many respects, have the same ideas of personal decoration as ourselves. Their gaudy feathers in the hair—their necklaces and bracelets of teeth and seeds—and even their lip appendages, were but the ruder modifications of our own fashions. The modern, highly cultivated European has certainly some artistic instincts in common with his brother the Botocudo, one of the most remarkable of which being the apparent necessity which both find of boring some one feature or another, and suspending something thereto.

Though we had captured the Botocudos so easily, it was evident that they were not unprepared to fight. No less than four bows were found already strung for use in the *rancho*, with a number of arrows ready beside them. Besides these, there were two heavy clubs which would have made formidable weapons in practised hands. These clubs the Botocudos used for making paths through the forest. They were each about four feet long, and from two to three inches in diameter, and were exceedingly strong and heavy for their size, being made of *piroba* saplings. The great mass of the undergrowth of this part of the forest consisting of bamboo or cane, a club, skilfully used, is almost as efficient a path-maker as the *facão* of the Brazilian. The phrase " beaten path " thus becomes very literally correct when applied to the *picadas* made by these Indians.

The two men whom we had just captured each wore in addition to the ornaments already mentioned, the half of a *cutia's* lower jaw suspended to their necks. All the teeth, with the exception of one incisor, had been extracted therefrom. This tooth had been brought to a fine edge, probably by being rubbed on a stone, and with it the handle of the stone axe, previously found by us, the bows and the lip appendages had all been cut and polished, the tooth marks upon each being plainly visible. The arrow heads had been fashioned by the same primitive implement. The shafts to which the arrow heads were fixed were formed of single pieces of bamboo from five to seven feet in length, and about five-eighths of an inch in diameter. The mode of joining the head to the shaft was very simple, and in all cases alike. One end of the bamboo was split in several parallel lines as far as the first joint, which was always about five inches from the extremity. Into this receptacle the lower end of the arrow head was inserted, and rendered tight fitting with bees'-wax, which was probably poured in in a melted state. Round the joint, narrow strips of the strong and imperishable bark of the black *cipó* were firmly bound, the ends being fastened off neatly by being inserted into splits made for the purpose in the bamboo stem below the joint.

Each arrow had two feathers, taken from the wing of the Jacu. These feathers were very roughly tied to the shaft by string made of fibre from the inner bark of the *palmito*. The bow-strings were very thick, and were made of the same material. It was a curious fact that all the string was made exactly on the same principle as our own cord or rope manufactures, there being always the three orthodox stages of yarn, strand, and final string or cord.

The articles I have now enumerated and described formed the absolute total of the arts and appliances of life of these wretched beings.

We gave them a portion of our beans and farinha to eat, which they devoured eagerly, and now, for the first time, we heard the sound of their voices. The sounds produced by the men, were, to our ears, of the most woeful and lugubrious description. Power of distinct articulation was almost totally lost by reason of the hideous distortion to which they had voluntarily subjected the lower lip and jaw; thus, no words containing such letters as b, m, and p, or sounds requiring the natural use of the lips, could be pronounced or produced with distinctness. Perhaps the most unpleasant effect in the speaking of the men, was the dribbling of saliva which constantly went on, down the lower lip and wooden appendage thereto suspended.

This was naturally suggestive of imbecility, and indeed the appearance of the men generally was that of the most repulsive form of idiocy.

We had now accomplished the chief part of our task. The objects for which the expedition had started were almost gained. It only remained to convince our captives, by kind treatment, that we were friends and not enemies, and to show once and for all by ocular demonstration to our remaining panic-stricken *camaradas,* how altogether ignoble were the objects of their dread.

By signs we made the Botocudos comprehend that they were to accompany us in our march back to the river. They showed neither willingness nor unwillingness, but obeyed passively. Each woman of her own accord took up one child to carry it. The remaining child was given to the bearded chief, and thus, with one of our strange companions between each of us, our backward trail was commenced.

The excitement which had hitherto borne us up being now past, I began to feel acutely all the varied petty annoyances which always accompany a forest march. First, the stooping position that we were forced to maintain for long stretches at a time, owing to the lowness of the *picadas,* was terribly fatiguing. Then the continual slaps in the face from some small twig or stem were a source of incessant irritation. Thorns that we had not noticed before also added their quota to the general discomfort.

We made no halt till long after noon, when we

rested for one delicious half hour by the side of a little
streamlet which crossed the *picada*. Towards evening,
when we were about two miles from camp, we found
that we were being trailed by a jaguar, whose deep
grating roar was at intervals heard in our rear. It
seemed to keep not more than a hundred paces
behind us, moving as we moved, and stopping as we
stopped. The Botocudos evidently recognised the
sound of an enemy, and for the first time seemed to
exhibit fear. In the parts of the forest inhabited by
Botocudos, jaguars are generally man-eaters, and will
often follow a man, as this one was now following us,
a whole day, waiting for an opportunity of pouncing
upon him when unprepared.

From having been by far the most heavily equipped
of our party, I was now the most tired of all. When
we reached the foot of the Serra d'Areranha, behind
the camp, and commenced the steep ascent, my
strength gave out altogether. Every few minutes I
was obliged to lie down and rest, and every quarter of
an hour or less, I had to moisten my lips with *cachaça*
to give me strength to proceed. When we at length
reached the top of the Serra, and started to take a
short cut down it through the open forest of the
summit, we were unlucky enough to disturb a hornets'
nest, and several of us, including myself, were stung
severely. This put the climax to my woes, and the
remaining half mile or so into camp was performed by
me in an almost stupified condition from the pain of
the stings and intense fatigue. Luco was right when

he had said " The doctor does not know what these expeditions are."

We announced our safe return by a blowing of *buzinas* and a salvo of pistol shots, and the last thing I saw, before entering my comfortable *rancho* and tumbling exhausted into my hammock, was a crowd of Brazilians surrounding our new guests, talking and gesticulating as though they had gone out of their minds at the strange sight presented by the wild Botocudos.

CHAPTER XVII

On the 24th of August, that is, about one week after the events of the last chapter, Luco, who had gone out again with a small party to explore the forest in a different direction, returned with another batch of fourteen Indians, similar in all respects to those previously brought to camp. There were now, therefore, twenty-six Botocudos in our camp, and these probably represented the whole Indian population of the forest for at least ten miles round us.

Panic had disappeared, for our strange guests had proved themselves the mildest and most submissive of human beings, and had, moreover, speedily become friendly and at ease with us, exhibiting no desire to return to their forest life. A certain amount of watch was kept upon them, and one or two of the more important *ranchos* were kept as forbidden ground. With these exceptions they were allowed to wander about the camp at their pleasure. We made them build a couple of small *ranchos* for themselves at one extremity of the camp, in which they slept at night, and where the women and younger children remained most of the day.

Though we had no intention of keeping, or even of allowing our wild guests to remain beyond the time necessary for them to become thoroughly familiar with us, yet for our own sakes we early commenced the process of civilisation upon them. Thus, immediately upon the arrival of each party in camp, two of our men were told off to wash each man, woman, and child in the river, this first operation being urgently needed.

In anticipation of some such intercourse with Indians as we were now having, our staff had been supplied at the outset with about £30 worth of gaudy calicos and red cloth, besides such nick-nacks as beads, looking-glasses, knives, and scissors in abundance. The former now came in useful, and, within a very few hours of the first arrival of the *Bugrés*, each adult, after having been thoroughly washed and scrubbed in the river, was supplied with some sort of garment, either cloth or calico. It was curious to notice that, when the clothing was first given to them, they seemed to have no idea of what use to put it to, but, after wearing it for a little time, would drop it unconcernedly here and there about the camp, and return to their primitive nakedness. By the second day we had taught them better manners, and after this it was rare that one appeared outside his own *rancho* except apparelled with some decency. Within their own quarters, however, all garments were invariably discarded.

On the third day after the arrival of the first party of the Botocudos, an addition was made to their number by the birth of a little *Bugré*. In a book such as this, intended for popular perusal, it would not be convenient to enter upon a description of the ceremonies and customs which, as exemplified in this instance, accompany the advent into the world of a young Botocudo. Some of these customs are, however, very curious, and, as far as I know, altogether unique.

I have already spoken of the long matted hair worn in common by all the Botocudos. It may certainly be taken for granted that this hair of theirs had never been either washed or combed since the day of their birth. In most cases it was so matted and tangled that we found it quite impossible, even after many hours' labour, to get a comb through it. Naturally it was straight, and in the majority of cases black. There were, however, two exceptions, in which the hair, when washed, came out dark brown. For the sake of cleanlinesss, we cut the hair of the men short, while that of the women was gradually got into a "combable" state by working upon each individual head for perhaps an hour or so every day for many consecutive days. With the children, as was to be expected, we found less difficulty in reducing the hitherto untamed locks into some rule and order.

Amongst the twenty-seven individuals comprising

the total of our Botocudo guests, there were two in whom, from their age and from the projects formed in reference to them, I took an especial interest. These were two children, a girl and a boy, aged about eight and nine respectively. They appeared to be brother and sister, and had been brought into camp with the second party of Botocudos. In view of future possible entanglements with other Indians of the same tribe, it would be of the greatest importance to us to have the means of conversing with them to prevent perhaps unpleasant misapprehensions on one side or the other. It was also certain that we should never get a better chance of supplying this desideratum than the one now afforded.

The choice lay between these two children and one or more of the adult men. It was more than doubtful whether it would ever be wise to put ourselves at all into the power of any one of these latter, whose natural sympathies with his own people would always render him a standing object of distrust and suspicion, notwithstanding the apparent guilelessness of his nature. This distrust could not be felt for children of such a tender age as eight or nine years, who would probably make themselves thoroughly at home with us in a very short time, and learn our language sufficiently to act as interpreters with far greater rapidity than any one of the older Indians. The choice fell then on these latter; and the process of adaptation to our purposes was at once begun by separating them from their brutish kindred, and placing them in a *rancho* attached to our own, under the especial charge of our own servant.   The separation produced no sign of disapproval from the parents or kindred of the two children.   I think it likely that the degradation of humanity in the adult Botocudo is so great as to have left almost nothing of the affection of parent for off-spring beyond that natural instinct felt by the brute creation, which of course only lasts till the offspring has arrived at an age when it can take care of itself.

It was a strange sight to see the Botocudos wander-ing about the camp with dull, downcast looks, stopping now and then to pick up from the ground some frag-ment of food that had been dropped, and beyond this exhibiting no curiosity and no wonder at any of the strange things that surrounded them.

The only occasion on which I observed them stirred to any excitement was once, when one of their number in his wanderings about the camp, happening to come across a pile of worm-eaten fire-wood that had just been brought in from the forest by the cooks, found in it one of the large white maggots which Indians, monkeys, and *coatis* * are all alike immensely partial to.   On making the discovery he gave a loud " ugh ! " which was taken up by the other Botocudos scattered about, and thus transmitted to their distant *ranchos*, where ten or a dozen of them were as usual reclining

---

* *Coati*, an animal something between a monkey, a pole-cat, and a pig.   Curling possessed a tame one for some time.   Its tricks were most amusing.   It became an adept at everything, from cleaning ed hot ashes out of pipes, to standing on its head in a swinging hammock.   In its wild state it is most destructive in the plantations.

in indolent sloth. The effect was electrical. A regular
stampede of them took place from one end of the camp
to the other, where the pile of wood was. The maggots,
which were about an inch and a half to two inches long
and very fat, were eagerly pulled out of the rotten
wood and devoured *alive*, save only their little black
heads, which were thrown aside as being, I suppose,
too hard for even Botocudo digestion.

On the evening after this occurrence the Indians
got up an entertainment in their *ranchos*, which we
imagined was a sort of thanksgiving after the unexpected feast of maggots. The entertainment was, as
might be expected from the whole nature of the Botocudo, of a most monotonous and lugubrious character.
It consisted in a chaunt upon two notes, wholly made
up of vowel sounds, the even flow of which was unbroken by a single consonant. This performance was
given by the men alone, who stood in a circle round
the women squatting on the ground, and beat slow
time with the feet. This not very amusing entertainment was continued half through the night without
intermission.

One day I happened to witness a curious mode of
curing a temporary ailment practised on one of the
women by her husband. The woman was apparently
suffering from the effects of over-indulgence in eating,
as by signs she kept signifying that the seat of her
complaint was the stomach. Her husband presently
rose up from the floor of the *rancho*, where he had
previously been lying half-asleep, and approaching his

sick spouse, who was squatting upon the floor moaning,
took off his necklace of Bugio's teeth, and began to
comb her vigorously therewith, like a man grooming
a horse, from the neck to the waist, both down the
back and in front. So powerfully did he use his formidable implement that even through the abnormally
thick skin of his patient blood began to flow in several
places. Every two minutes he would stop to dash a
gourd full of water over her body, and then once again
vigorously resume the rough combing operation.

The whole process occupied about a quarter of an
hour, and, notwithstanding that the pain must have
been considerable, the woman submitted to it with the
utmost stoicism. An hour later she was walking about
the camp to all appearance perfectly recovered. No
doubt the effect of this curious treatment was merely
to restore the proper circulation of blood throughout
the body, which had been temporarily retarded by
over-indulgence. It probably combined in an inex-
pensive form the merits of a brandy and soda and a
Cockle's antibilious pill.

It cannot be said that the better acquaintance with
our rude guests which we gradually made did more
than increase the loathing which their first appearance
had so naturally excited. Perhaps this appearance,
repulsive as it was, more especially in the case of the
adults, was the strongest link that connected these
Indians with the human family. Their habits, as far
as we had opportunities of observing them, belonged
far more to beasts than to men.

Unfortunately for us, and, as it afterwards proved, for the *Bugrés* also, we found that it was far easier to bring them into camp than to get rid of them again. Two attempts were made to send them back under escort to their old forest homes, but in both cases they returned to us the following day. It was impossible to keep them with us, if only on account of the cost of feeding them; we therefore, after keeping them for nearly a fortnight, despatched them up to Colonia Thereza by one of our returning fleet of canoes, begging the director of the colony to put them under the charge of the tame Coroados Indians to be housed and fed in their village. At parting the bearded chief made me a present of his own lip ornament, represented on the next page.

Poor *Bugrés!* their end was sad. One by one they died, some even before reaching the colony. A kind of epidemic dysentery broke out amongst them, caused probably by the change of food, and especially by the salt, to which, in their wild state, they were wholly unaccustomed. The malady commenced with the children, who were its earliest victims, and then rapidly extended to the adults, who died off one by one, till, when a month later I went up to the colony, I found but two of them alive out of twenty-five who had started from our camp.

There yet remained the two children, whom we had picked out to remain with us to be trained as interpreters, and they formed a far more pleasing study than their brutish kindred.

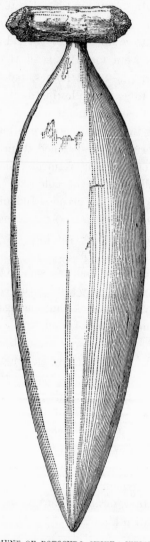

LIP ORNAMENT OF BOTOCUDO CHIEF; WEIGHT, $\frac{1}{4}$ LB.

I was at this time much engaged in preparing plans and reports, and was consequently for most of the day occupied in the engineers' *rancho*, which in Curling's absence, I now occupied alone. Being of ample dimensions, a large fire was always burning upon the floor in one part of it, and I accordingly encouraged the two Botocudo children to spend as much of their day as they liked in the *rancho* with me. Their favourite occupation was the cooking and eating of small fish or birds, such as parrots and toucans, that were from time to time brought into camp by the Brazilians for their use. This cooking was generally done in the ashes. They seemed to know every joint in the body of a bird, or other animal, dissecting it surely and rapidly, with the aid only of a piece of split bamboo stem.

It was easy to tell that they had been accustomed to hard times in their former state of life. Not the smallest particle of anything that could possibly be eaten in the birds or fish, would they waste. Each bone was picked absolutely clean, and even the entrails were devoured.

While birds and flesh generally were always baked in the ashes, fish they occasionally roasted, which they did in the following manner.

Two small forks of wood were stuck into the ground close to the red hot ashes, arranged at such a distance apart, that the head of the fish rested on one fork, and the tail on the other. Beneath the fish, thus suspended, a tray, usually consisting of a piece of the inner bark of a *palmito*, was placed to catch the moisture that dropped in the course of the roasting. By means of a feather dipped into this liquid, they kept the fish constantly basted throughout the operation, putting their whole mind into the work. When one side of the fish was done they turned it, transferring its head to the fork where its tail had previously been, but never laying the fish on its side or on its back, the reason of this probably being that the fish were cooked without being first cleaned.

Both the children were first rate mimics, and were keen to pick up any familiar cry of bird or beast in the forest behind the camp, imitating it and then telling its name to anyone who happened at the time to be taking notice of them. The various melancholy notes of the *pombas* they were especially fond of imitating. Evidently they had learnt to produce these sounds almost as soon as they had begun to talk. By hearing the two children imitate sounds, and then repeat the names of the animals to which they belonged, I soon began to know a number of Botocudo equivalents. The boy especially was not only a quick scholar, but an apt and persevering teacher, never resting till his listener had caught from him the exact pronunciation of the word he was teaching. Both children were very lively, as well as intelligent. In these respects, therefore, they differed greatly from the adult Botocudo, who, according to our experience, was dull and stupid to the verge of idiocy.

We had taken some pains to improve the external

appearance of our young guests. Our servant, the Swede Oberg, who had been a tailor in former days, made frocks for the girl, and suits of clothes for the boy. Both children were regularly washed every morning, and their hairs combed. We had at first some difficulty with them at night, on account of their not understanding the use of blankets. On one occasion, I was startled on awaking suddenly, to see both of them in the *rancho,* lying down upon the ground with little fires put all round them. This was their only idea of keeping themselves warm in the night.

On the 28th of August, three days after the main body of the Botocudos had been despatched to Colonia Thereza, the little girl became ill, and on the following day, the boy became similarly indisposed. I first observed that the girl was not well, by noticing that she had bound her forehead round several times with a long piece of string, so tightly that the string seemed to have actually cut into the flesh. This is the common habit of the Botocudos when suffering severe pains in the head. She ate nothing during the day, but kept constantly scraping her tongue with a strip of bamboo. When the boy became ill, he behaved in an exactly similar manner, binding his head and scraping his tongue. It soon became evident that they were both suffering from the epidemic which was even now, though unknown to us, beginning to commit havoc with their kindred, who had gone up the river.

After the fourth day, the boy began to improve, but

the girl continued to grow worse. On the seventh day, it became evident that she would die, and her brother was therefore removed from the *rancho* which the two had hitherto occupied together. Her constant cry was for "uch" (water), and "Oita," which we supposed was her brother's name.

On the evening of the eighth day she died, and the following morning she was buried just without the boundaries of the camp, close to the bank of the river. The boy by this time was nearly well, and it was pitiable to see him constantly coming to the *rancho* for the next few days, to look for his sister, and, not finding her, wander about the camp repeating the word *Oităna* to everyone he met. We did not let him know that his little companion was dead, for fear of the effect that it might have produced upon him. It was therefore a long time before he ceased asking for her. However deadened and brutalised the feelings of the full-aged Botocudo may have become by reason of his hard life, it is certain from the affection which these two children displayed towards each other, that in childhood there is not much innate difference between their nature and our own.

The death of the little Indian was soon to be followed by another very sad event, which came about in this wise :—On the 7th of September, the day being Sunday, most of the men, and there were but nine now at the Areranha, had gone out to amuse themselves either by hunting or fishing; myself, Oberg, and the Brazilian cook alone remaining in camp.

Even the Botocudo had been taken out hunting with the Brazilians.

Johanne, our Swedish carpenter, I could see from my *rancho,* quietly engaged in fishing from a canoe moored to the opposite bank of the river, about 200 yards distant. From the holloaing and shouting proceeding from a little distance down the river, it was evident that some noisy Brazilians were, according to custom, venting their exuberance of spirits on the water in that direction. I envied them their careless enjoyment of life, for hard fate compelled me on this day to submit to the torment of the Borrachudo fly,—which pest was at this time rampant in camp,—and remain in the *rancho* writing letters and instructions.

I noticed after one shout, perhaps a little more vigorous than usual, that the holloaing abruptly ceased; but I thought nothing of this, and went on alternately writing, and giving vent to maledictions upon the blood-thirsty Borrachudos.

Suddenly I was astonished by the apparition of Johanne, who now for the first time I observed had left his station on the opposite side of the river, rushing into the *rancho* with excited manner, and in his broken English saying the words, " *One Brazilian has drown!* "

Comprehending him in a moment, I waited but to give directions for hot bottles and cloths to be got ready. I then ran down with him to his canoe, and getting in, we paddled as hard as we could towards the spot where the shouting had been.

Two men, with white faces and dripping garments, were standing upon a rock in shallow water, endeavouring to bale out the water with their hands from a canoe that showed unmistakeable signs of having been recently upset. There had been three men, and one was beneath the water. None of the three could swim. The two on the rocks said their companion had been under the water more than a quarter of an hour. They showed the spot where they believed he had gone down, and I hurriedly took off my boots and clothes and dived down to search for him.

The water was barely seven feet deep, but it was not till I had dived four or five times and searched the bottom over a considerable area that I succeeded in finding the body. The moment we had got it on board we poled quickly up to camp, and, having landed, for a full hour tried all the remedies with which I was acquainted for restoring life in such cases. Then we gave it up as hopeless.

The unfortunate victim was Pedro Baptista, one of the men who had been with me on the first Indian hunt. The three, according to Johanne's account, were larking in the canoe, which was but a small cranky affair, when all at once he saw it turn over and precipitate them into the water. This was when the last shout was given. Pedro Baptista alone of the three had failed to catch hold of the overturned canoe, and, after struggling a few seconds on the surface, had gone down like a stone to the bottom, reappearing no more. The other two having clung to the canoe had been rescued by Johanne. All three were men from the prairie-town of Guarapuava, which accounted for the fact of their not being able to swim, there being no river there.

Pedro was a finely-made, powerful young fellow, of about twenty years of age. His father was engaged in making canoes for us near Colonia Thereza, and his brother was one of the men who on this day had gone up the river to hunt.

In the evening this party returned, shouting and singing, having bagged a tapir.

The sudden change from joyous shouting to silence told more eloquently than any words that the brothers had met again, for the body was still lying in the *rancho* nearest the landing place where it had been first brought.

On the following day Pedro was buried, not far off the grave of the little Indian girl, which was itself not yet three days old, and later on a rough wooden cross and railing were put up to mark and protect the spot, which had now become the burying-ground of the camp.

This sad accident lost us three good men to the expedition, for we could not refuse to allow the father and brother to go away when they requested permission to do so. Many other men, relations of Pedro, were, at the first sudden shock of the occurrence, also anxious to leave, but by persuasion they were ultimately induced to remain.

The events which had happened had, for the time,

sickened me of the Areranha camp, and I rejoiced
when, a week or two later, it was decided that I
should go on an expedition to a distant part of the
province of Paraná, where fresh scenes and an entire

OUR GRAVEYARD AT THE ARERANHA CAMP.

change of life would be open to me, and the memory
of the past melancholy days somewhat obliterated.

It is with a sore heart that I have now to request
the reader to bid a long farewell to the Ivahy river, as
far at least as these present pages are concerned.
The inexorable natural law that decides the exact
limits of relationship between volume and space cries

" stop " ; and no friendly genii of Arabic fame is forthcoming to demonstrate on my behalf how *something* can
go into *nothing*.

To me this is the more trying, because, whilst engaged in writing the foregoing pages, I ever consoled
myself for their numerous defects, of which I am only
too conscious, by fond indulgence in the belief that I
was but kneading the *dough* of the pudding, while the
plums that were to render it attractive for literary consumption were merely being held in reserve for a little
while, to be brought in at the last as a *bonne bouche*.

To the reader, the narrative thus cut short in its
career, may seem but a case of " happy release."
Should such be his verdict, I shall at least be able to
extract therefrom the consolation not denied to the
heretic of the dark ages, who, when his persecutors cut
off one by one his fingers, his nose, and his ears,
thanked God on each occasion that there was so much
the less of him left to suffer the final torture at the
stake.

In the less probable event of the reader sharing my
regrets at the abrupt conclusion of this portion of the
narrative, I may then not the less console myself with
the hope of some day taking up the lapsed thread and
continuing it to the end, through the final, and, to us
who were engaged in these events, most stirring scenes
of our life in the wild valley of the Ivahy.

It is because this book has a somewhat wider
purpose than that of being a mere record of personal
adventure and wild living, that space has now to be

afforded to the description of other scenes and modes
of life than those which have hitherto filled the lion's
share of its pages.   There is work to be done
and there are intelligent sympathies to be enlisted in
other directions also.   To these, then, I would now
pass on.

PART III.

—◆—

CHAPTER I.

Bound to the Ribeira.—The camp of No. 1 Staff.—The Pass of the Ivahyzinho.—The delights of the prairie.—Palmeiras *versus* Ponta Grossa.—"Herva-mate;" its preparation and its commerce.—The Barrigui.—Fact and fiction.—A mistake.

IF the reader will turn to the map accompanying this book, he will see there a river, running nearly due east and west, its nearest point being about forty-five miles northward of the town of Curitiba. This is the river Ribeira, as it is commonly called: or, to give it its full name, Ribeira de Iguape.

It will be seen that this river runs through a very mountainous country, which is indeed perhaps the most generally mountainous district of the whole province of Paraná. Unlike that of the Ivahy, of which we have just taken leave, the valley of the Ribeira and those of at least two of its leading tributaries, namely, the Ribeirinho and the Assungui, are all more or less thickly populated, and are connected with each other by mule tracks, as well as by waterway.

As might be expected from the rough nature of the country through which it passes, the Ribeira in its upper course is an impetuous torrent-like river, full of corredeiras, and other such-like obstructions to navigation. Below the last point marked on the map— the Porto de Apiahy—the river begins to change its character, and sobers down to a more equably flowing stream. About seven leagues beyond this point again, at a settlement called Iporanga, every obstruction to free navigation entirely disappears, and from here steamers of light draught can run right away to the Atlantic without fear of either being broken in a rapid, or stuck in a shallow in their course.

A not inconsiderable trade in agricultural products is carried on both eastward to the Atlantic, and northward and westward to the prairie towns, from the whole district surrounding the head waters of the Ribeira. Thus it is that every Caboclo inhabiting this district, is a canoeman born and bred; for the mule tracks, as usual in all these mountainous and wooded parts of the country, are but the most miserable apologies for roads, to which even the most risky waterway, such as that afforded by the Ribeirinho, the Assungui and the Ribeira, is generally preferable for the transport of cargo.

Hither, then, I was now bound in search of men courageous and skilful enough not to be appalled at the long series of tremendous cataracts, forty miles in length, which obstructed the middle course of the Ivahy river.

' En route ' I stopped two days with the members of Staff No. 1, who were now camped on the "Campinas," on the banks of the Ivahyzinho, within a day's ride of Colonia Thereza. They entertained me luxuriously on the choicest viands of the prairies, such as I had long forgotten the taste of. Bread, milk, eggs, roast beef—all these gave a veritable flavour of Old England to our repasts. Tents too they still inhabited. The dry and breezy prairies upon which their lines had hitherto chiefly fallen being the very antipodes to the damp and dripping forests that, within the first three months, had caused our coverings to rot and fall away like autumn leaves, and even our very garments to turn to mould upon our backs.

Poor fellows! they little anticipated at this time, when they were almost within sight of the goal, what troubles were in store for them before they were destined to reach it.

They were now upon the summit of the great watershed between the Tibagy and Ivahy rivers. In a straight line their distance from Colonia Thereza was but fifteen miles, the village lying about 1600 feet below them. Yet this short distance occupied almost exactly five months to overcome; bad weather, sickness and climate sores all adding their quota to retard the accomplishment of the work.

The route chosen was by the valley, or rather "gorge" of the Ivahyzinho, which, in its course from Campinas to Colonia Thereza, passes through some of the grandest and wildest mountain forest scenery that the province can anywhere boast of; leaping over cataracts and saltos of 50, 100 and 150 feet in height, between mountains rising 1,000 feet almost perpendicularly on either hand.

So deep and steep are the gorges through which this tyrant little river flows in many parts of its course, that the sun never enters them from one year's end to another; and after a moderate spell of dry weather the stream runs almost dry, the water that remains in it collecting in the deep rocky pools between the saltos and becoming stagnant and putrid. From drinking this water a kind of epidemic jungle fever was brought on amongst the members of the Staff, which attacked both engineers and workmen, Europeans and Brazilians indifferently. Though fortunately not attended in any case with fatal results, the epidemic thus caused was of sufficient importance to seriously interfere with the due progress of the work, scarcely half-a-dozen men escaping without one or more violent attacks at different times. When the Staff ultimately emerged from their long residence in this confined valley, they were bleached a sickly yellow and white, though on entering it their complexions had been of a deep ruddy brown, the result of a year's exposure on the healthy open prairies.

For the last mile or two, however, of its course, the Ivahyzinho may be said to have been quite a placid stream, in comparison with the wild passion of its youth. Its fury had been spent amongst the moun-

SCENE ON THE IVAHYZINHO: INDIAN SHOOTING FISH.

tains which then endeavoured, though vainly, to bar
its onward career.

The accompanying illustration is from a sketch
taken at a point in its course not far above Colonia
Thereza, where the mountains have given place to the
flat rich forest land, and the mad falls to gentle,
picturesque cascades. The particular cascade here
represented was a very favourite place of resort for
the Indians of Colonia Thereza, who used to frequent
it for the purpose of shooting fish. The arrows used
for this purpose are of extraordinary length—generally
seven feet—all, with the exception of the tip, which
is formed of a piece of *pao d'arco* about ten inches
long, pointed and barbed, being made of the lightest
bamboo, so that when a fish is transfixed the shaft
of the arrow tends to remain above water, and thus
the finny prey is more readily followed in the water,
and is ultimately secured without difficulty. Some
Brazilians are even more expert than the Indians
themselves in shooting fish with bow and arrow, and,
at our camp at the Salto d'Areranha, we were often
kept supplied for days together by one of the younger
camaradas, who used to bring in thirty or forty pounds
weight of *dourados* in the course of a morning's shooting in the falls.

On the 3rd of October, two days after having left
the jovial and hospitable camp of the 1st Staff, I
passed through the last strip of forest that marked the
boundary of the Great Prairie.

Ye Gods! how my heart bounded within me at the

long forgotten sight of the great rolling plains, stretching far away to the dim horizon, to the very boundaries
of Heaven.   In the excitement and enthusiasm of the
moment, I left the path and galloped up to the summit
of the nearest wave crest, and there stood for the space
of full five minutes, with chest expanded and arms
outstretched, inhaling the glorious breeze that came
sweeping over the plains direct from the Atlantic.   I
felt like a prisoner just released from his dungeon.
For thirteen months I had not known what it was to
feel a breath of air on my cheek—nor to see farther
than the sound of my voice could reach.   I shouted
with delight, so that my attendants, Pedro and Messeno, thought I had suddenly gone mad.

Presently, when my first exuberance of spirits had
been somewhat relieved, I subsided into a quieter
enjoyment of the new surroundings.   I felt astonished
when I thought of how long I had been able to endure
life in the tropical forest below, which, in comparison
with the prairie, I now looked back upon as a sort of
earthly "Inferno."

Apart from the insect plague and the minor miseries
of life in these forests, there is something in their
everlasting stillness, in their gloomy shades and contracted horizons, which must and does act sympathetically upon both mind and body, dwarfing both
into a narrower compass.   Thus it is that on first
emerging from them after a long residence therein,
one's whole being, moral as well as physical, bounds
all at once into a fuller life, just as a shrivelled apple

will, at one stroke of the air-pump acting upon the surrounding atmosphere, as if by magic distend and regain for the time its original youthful plumpness.

This subtle but potent influence, acting through several generations, is probably one of the causes which make the forest Indian generally so much inferior in spirit and enterprise to his brother of the prairie.

The first night after leaving the forest I passed in a tiny prairie village, by name Capella do Pinheirinho, situated about three leagues from Ponta Grossa. At this time of the year (October) the fogs, which during the height of the dry or winter season every morning envelope the whole prairie from its lowest valley to its highest crest or summit with a thick white blanket, concealing everything till perhaps 9 or 10 A.M., have lost a part of their power, deserting, therefore, the higher ridges, though still forming densely in all the hollows and valleys. This is the season when the traveller may witness dissolving scenes of the most surpassing loveliness.

By sunrise the following morning I was up and out, enjoying the delicious freshness of the highland air, to which I had been so long unaccustomed. But for the temperature, which, even at this early hour, must have read from 58° to 60° Fahr., I could have imagined that it was a bright Christmas morning, and that all around me lay a wide extent of snow-clad country glistening in the bright rays of a winter's sun. The Capella stood on one of the most commanding elevations of the whole prairie, having an uninterrupted view both northward along the valley of the Tibagy, and southward over that of the Iguassú, of more than eighty miles in either direction.

The white morning fog was just beginning to move upwards in the hollows where it had been resting. It had not yet risen high enough to obstruct from view the wide range of rolling plain, which to the south first dipped down to the Iguassú, and then gently rose again billow after billow on the opposite side of the river, till, at a distance of full eighty miles from where I stood, the ground, again reaching its former level, concealed the farther prospect. As the sun rose higher, from behind each billow, the mist, now in the guise of snow-white clouds, rolled upwards from its resting-place in the hollows between, covering, for a time, the whole face of the country as with a glittering snow-field; then, rising still higher, it slowly split up and gradually melted into the blue ether above, and the new day was fairly begun.

These lovely transformation scenes are of almost daily occurrence in the months of September and October. When the sun has risen an hour or two, the atmosphere loses some of its clearness, and the southeast prairie breeze springs up, gradually increasing in force till about 4 P.M., after which hour it slowly dies away and sinks with the sun. In the morning the same lovely snow picture is again renewed, and thus the prairie world goes round.

Passing through Ponta Grossa on the afternoon of

the 4th, I found that it had risen to the dignity of possessing an hotel of its own, an enormous boon to the independent traveller. On a subsequent occasion I stopped a day or two at this new hotel, and found it to be a very decent specimen of its class. If it had a fault it was to be found in the abnormal civility of its proprietor, which was indeed painful to one's own self-respect. He seemed, in fact, servilely anxious to offer his moral person to be kicked on all possible occasions. Be it noted, however, that he was *not* a Brazilian but an Italian.

Seven leagues from Ponta Grossa, after crossing *en route* the Tibagy by a well-built wooden bridge standing on piles, we came to the town of Palmeiras, the destined rival of Ponta Grossa, whose population at present, however, does not exceed 3,000. This town is the centre of a somewhat rich producing district, and possesses cattle and timber in abundance. Water power, which is totally wanting at Ponta Grossa, is here used for driving saw-mills and *mate*-mills. Lastly, a carriage-road, which is already more than half completed, will in a short time connect it directly with Curitiba and the sea coast, while no such scheme has yet been spoken of in connection with Ponta Grossa.

Leaving Palmeiras on the second day, we descended the Serrinha at a point twenty-five miles south of the track up which we had marched fifteen months before. A good carriage road had here been constructed, being a portion of the new road just referred to. Our

animals, not being shod, could not stand the hard
metalling of quartz and granite upon the road; we
therefore soon deserted it again, preferring to follow
the old mule-track.

Skirting the town of Campo Largo, we came a
league beyond to a *mate*-mill, being the second we
had passed on this day. I sent Messeno in with a
request to the proprietor that I might be permitted to
go over it. The permission was readily accorded, and
I went in.

The process of the preparation of *herva-mate* has
been so often described that I will not here do more
than give a slight general description.

There are really two processes, entirely distinct from
each other. The first is the gathering of the young
shoots and leaves, which are dried on the spot over a
quick fire; and the second is the crushing or stamping
of the dried materials, which process alone is carried
on in the *mate*-mills. It was this latter that I now
saw in operation.

This particular mill had twelve wooden stampers,
worked in the usual manner by teeth or studs, placed
spirally round the circumference of a revolving cylinder.
The motive power was derived from a tiny streamlet
working intermittently from a small reservoir over a
very narrow overshot wheel of sixteen feet in diameter
and but two feet six inches in width. Yet with this
power and with these appliances, 150 arrobas or more
than two tons weight of *mate* could be turned out per
day. When it is remembered that the *herva-mate* tree

requires no cultivation, but grows wild very abundantly on the borders of the forest, it will not be surprising to learn that but a very few years ago the manufacture and sale of *mate* by the mill-owners, who buy the material ready dried from the cutters, yielded more than cent. per cent. clear profit.

The chief consumers were, at this time, the Argentine Provinces, Chili and Peru. Suddenly these States refused to buy any more Brazilian *mate*. Owing to the high price it had been commanding, manufacturers and dealers had taken to largely adulterating it with worthless rubbish in order to secure greater profits to themselves. In consequence the trade, which at one time had bid fair to enrich the province of Paraná, was suddenly stopped, prices having fallen to such an extent that it now barely paid to produce the article. Never was the truth of the time-honoured motto, "Honesty is the best policy," more abundantly proved than in this case.

A year later I heard that the trade was again showing some symptoms of revival. It would be a pity indeed if so great a source of legitimate profit were to be thus summarily taken away from the province.

Paraguay, before the great war in which that country was utterly ruined, had been the chief *mate*-producing State in South America. Upon her downfall, the centre of the trade was removed to the southern provinces of Brazil, whence again it has been partially driven away by the fraudulent policy pursued by the manufacturers and merchants in order to increase their gains.

On the evening of the 8th of October, I camped on
the bank of the little river Barrigui, a tributary of the
Iguassú, which runs past within a league of Curitiba.
It has been stated in a "prospectus" recently issued,
setting forth the advantages of a certain colonisation
scheme to which reference has once before been
made,* that a great navigable highway exists, by
means of this very river, the Barrigui, to a point about
fifty miles below its junction with the Iguassú.   In
the face of this statement, which is calculated seriously
to mislead intending emigrants as to the value of the
proposed settlement, I may remark that the surveys of
our expedition prove that there is a total fall of nearly
200 feet on this so-called water highway between
Curitiba and the settlement.   As a matter of fact this
"highway" is no highway at all, the rivers between
the two points referred to being obstructed by a great
number of rapids and cataracts.

Curitiba had grown out of all remembrance in the
interval of fourteen months that had elapsed since I had
last seen it.   To right and left of the new road leading
to Palmeiras long lines of houses had sprung up where
before the prairie rolled.   On the right a gigantic
building more in the modern London hotel style than
anything I had yet seen even in Rio itself, was in
course of erection, and on all sides unmistakeable
signs of progress were manifest.

The German element seemed to have multiplied

* See Appendix, Notes F 1 and F 2.

exceedingly in the place, and the dark skins and black hair of my two Brazilian companions seemed all out of place in the capital "city." People turned round to stare at us as we rode through the streets, wondering no doubt from what remote part of the globe we had come, for our backwoods costumes and travel-stained appearance betokened strangers.

Presently two black fellows in uniform, carrying short swords, came up and stopped us; and then, for the first time, we remembered that we were armed to the teeth, with pistols, revolvers, and long knives stuck all round our waists. No wonder that the people had stared at us, for the carrying of arms is forbidden in Curitiba. The mistake was soon explained, but the black fellows would not leave us till we had reached the door of Leitner's hotel, at which I intended to put up, being evidently afraid that we might at the last moment turn out to be desperate ruffians bent on some murderous outrage.

Herr Leitner received us with outstretched arms, and it was pleasant to find oneself not altogether forgotten amidst the many changes that had taken place in the town.

CHAPTER II.

THE colony of Assungui has earned of late years at home a name of some notoriety, not perhaps of a very favourable kind, in connection with emigration. Hapless colonists have returned from it to England, the bearers of very woeful tales of the disappointments and even sufferings which they there encountered. Seeing that in the year 1864 its population was officially given at 208, and in the year 1873 only as 440, notwithstanding that, in the interval between these dates, a more or less constant stream of immigration had been pouring into it, there can be little doubt that there has been all along a screw—possibly a good many screws —loose somewhere.

Assungui stood directly on my route to the Ribeira, almost on the banks of which river indeed, the colony is situated. Owing, however, to there being two Assunguis—a Colonia and a Freguezia, some thirty miles apart from each other—of which fact I was not aware at the time, I found myself on the road to the latter when I had intended to go direct to the former, after leaving Curitiba. As the event proved, the mistake was rather of advantage than not to the objects of my journey; for I was thus enabled to visit a district which gained for me some of the most valuable canoe-men that could be found anywhere in the province ; and, had it not been for certain unexpected obstacles, I need have gone no farther than this to have obtained the full supply required for the Staff.

The Freguezia de Assungui then, to which village I found myself wearily plodding along on mule back, on the 12th of October, over vile clay roads, rendered still viler by a constant drizzling rain, is situated about fifty miles N.N.W. of Curitiba on the river of the same name, a tributary of the Ribeira, while the Colonia de Assungui, the centre of the English settlement, lies about sixty miles from Curitiba in a direction slightly east of north, one and the same mule track for the first half of the distance leading to both settlements.

We had enough to do in attending to our mules, which were performing erratic slides on the slippery surface of the steep paths, and threatening momentarily to bring one or other of us to grief, to think of any-thing else ; though the country through which we were travelling was remarkable enough, both in appearance and geological character, to have merited more than ordinary notice.

My note-book records the fact that on this day my
mule tumbled down five times, whereas once or twice
per diem was generally the average on bad forest
tracks.   It must not be thought that when a mule
tumbles, its rider necessarily tumbles too.   On the
contrary, he merely spreads his legs apart to avoid
having them crushed—for the fall is more often caused
by a side slip, than a direct forward tumble—and waits
in the saddle till the animal gets up again.   Sometimes, however, the shaking that he receives is very
severe, for the mule, if it be a plucky one, will make
the most frantic efforts to regain its footing, which
efforts frequently render matters worse, and culminate
in a rib-breaking fall which jars the rider's backbone
to its very core.

On the 13th, we got on much better, as the roads
were drier, the rain having then ceased.   About ten
miles to the north of Curitiba, the boundary of the
raised plateau on which that town is situated, is reached.
This boundary or line is marked by great distortion
of strata, and a general sinking of the whole area of
the country northwards as far as the eye reaches;
while at the same time, short choppy hills, densely
wooded, take the place of the long prairie-wave and
grassy plain.

From every point from which a view could be obtained, I observed that these hills had at one time or
another been " roça'd " or cultivated up to their very
summits, a great many patches being still under cultivation.   The bye-paths leading to the roças were so

numerous, that we, on two or three occasions, lost our way amongst them, and had to retrace our steps for considerable distances. The only fault to be found in the land from an agricultural point of view, was that it scarcely possessed a square yard of level surface anywhere. So steep were the slopes, that it was impossible to keep the complicated Brazilian saddles, with which Messeno and Pedro were riding, in proper gear for any length of time, and the men were constantly having to dismount in order to re-adjust them.

This general steepness of contour is a fatal objection to the introduction, in these parts, of any improved system of farming, other than the " roça " ; for, in the first place, a plough cannot be used, and in the second place, the annual deluges of rain would speedily wash away all goodness from the rich slopes, were they exposed, unprotected by forest or *Capöeira* (second-growth forest), for more than a year at a time. Practically, the land loses at least three-quarters of its value for agricultural purposes by this one fault alone.

About mid-day on the 14th, as we were approaching within a more hopeful distance of the Freguezia, the last *Caboclo* we had met having told us that he himself had only left there three hours before, we overtook a horseman riding leisurely in the same direction as ourselves, with whom we entered into conversation. He turned out to be one of the chief *fazendeiros* of the place, by name Sr. Cordeiro.

Hearing what was the object of our journey, and

that we were bound for the Freguezia, he obligingly
offered to accompany us, and to give me a personal introduction to the chief employer of labour there. His
own *sitio* was about seven miles outside the village to
the left of our course, so that he was going some distance out of his way on our behalf.

At about 2.30 we came in sight of the village, and
soon after waded across the swiftly rushing Assungui,
here about thirty yards wide, going straight to the
house of a *fazendeiro*, whom our companion introduced
as Sr. Nobrega, the wealthiest and most influential
man of the whole district round, and as such, the
most able to further the object which I had in
hand.

The Freguezia itself was a very small place, scarcely
so large as Colonia Thereza, for most of the inhabitants of the district lived the whole year round upon
their *fazendas* or *sitios* outside.

Sr. Nobrega was hospitality itself, and most courteous in his conversation and expression of desire to be
of service, but I was not long in finding out that his
words were very remote from his intentions. Instead
of using his influence, which was evidently almost
autocratic, amongst the surrounding *Caboclo* population to further my objects, he, whilst ostentatiously de-
ploring the unsuccessful result of his pretended efforts
to induce men to enter into contracts with me, was
secretly spreading bad reports about the expedition,
its hardships and dangers; and even insinuating that
the high pay promised was nothing but a false lure.

Finding that he, for some reason of his own, which I did not at this time quite understand, was bent on thwarting my object of obtaining men, I sent Pedro in one direction to make a house-to-house visitation amongst the *Caboclos,* whilst I went with Messeno to beat up in another direction. Sr. Nobrega had, however, been beforehand with us, and the *Caboclos* were difficult to persuade.

In the course of my inquiries I was struck with the number of men who gave as a reason for not accepting our service, that they could not get away, because they owed money. Becoming curious to find out the cause or meaning of this universal indebtedness amongst the *Caboclos,* I went a step farther, and collected particulars of some of these debts.

The result of these inquiries gave me the key to Sr. Nobrega's conduct which had before been so unaccountable, and led me to the discovery of the existence of a wide-spread system of " white slavery," such as formerly ruled in the northern counties of England.

A *Caboclo* wants a certain sum of money, say a hundred milreis—a large sum in these parts, where wealth exists chiefly in kind, and where money is so scarce as to be worth 24 per cent. per annum on the best security. He goes to the head man of the village, in this case our friend Sr. Nobrega, and begs the loan of that amount, promising to pay it back by a certain time.

From this moment the wretched *Caboclo* becomes, to all intents and purposes, a *slave.* How can he earn

money to pay back his debt, except from his *patrão*—
Sr. Nobrega? What can he do, supposing his *patrão*
is very sorry, but has no particular need of his services
just yet? Meanwhile the time for re-payment of the
debt arrives, and the poor wretch of course cannot pay.
"Never mind," says Sr. Nobrega, "you shall work
it out, I won't press you for the money." Work is
given him, and he goes into the roça to cut or plant or
gather, as the case may be, for a certain number of days
at a milreis per day. He is happy, and thinks he will
soon be able to pay off his debt at this rate, when suddenly the work is stopped for the season, and with it his
earnings. Interest, however, goes on accumulating,
and when the next season of work commences, he finds
his original debt as big as ever, and again he works
away to earn money to pay it off, which, however, he
never can do, because it is not to the interest of his
creditor that he should do so. Thus year after year
he gives his labour for nothing, and yet remains a
debtor, and the *patrão* grows prosperous and rich.

This is the system which prevails at the present day
in the whole agricultural district of the Ribeira, and
thus it was that at this time not one man in ten was
his own master, the great majority being completely at
the beck and call of the large *fazendeiros* such as Sr.
Nobrega and others with whom I afterwards became
acquainted. I do not know what the precise law of
Brazil is, between debtor and creditor; judging, however, from its results, I should say it must be of a
somewhat harsh nature as regards the debtor.

Learning that there was another Freguezia about three leagues distance from that of Assungui, situated on the river Ribeirinho, I rode off there with Messeno to see whether better success could not be obtained in a different locality. The mule track connecting the two places was villanously bad, and the journey took us four hours to accomplish. The country through which we passed was of the most fertile description, and roças were numerous on every hill side.

I had brought a letter of introduction from Sr. Cordeiro to a certain Sr. Garses, whose house, after some difficulty, we found. As usual, we found we were received most hospitably, liberal accommodation being provided for both man and beast.

The house was of a class which I had not yet seen, but of which I afterwards, in the course of many months' travelling about the province, saw many specimens. Its chief feature, in which it differed from other houses, was the large wide verandah which ran along the whole length of one side of it. This verandah was used as a reception hall and dining room, the whole of the rest of the building being devoted to the sleeping apartments and domestic offices.

For the first time I saw attached to a Brazilian dwelling, a large, well arranged and well cultivated kitchen garden. The owner took pride in it, as was easy to see, and was delighted at being asked to show it to us. Besides the kitchen garden, on the other side of the house there was a well-kept coffee plantation, which Sr. Garses said yielded him a small fortune every year.

Though, in a straight line, the distance of this Freguezia from Curitiba is only forty miles, yet the climate of the district surrounding it is totally different. Frost, for instance, is here entirely unknown, and both sugar and coffee are cultivated with great success.

Being situated so high up the Ribeira valley, the chief outlet for the products of the district is to the prairie towns of Castro, Ponta Grossa, and Curitiba; these products being Indian corn (from which *farinha* is made), beans, coffee and sugar. As this is essentially an agricultural, and not a pastoral district, cattle breeding is not carried on except for home consumption; but pigs are very largely bred for their fat or *toucinho*—an article also of an extensive trade.

From want of proper roads, the whole traffic with the prairies has to be carried on by means of pack mules alone. In order that this may be done profitably, it is necessary that each *fazendeiro* or farmer shall have a sufficient pasturage on which to keep a troop of these animals. Hence it is that small landed proprietors are heavily weighted in the race for prosperity; because, not being able to keep a mule troop, from the want of a sufficient extent of pasturage, they are forced to sell their crops *in situ* to the larger *fazendeiros* at their own price.

This is a point of some importance, as bearing upon the question of English colonisation in the neighbouring Assungui district, where the inhabitants are likewise dependent upon this expensive mode of conveyance in all their commerce with the prairie towns.

Notwithstanding the great civility which Sr. Garses showed to me, I found that he was quite as unwilling as Sr. Nobrega to give me any aid in obtaining canoe-men; and I had every reason for believing that the " white slavery " system was as rampant here, as it was in the district under the sway of Sr. Nobrega.

I slept one night under Sr. Garses' hospitable roof, and, resisting all persuasions to remain another day, started soon after sunrise on the following morning to return to the Freguezia de Assungui.

More advanced in social civilisation than Sr. Andrade, the *fazendeiro* of Campinas, Sr. Garses did not keep his family tightly bottled up from public gaze. His daughters all appeared in the outer verandah, and also sat down to meals with us. Two of them were rather pretty girls, very shy but not *gauche*.

Sr. Garses himself was the most intelligent specimen of the *fazendeiro* class that I ever remember meeting with in this province. He was, to a certain extent, an educated man, and knew something about European history and geography. The majority of the *fazendeiros* that I have met with in the province are totally ignorant of the outside world. Many even could not sign their own names to save their lives, and yet they live and prosper! This is one evidence of how little mental capital a man needs to become prosperous in this country.

CHAPTER III.

AFTER four days' work in this district I succeeded in obtaining five men, a scanty success, achieved, however, against powerful opposition.

All the animals belonging to my little party were more or less knocked up, for up to this time they had travelled more than 250 miles since we had left Colonia Thereza, about eighty miles of which had been by mule tracks of the worst description.

Sr. Cordeiro having given me a pressing invitation to pay him a visit at his *sitio* before leaving the district, I went there, hoping to be able to renew my tired troop by purchases and exchanges from his stock.

I was surprised to find there a little English boy, whom it appeared Sr. Cordeiro had adopted a year before, on his parents deserting the colony of Assungui. This little boy was a bright little fellow, about eleven years of age. He told me he never expected to see his parents again, and that he had never been happier in his life than he now was. His christian name was Henry, his surname I have forgotten.

Cordeiro himself, seen in his own house, was the type of a jolly farmer. His cattle, his horses, his mules and his pigs, were all fatter than any I had ever seen in the province. His house, situated in the midst of a large piece of pasture land, which had been reclaimed from the forest, was of palatial dimensions. A small stream, by name Coriolo, flowed past just outside the stockyard.

Sr. Cordeiro told me that his roças were scattered about over an extent of many miles of country, and that his only difficulty was the scarcity of labour to plant and to gather them. In the face of this scarcity of labour in this district, it may seem at first sight astonishing that the *Caboclos* are never paid higher than one milreis a day for their labour, and generally only two patácas (two-thirds of a milreis). If it were not that the great majority of them are more or less in the power of the large *fazendeiros*, by reason of their debts, this low rate would not stand for a day. Whether Cordeiro himself practised the system of "white slavery," I could never find out; it was, however, partly through his aid that I succeeded in obtaining the few men I did. I imagine there was considerable rivalry between him and Nobrega, and that the former had no scruples in aiding to draw away the men of the latter.

A rather alarming incident occurred on the night of my stay at this *fazenda.* I was suddenly aroused from a deep sleep by loud shrieks in a woman's voice, coming from a room not far off mine. The shrieks were so terrific that I thought murder or some other fearful outrage was being committed, and I rushed out to see what it was. Groping my way in the darkness towards the sound, I found a door, through the chinks of which light was proceeding. It was fastened, but on my calling out, it was at once opened, and Sr. Cordeiro himself appeared in the way, blowing and panting as though from some severe exertion.

I went in and beheld a young negress strapped down to a bed, and crying out at the top of her voice to the effect that ten thousand devils had got hold of her, and were tearing her to pieces. Another man was in the room, a son of Cordeiro, besides an old negress.

The negrinha was mad, and the three had just succeeded in strapping her down, in order to prevent her doing herself some injury. Her madness was periodical, and generally came on about every three weeks, lasting for a day or two each time, on which occasions she was always fearfully violent. Her screams went on half through the night and were horrible to listen to, effectually spoiling my repose.

The following morning, while we were sitting at breakfast, the door of the room in which she was confined suddenly burst open, and she rushed franticly out into the stockyard, and threw herself over the seven-foot fence surrounding it, and raced away down the grass slope to the Coriolo, shrieking *diabos! diabos! diabos!* No one followed her, and she was left to vent the last dregs of her madness, free and undisturbed, under the open vault of heaven. Before I left on that day, I saw her walking about the house quietly and sanely as other people.

I bought from Sr. Cordeiro a strong horse for my own use, a riding mule, and two pack-mules, all in superb condition, for a total sum of £41. Besides this, Sr. Cordeiro agreed to keep my own worn-out animals free of charge till my return, which might not be for some weeks.* Horseflesh and muleflesh is thus cheap enough in these parts, and indeed my own *camaradas* told me privately, that even £30 would have been a fair price to have given for the four animals.

A day and a half's riding, after wishing good-bye to the *fazenda* of Sr. Cordeiro, brought me to the out-

---

* One of the mules, thus left at Sr. Cordeiro's, died there. This animal was not my own, but one that I had hired at Colonia Thereza. The unwritten law in these cases is, that if the hired animal die, its loss falls on the *owner*, but the hirer must produce its mark, that is, a piece of its hide having the owner's brand stamped upon it, as a proof of death. If a hired animal is lost on the road, as is sometimes the case, the *hirer* is responsible for its value in money, which the owner then claims.

skirts of the English colony of Assungui. Let me
here remind those of my readers who have not read,
or who have forgotten, the correspondence that has
appeared in the papers from time to time, with
reference to this and other English colonies in Brazil,
that there are two distinct and opposite theories, by
which it has been attempted to account for their
non-success. One theory lays the blame entirely on
the Brazilian Government, asserting first that the
sites of the colonies are badly chosen, and secondly,
that faith has not been kept with the colonists; whilst
the other theory affirms, that the cause of failure is to
be found solely in the bad character of the emigrants
themselves. In my mind no doubt whatever exists as
to the cause, or rather causes of failure in the case of
the colony of Assungui. I will, however, first give
some of the results of my own observations and
inquiries, and then the opinions which I formed therefrom.

The habitations of the colonists begin to be encountered about two leagues on the Curitiba side of
the nucleus of the colony. These habitations are palm-
built huts, constructed very much in the style of those
we had been accustomed to build for our big camps
on the Ivahy. Each hut is situated upon a clearing,
about 100 yards by fifty in extent, the clearing, be it
noted, not being grubbed, but merely cleared super-
ficially of forest. These plots of land have attached
to them a certain number of acres (the minimum
allowance being thirty-seven, and the maximum 150)

of uncut forest land belonging to and sold with the lot on which the hut stands.

The lowest price for which these lots are sold to the colonists, is about £1, and the highest price £4 per acre; besides this the colonist has to pay for the building of his hut £3, and the clearing of the plot on which it stands, £1. Other liabilities have also accumulated upon him before he can take possession, such, for example, as a certain share of the cost of his passage out from England, and of his keep whilst in the country. Also, unless he pays ready money for his land, twenty per cent. is added to its cost price as given above, and he is bound to pay off the whole debt within six years of his coming into possession, under pain of forfeiture. Thus to begin with, the emigrant, unless he be a man of capital, starts weighted with a debt of, at the very least, £50, and which may amount to three or four hundred pounds or more. He has no right however to complain of this, as he is supposed to agree to it with his eyes open, before deciding to go out as an emigrant. It may be questioned, however, whether the information is put before him in so bald a manner, stript of all disguises, as I have given it here.

The system by which all this preliminary debt is accumulated, certainly appears on the face of it to be bad, for it puts a sort of premium on idleness, which badly disposed emigrants soon discover, and make use of. For example, many emigrants whom I met at Curitiba, boasted that having got all that they could out of the Government, namely, a free or rather a lent

passage from England, and all expenses paid up to
Curitiba, they would now start on their own account,
when their identity would be soon lost, and thus they
should get off having to refund their passage money
and other expenses. I know several emigrants by
name, who have done this very thing.

To return however to the Assungui settlers. What
are the advantages that they are to gain which is to
make it worth their while to saddle themselves with
this debt? In the case of those who have settled
down on the lots to which I first came, situated on the
south side of the colony, the land they have bought is
undoubtedly very rich and fertile, and capable of
producing all the staple food products of the country,
but, before it can be utilised, it has to be cleared of
forest, and the cost of felling and burning the timber
on one acre alone, even when done in the rough,
slovenly Brazilian roça fashion, would come to nearly
£1, or nine days' labour for one man; and if grubbed
and made ready for the plough, the cost would be at
least five times as great. But the contour of the
ground is such, that the plough could not possibly be
used, the lots being laid out on the steep slopes of a
narrow mountainous valley, something like those we
are accustomed to see in the higher Swiss valleys.

Thus, then, the English settler is necessarily re-
stricted to the roça style of cultivation, as practised by
the Brazilians around him, and with whom therefore he
has to compete, with absolutely no advantage, but on
the contrary, with all the disadvantages of ignorance

of the country, and a millstone of debt hanging round
his neck. The Brazilian is not a hard worker, and
therefore even with these weighty obstacles to success,
the English colonist might manage to obtain a good
footing, were it not for the existence of the large *fazendeiros* such as Cordeiro, Nobrega, and Garses already
mentioned. He has no mules, and no possibility
of keeping any if he had them, his property having
no pasturage upon it. Thus he at once sinks to the
very self-same position which, as I have already shown,
is so detrimental to the success of the *Caboclo*. He
must perforce sell his produce "in situ," or else pay a
large price for the hire of mules to take it to the
market at Curitiba.

Neither is he any better off if he tries to send it
down the Ribeira to the sea coast. In the first place
he is several miles from the river, and in the next
place he has no canoes, and to hire a canoe with men
to work it, is as ruinous as the hiring of mules would
be, for he has large competitors 100 miles or more
nearer the coast, that is to say on the very banks of
the lower Ribeira, not twenty miles perhaps from the
point up to which steamboats can come.

So much for the prospects of the settler on the
Curitiba side of Assungui, and those on the Ribeira
side are scarcely more favourably situated.

I do not know how many years it is since this
colony was first attempted to be established, certainly
more than ten, and yet it does not contain one single
successful emigrant; for the simple reason, of course,

that success under the given conditions is next to impossible to be attained.

I dismounted at many of the settlers' huts by the side of the mule track, and went in to talk to the people. In answer to my questions as to how they liked their new homes, the invariable reply was to this effect, "Would to God we had never come here, but we were misled by false promises." That the agents had lied to these poor people in England, I have not the slightest doubt, the testimony of the settlers being overwhelming on this point, but that the Brazilian Government itself in any way connived at the deceptions practised, I can scarcely think likely. Official morality in Brazil is certainly not held in very high esteem, according to vulgar report, but in the case of the English emigrants, the Government must long since have discovered that a man inveigled out to the country by misrepresentations, represents so much money thrown into the sea, and more than this, for he becomes the instrument by which the name of Brazil, as an advantageous emigration land, is brought into ruinous disrepute.

It is probable that most of the emigrants had been only too willing to have their ears tickled by such high sounding phrases as "landed proprietors," "freehold estates," &c., &c., and in consequence have themselves greatly to blame for the reality having proved so much harsher than the picture they had drawn in their own mind's eye.

The colony or village of Assungui is very prettily

situated, near the mouth of the little river Ponta Grossa, a tributary of the Ribeira. Here, the valley, hitherto most contracted, suddenly widens out to nearly a mile in breadth, a large piece of flat ground, on the right bank of the stream, being appropriated to the village.

About a mile outside the village there is a piece of macadamised road a few hundred yards long, the miserable result of many long years of expectation for the promised highway to Curitiba. This piece of road, I was told, represents the total amount of Government work that has been provided for the colonists since the foundation of the colony; though by the terms to which the Government has agreed, it is bound to find ninety days' work within the first six months, at reasonable wages, for any and every colonist who may choose to apply for it. Many of the settlers whom I conversed with, affirmed that this promise had not been kept, and their assertion was strongly supported by appearances, as well as by some independent Brazilian testimony.

Learning that the director of the colony was temporarily absent, I went to the house of the chief merchant of the place, a Brazilian, by name Sr. Serivera, and introduced myself to him. Though styling himself "merchant," after the custom of the country of calling little things by big names, Sr. Serivera was, in reality, a shopkeeper, selling everything, from a Brummagem tin kettle to Manchester cotton goods. Here we were willingly received and accommodated, and I found that I could not have gone to any better place if I wished to obtain varied and detailed information about the colonists.

Sr. Serivera brought out his big ledger, wherein were written the names of, probably, every male adult colonist who had ever visited Assungui. Turning over the leaves containing the record of their transactions with him and their many debts, he delivered a running commentary upon each name. I was surprised to see, by the names he read out, that, at different times, there had been many Frenchmen in the colony, and for these the merchant had but one word to say, "*ladrões todos*," literally "thieves all." The word *ladrão*, however, as commonly used amongst the Brazilians, implies something much stronger than this. It is an expression intended to convey the idea of the person being utterly worthless and despicable. Such was Sr. Serivera's verdict upon the Frenchmen, who, he said, never paid a single debt, if they could possibly sneak out of it, whereas the English were *boms rapazes*, good boys, who got drunk and fought, but seldom forgot their debts when they had money to pay them, which was, unhappily, not often.

No sooner was it known in the colony that an English engineer had arrived, and was seeking men, than I was besieged both in the house and out of the house, by numbers of colonists eager to be engaged. One glance was sufficient to give a very good notion of what the majority of them really were. Two thirds were evidently town roughs and rabble, both their speech and their appearance amply betraying them;

yet the Brazilian Government innocently imagines that it is importing English "agriculturists, well acquainted with the improved modes of farming as practised in their own land!" Poor deluded Government!

Hitherto, in my own mind, I had blamed solely the Government for its hard conditions, whereby success could not, without great difficulty, be achieved by the emigrants. Without retracting this opinion, the arguments for which must, in any case, hold good, it was yet abundantly evident that with such men as these, a colony established on the very best site, and on the easiest conditions, must be hopelessly damned from its very commencement.

The question naturally arises, why and wherefore were such emigrants as these brought out? The answer I must leave to the agents of the Brazilian Government in England. They best know by what reasoning process they were able to salve their consciences for passing men, who, as they could not but have perceived at the time, were utterly worthless, and in no degree answered to the requirements of the Brazilian Government.

On the second day of my stay at the colony I went round the village on a tour of inspection. The public receiving houses, where the newly arrived emigrants are sheltered till their own plots and houses are ready for them, were of the most interest. In these houses I found families herded together with considerable disregard to decency; two married couples often occupying one room.

It may be interesting to relate the history of the journey from England to Assungui, as told to me by one of the emigrants whom I found in the receiving houses, the main points of whose story were corroborated by others. The story points to very injudicious management on the part of the Government. The substance of it, which I took down in writing at the time, was as follows :—

" We sailed from England in the ship 'Santa Rosa,' which brought us to Rio de Janeiro on the 4th of February of the present year (1873) ; there were 120 of us. Yellow fever was very bad in Rio when we arrived (it will be remembered that Captain Palm died of this scourge on the 12th of the same month), and so we were sent on next day, by rail, to the Barra Piauhy, eighty miles up country, where we were kept nine days. We then went back to Rio, and were sent at once on board a steamer, which took us down to the Ilha das Cobras (?) near Paranaguá. Here we remained for five weeks idle. Many of us got ill, and some of the children died. From this place we were taken on to Antonina, where we stopped two weeks. Better food was given us here, and those who were sick before, now recovered. Early in April we were moved on to Curitiba, and from there were taken to ' receiving ' houses at Barrigui (a small place five miles out of Curitiba). These houses were very bad, and the rain came in through the roofs. We stopped here some time, and then we were brought on in small parties to this colony, the men having to march on foot (sixty miles),

but mules being provided for the women and children.
Four milreis were given to each of us for food on the
way.   The food on board the ' Santa Rosa' was very
bad.   At the Ilha das Cobras it was not very good,
but at Antonina it was quite good enough."

The point to be noticed in this brief story, is
the immense time—nearly three months—which the
journey from Rio to the colony had occupied, and
which had resulted in sickness, disgust, and, as was
to be supposed, the demoralisation of the emigrants
generally.   Instead of three months, three weeks
would have been ample and more than ample time to
have allowed for this part of the journey.   A single
traveller, not over-burdened with baggage, can easily
accomplish it in six days.

To sum up, then, briefly, the causes that have
hitherto militated against the success of the Assungui
colony—they are these :

1st. The injudicious choice of a site, where, from
the steepness of the ground, the plough and other
improved implements of agriculture cannot be employed, and where there is no pasture land within
reasonable distance, for the keeping of mules for
taking produce to market.   2nd. The high price
charged to the colonists for the land allotted to them ;
the best proof that this price is too high, being, that
Brazilian colonists are not excluded from settling on
the allotments, but yet do not do so.   3rd. The carelessness or dishonesty of the agents of the Brazilian
Government in England, in passing applicants as fit

and proper persons for an agricultural colony, many of whom are really altogether unfit. 4th. The weakness or carelessness of organisation, which can allow of the journey from Rio to Assungui to be so unnecessarily protracted, resulting in the demoralisation of the emigrants, even before their work is begun, and which also permits the newly arrived emigrant to frequently remain many weeks in the receiving houses at the colony, without the opportunity of work being afforded him, waiting till such time as it may be convenient to the officials to have his lot of land and his house prepared for him. 5th, and last, the bad character of many of the emigrants themselves.

With reference to number 4, even granting that the full ninety days' work in the first six months is given to each new arrival who applies for it, which the colonists deny, this is not sufficient. It would be better for the colonist and better for the Government, that, for the first year at least of his time at the colony, he should be able to obtain work on the public road whenever he might choose to apply for it. Conditions might be attached to this granting of work, for instance, the obligation on the applicant to plant not less than a certain definite amount of his own land in the year.

The Government may say to this, " Oh! but we cannot afford to give unlimited work to the colonists." The answer to this is obvious. " Import no more colonists than you can properly provide for." Another answer might be given to the effect that, at the present rate of work, the promised road to Curitiba will take something like 200 years to complete, which delay constitutes a distinct breach of faith on the part of the Government towards the emigrant. No better example of the success which may attend colonisation in the province of Paraná, provided that *unlimited* work is provided for the strangers for the first few years after their arrival, can be pointed to, than that which the Germans have achieved in the neighbourhood of Curitiba.

Although there are such great natural causes which will always prevent the colony of Assungui rising to the rank of a great agricultural centre of English industry and science, there are none sufficient to prevent its becoming a moderately prosperous self-supporting settlement. Radical changes both in its organisation and administration are, however, essential before even such moderate success can be hoped for.

On the whole, Assungui cannot be said to be a suitable spot for the establishment of any English colony.*

* See Appendix, Note F, "State Colonies and Private Colonies in the province of Paraná."

CHAPTER IV.

Down the valley of the Ribeira.—The bell-bird.—The Capella de Ribeira.—Opposition of the *fazendeiros*.—Brazilian farmers' life. —The " Puxerão."—The march back.

LEAVING the Colonia de Assungui after a stay there of two days, I pushed on with my two faithful *camaradas*, Pedro and Messéno, down the valley of the Ribeira to visit the various little villages and Brazilian settlements situated on the banks of that river. It was somewhat of a relief once more to get away from the atmosphere of noisy discontent and unsavoury Billingsgate of this hapless British colony, to the calm solitude of the forest.

Probably the best mule-track existing in the whole province is that which, commencing at Votuverava, half-way between Curitiba and the colony, runs down the valley of the Ponta Grossa, and thence down the left bank of the Ribeira to the Capella of the same name, twenty-five miles below Assungui. It is a path regularly cut out of the sloping valley side for the whole distance, with due and proper regard to gradients, such as is never given to the common *picada* mule-track.

Enormous fig trees and garlic trees bounded each side of the path, throwing out immense flying buttresses, the better to support their huge ungainly trunks and the weight of their massive branches above. A whole forest of slender palms and tall tree-ferns grew beneath the spreading tops of these great giants of the forest, adding marvellously to the beauty of our road. Frequently we obtained glimpses of the Ribeira itself on our left, racing down its steep rocky bed over a series of small though powerful *corredeiras.*

For many hours we plodded along through the midst of this lovely scenery of mountain, forest, and cataract, without meeting a living soul. A flock of screaming parrots now and then enlivened us for a moment with their harsh music as they hurried past in full flight towards some favourite feeding-ground. With this exception the forest through which we were passing seemed to be given up entirely to the dominion of the *ferreiro* or bell-bird, whose note, resembling much the shrieking of the ungreased axles of a bullock cart, sounded far and wide on either hand.

The bell-bird is not known in the Ivahy valley, and I had not heard it before. It is almost impossible to do more than catch an occasional glimpse of it when it is in its wild state, for, in the first place, it is, like the musical frog of the prairie, a ventriloquist of very high powers, and, secondly, being a sun-loving bird, it frequents only the highest tree-tops, where, in the bright sunlight, its snow-white plumage and transparent wings render it almost invisible, even when in motion.

In size it is but slightly bigger than a starling, while its voice is fully as powerful as that of a peacock.

I once saw a bell-bird in captivity at Antonina, where the cage in which it was confined was suspended outside a window of a house in one of the streets. The cry of this bird could be distinctly heard in every quarter of the town, and even at some distance beyond its outskirts. For a long time I used to think it was a wild one, for its notes sometimes seemed to come from the mountains at the back of the town, fully a quarter of a mile distant from where the bird was actually encaged.

Just before sunset, as we were on the point of camping for the night, a canoe, manned by three stalwart *Caboclos,* shot past us on the river down a series of swiftly-rushing *corredeiras.* We shouted to them to stop and join our camp for the night, but we might as well have spoken to the wind, for they were powerless to hinder their course. We watched them for the next half-minute as they shot rapid after rapid in quick succession, their bodies, naked from the waist upwards, glistening with the spray that kept dashing over them, and their long hair streaming behind like the tail of a race-horse. They gave us a fiendish yell as they flew past, and in half-a-minute they were out of sight round a bend of the river. These were the kind of men I wanted to get hold of for our Ivahy rapids.

On the following day we arrived at the Capella de Ribeira and found the three men there before us. Learning from them who was their *patrão,* and that, 'or a wonder, they were only bound to him for a short-time contract, and owed very little money in the place, I managed to enlist all three for our service by advancing a month's wages to enable them to satisfy all their creditors in full.*

The Capella de Ribeira proved to be a tiny agricultural village, numbering perhaps a hundred inhabitants. The chief products of its district, besides the inevitable Indian corn and beans, were sugar and coffee, both of which grew luxuriantly on the stiff red and yellow clay soil of the hills around. I here met a *Caboclo* who showed me some gold which he said he had washed from the river, at a point a short distance above the village. I have no doubt that he spoke the truth, for the sand of the Ribeira, in certain localities, is almost identical in appearance and doubtless also in constitution with that of the Tibagy river, in which latter I myself subsequently found gold as well as diamonds.

Two leagues beyond the Capella de Ribeira stands another little village called the "Porto de Apiahy," also

---

* I must here pay a well-merited compliment to the *Caboclos* of the Ribeira district as a whole. I engaged fifteen of them in all, from different parts of this district, and for three months, during which they were working immediately under my orders, they formed the very backbone of the most important section of the Ivahy river service. With but one exception, they were trustworthy, hardworking, and courageous fellows, much superior to the general run of our Ivahy men, notwithstanding that, amongst the latter, there were ten or a dozen, who, as a Yankee would say, "I guess would beat all creation." Such men, for example, as the two brothers Miguel and Hypolito, could not have been surpassed by any.

situated on the bank of the river. The mule-road connecting the two, passes over a break-neck mountain of a thousand feet in height, though why it should do so in preference to the far easier mode of skirting the river is a mystery to the uninitiated. I took Messeno there with me to try our luck in obtaining men, while Pedro remained behind at Capella to complete the work already commenced in that district.

Once more I found "white slavery" rampant. The *fazendeiros*, though courteous and hospitable in the extreme to us personally, did not shrink from using underhand means in order to dissuade the few independent *Caboclos* who showed any inclination to do so from entering our service. They industriously spread reports to the effect that many men of the expedition had died of fever and even starvation; that the Ivahy valley was infested by wild Indians, by whom many Brazilians had already been killed; and lastly that the mosquitos in that valley were as big as hornets, and no one could have an hour's peace from them at any time. There was just enough truth in these reports to render them very prejudicial to our success. It was in vain that we pointed to ourselves as men who had been with the expedition for the last twelve months, and had neither been starved to death nor slain by Indians nor devoured alive by mosquitos. Such negative logic fell flat in the majority of cases. What men we did succeed in obtaining, succumbed to the tempting bait of 300$000 (say £30) offered for a six months' service,—such a sum being enough to set a careful *Caboclo* up for life, and, as we told them, to get for them the prettiest wives in the country.

Irritating as was all this constant opposition that everywhere I met with, it yet had its good, for it gave me an endless variety of opportunities, such as I should not otherwise have obtained, of becoming thoroughly acquainted with the general character and modes of life of the two great classes of Brazilians inhabiting these remote districts—the *fazendeiro* and the *Caboclo.*

With this object I never refused an invitation to sleep in a *fazendeiro's* house or even in the humbler *rancho* of a *Caboclo,* whenever such hospitality was offered. After a time I began to feel quite a Brazilian myself, so thoroughly accustomed did I become to their ways and customs of life.

It is almost impossible not to feel a hearty liking for a people who universally throw their houses open, not only to their own kith and kin, but even to the passing stranger and foreigner, not proudly, as though they were conferring an honour, nor obsequiously as to a superior from whom they expect to receive some return, but from sheer goodwill, kindliness of heart, and custom of the country.

The *fazendeiro* will give you coffee and cigarettes on your first arrival, and give up to you the place of honour—the hammock ; his slave will come and take your boots off, wash your aching feet, and give you a pair of his master's *chinellas* or slippers to wear for the evening. You will then sit down to a substantial supper of chicken and rice, with unlimited *cachaça* and milk. At night your host will even supply you with a blanket or *poncho* for a covering, should you chance not to have got your own with you. He will talk to you and entertain you to the best of his ability, as though you were his bidden guest.

The *Caboclo*, more humble in his establishment, but not less hospitable, will, according to his means, give you *mate* in lieu of coffee, and beans and *farinha* instead of chicken and rice. He will give up his own bedstead to you for the night, and himself sleep on the hard mud floor of his hut. Payment is always made for corn given to your animals, and a poor *Caboclo* is not above accepting a small present when you leave him in the morning, but even this is rarely expected and never asked for.

There is, however, one virtue in which both wealthy *fazendeiro* and poor *Caboclo* are alike deficient, comparing, in this respect, unfavourably with even the despised Coroado *Bugré,*—personal cleanliness is not cultivated to the extent that the climate demands.

For example, the house of a large *fazendeiro*, who employs, perhaps, from one hundred to two hundred *camaradas* during the planting season, has for its lavatory paraphernalia usually but *one* tin basin, in which the feet of the guest are washed in the evening and in which every male member of the household washes his eyes and the tips of his fingers in the morning. With the temperature up to 90° Fahr. in the shade for half the day, neither *fazendeiro* nor *Caboclo* dreams of taking a bath in the cool inviting waters of the river before him. In all those cases when the first thing to which an Englishman's thoughts naturally wander is a tub, the Brazilian finds full solace in a cigarette. With him in fact the fumes of tobacco always stand in the stead of personal ablutions.

One of the customs common to this essentially agricultural district of the Ribeira valley is so curiously like our own " harvest home," that it will be interesting to give a short account of it in this place.

It consists in an entertainment, given annually by the *fazendeiro* to his *Caboclos.* This entertainment goes by the name of *puxerão*, an expressive but untranslatable word, feebly rendered by the words " big gathering." The object of the *puxerão* is not alone to induce friendly relations and a good understanding between the *patrão* and the *camarada,* as in the old country between the . squire and his labourers or tenants, but more especially to give all parties the only chance perhaps that they have in the year of meeting together at one time and in one place.

The *patrão* who gives the feast more especially benefits by it, for it saves him an enormous amount of time and labour in riding about the wide extent of country through which his workers are usually scattered. Almost all the business arrangements for the ensuing season are put on a footing at the *puxerão*. Men are re-engaged and told off to this or that *roça*. Accounts are adjusted, debts being paid off or carried

on to the next half year.   Or again, new debts are
contracted by some silly *Caboclo*, who knows not that
he is selling himself into bondage, and the day is
finally brought to a close to the satisfaction of all.

I chanced to be a guest at two of these *puxerões*, and
their business-like character was sufficiently evidenced
by the absence of all women-kind from them, for
women in these remoter districts of Brazil do not hire
out their labour as in the more civilised parts, but
remain all day shut up at home, on household cares
intent.   Though at the feast, which forms a main
feature in the *puxerão*, there is always an unlimited
supply of *cachaça* on the board, I never saw a case
of drunkenness on these occasions.   The natural pride
of the Brazilian is sufficient to prevent him giving
way on these public occasions, even though his in-
clinations may strongly tend towards the indulgence
in strong spirits.   In this respect the lower class
Brazilian is somewhat superior to his brother of
England.

I was anxious to go down to Ipiranga, the point on
the Ribeira to which steamers can come up from the
coast, in order to see with my own eyes what was the
extent of trade carried on from this valley.   Time
however pressed, and men of the kind that I wanted
were not likely to be found there, I was therefore
obliged reluctantly to give up the idea of extending my
journey farther in this direction.

Returning by way of the two Assunguis, we once
more beat up the districts to right and left of our line

of march, picking up a man here and a man there, and wearing out our animals at a terrific rate. For many days together, I was in the saddle for twelve and thirteen hours at a stretch, accompanied by one or other of my two attendants. On one occasion the horse on which I was riding fell down, while descending a very steep path, and, not content with depositing me in a mass of jungle, itself rolled down the slope of the valley for several yards, not stopping till it was brought up by the mass of thorns and *cipós* which had then wound themselves around it. We were obliged to cut the poor animal free with our knives, so firmly was it entangled in the jungly growth.

At Cordeiro's we again picked up our original animals, which had now, to a great extent, recovered from the effects of their first long march, while, at the same time, those that I had bought at this place only three weeks before, had to be re-sold on account of their being worn out, and others bought to supply their places.

The newly engaged *camaradas* marched on foot, their scanty equipments alone being carried by the pack-mules. From the Freguezia de Assungui we marched direct to Ponta Grossa and thence to Colonia Thereza, a weary distance of nearly 200 miles. Once I was unfortunate enough to get a slight touch of sunstroke, which, however, was sufficiently powerful to prostrate me hand and foot for several hours, and to stop the march for two days.

In passing through the little *povoação* of Ipiranga,

mentioned in the first volume of this book, we were delayed another day by the loss of three of our mules. Ipiranga had already got an evil name from us, on account of the number of mysterious disappearances of

JOAO, THE MULE-STEALER.

animals belonging to the expedition, that had taken place in this neighbourhood.

There was a certain old "nigger," by name João, who was commonly credited with being the author of these otherwise unaccountable disappearances.

Whether he was so or not, certain it is that a mule, once lost at this camping ground, could never be recovered except by the aid of João, who, on these occasions, always came forward and offered his services in the search, at the price of 5$000 per mule recovered. If his assistance was declined, farewell to all chance of seeing again your lost animals. A veritable black mail was thus levied upon all passers by, though it was impossible to bring the matter home to its wary originator.

The accompanying woodcut, from a sketch taken by my friend Mr. G. Selwyn Edwards, is a speaking likeness of the original, who, in addition to his mule-stealing propensities, had a capacity for imbibing *cachaça*, such as only Africans can have.

On the 22nd of November, after an absence of two months, and a ride of not less than 800 miles, I found myself back again at Colonia Thereza.

Thus it ever is, in the carrying out of great enterprises or works in semi-barbarous countries. The most elementary arrangements, the most trivial details as would seem, requiring for their execution an amount of time, labour, and perseverance, which in more advanced countries would almost suffice to carry out to completion the whole work itself.

PART IV.

CHAPTER I.

Précis from November '73 to June '74.—A burning question solved.—
Sketches : present, past, and future.

SIX months had passed since the day mentioned at
the conclusion of the last chapter—six long and eventful
months. The great rapids of the middle Ivahy, so
long a terror to the Brazilians, had been overcome and
navigated again and again by a score or more picked
men of the expedition. The main body of the staff
had pitched its last camp 230 miles below Colonia
Thereza, while an advance party of fourteen, under
Curling, had penetrated ninety miles farther into the
lower valley of the Ivahy, as far as, in fact, the *Corre-
deiro de Ferrò*, or Iron Rapid itself—the terminal
point of our section of the exploration. Then had
come a sudden collapse. The men forming the
advanced party mutinied from fear of the Coroados
Indians, who, to the number of about 500, were collected in villages near the Iron Rapid. At dead of

night they plotted to desert their leader and chief (Curling) by taking the canoes, and leaving him and two other Europeans at the mercy of the Indians. Extreme measures alone prevented them from carrying their cowardly plot into execution.

Totally demoralised by fear and other causes, they hurriedly retreated upon the main body higher up the river. A large number of the Coroados Indians following by the banks, the panic spread through the whole Brazilian staff, and all efforts proved futile to induce the men to remain. Persuasions, threats, entreaties, all were tried in turn, and all ended with a like result.

The entire staff was thus compelled to retreat up the river, abandoning its work for the time. This was in the month of March. Even the elements now rose up against us, and from the day the retreat was commenced, the rains came down and continued almost incessantly for five weeks. The river rose, and the cataracts were roaring above, below, and all around us. The journey commenced on the 10th of March, and the last canoe in which I was travelling did not arrive at Colonia Thereza till the 15th of April. The provisions had rotted in the canoes, our clothing had rotted off our backs during this trying journey of five weeks. Canoes had been swamped daily, and baggage, containing invaluable instruments and documents, was in hourly peril of being lost in the floods. Such a journey, performed under such circumstances, was simply terrible, morally as well as physically.

At this time the 1st Staff, having completed their

original length, had just come on to the river to take
up the surveys of a portion reserved for them midway
between the two extreme sections. Fortunately their
Staff was composed chiefly of Europeans and men
already proved by eighteen months' previous work.
Ultimately it was decided that this Staff should be
made the nucleus of a larger staff, to be formed by the
combination of various members of the 1st, 2nd, and
3rd Staffs, and that to it, thus strengthened, should be
entrusted the execution of the whole remaining distance
of the Ivahy section.

There was still the possibility of failure, should the
Indians at the Corredeira de Ferro prove hostile.[*]
To meet this possibility, it was decided to make a
preliminary exploration of another route, namely, by
way of the sister valley of the Tibagy, by which the
desired object of connecting Curitiba with the Paraná
river could be attained. To my charge the carrying
out of this new exploration had been given, and now I
have brought the reader up to the date indicated in
the first line of the chapter.

On the 1st of June, 1874, the hour being about
10 A.M., I was standing on the bare summit of a hill

---

[*] The chief cause of the panic, which resulted in the mutiny of the
Brazilians of the 2nd Staff, was the unfortunate fact of a collision
having occurred between the Coroados Indians of the Iron Rapid, and
some members of the 4th Staff, who had come up to this point from
Paraná, eight months before. In this collision, if we could believe
our interpreters, two Indians had been shot and killed. For this the
tribe determined to have revenge. The interpreters, by their injudicious
communication of this to the Brazilians of our Staff, caused the disastrous panic above referred to.

looking down upon the tiny little town of Tibagy whose dimensions were rendered still more diminutive to the eye, by the depth and distance at which it lay below and away from the hill. Stretching far away beyond the town, and extending to the extreme limits of vision was prairie, with its slopes dotted here and there with herds of cattle or troops of mules. To the right, sparkling here and there between the rises of the grassy billows and the dark green *capões*, glimpses of white foam-coloured water were visible, marking the position of so many points of the river that I had just safely descended—for sixty miles of this, my new exploration, had already been accomplished. Behind the hill was forest and mingled forest and prairie, forming part of the neutral belt or zone referred to in some of the earlier chapters of this book. On the left lay a similar country of mixed forest and prairie, beyond which again the great *Sertão* held undisputed sway, in which latter direction it was that my further explorations were to lie.

Before, however, going so far, I must introduce the reader to a veritable prairie phenomenon—for so it seemed to me—lying immediately beneath my feet, comprised in a compact little area of about ten square miles. On this little tract of prairie all the signs of a thriving and well-to-do population were manifested. *Chacaras* and other small houses were thickly sprinkled about it. Gardens and orange orchards, cultivated patches of potatoes and *mandioca*, green paddocks in which mules and cows were grazing, struck the eye, offering altogether a sight so uncommon in the province of Paraná as to excite something more than ordinary surprise and wonderment.

With me was an Englishman, named Mercer, who, though having only lately settled in the district, had prospered so well that he was about to become a son-in-law of one of the wealthiest *fazendeiros* of the neighbourhood. The phenomenon in question Mercer explained to me thus. The *chacaras* and houses had formerly been the habitation of miners. After the abandonment of the mine (about which more here-after), these men had, contrary to usual experience in Brazil, found it profitable to remain where they were, merely to cultivate the soil, so marvellously fertile was it, as compared with other prairie lands, and, moreover, so convenient was its situation with respect to other essential requirements.

This situation, indeed, was perhaps the most important element in insuring the prosperity of this little handful of colonists, for such they really were. Its advantage lay in the fact of its being in close proximity to the Forest, but yet, at the same time, not actually within its borders. Each of these little farmers had his garden and his paddock of twenty or thirty acres on the prairie, close to his house, on which he kept his mules, his cows, and his pigs, while at the same time, within an hour's walk or ride, he had his forest *roças*, where he could grow corn and beans, without which his mules would not work, his pigs would not fatten, and he himself could not live. While the prairie enabled him to keep his half-dozen mules or so with profit, the forest was the reservoir from whence, by means of his beasts of burden, all his chief necessities of life were drawn. The surplus produce of his *roças* he was able in like manner to convey profitably to the neighbouring markets of Ponta Grossa, Castro, and Curitiba, where fair prices were always obtainable.

Here then was a case of the vexed problem of colonisation in Brazil solved. A class of small proprietors had sprung up, without petting or nursing either by government or by well-meaning enthusiasts such as Dr. Favre, and the evidence of the prosperity to which they had attained was there before our eyes.

Just as the forest district of Assungui can never hope under its normal conditions to produce a thriving class of small proprietors, whether foreigners or Brazilians, so the prairie district we were now overlooking would inevitably have been merged long since into the wide and wasteful cattle-breeding estate of some large *fazendeiro*, had it not been for this main condition of proximity to the forest.

No observing traveller in this part of Brazil can fail to notice the entire absence of *small* farmers throughout the prairie districts, the fact being that only huge estates can yield any profit at all when there is no forest at hand. The same law holds good for purely forest estates, as I have already shown.* The large *fazendeiro* alone can live independent—the smaller fry

* Vide Part III. Chapters ii. and iii.

must either sink to abject poverty, or be content to
become hired labourers. Only on the verge of both
forest and prairie, where both are equally accessible, can
the *small* proprietor, or, in other words, the colonist,
hope to preserve his independence and win success.

This truth cannot be too widely known amongst
those who are in any way, either as capitalists or as
emigrants, likely to become connected with schemes of
colonization in this province of Brazil. No exclusively
forest (or agricultural) colony, such as that of Assungui
can be a success, and with equal certainty it may be
affirmed that no attempts to establish an exclusively
pastoral colony on the prairies, by means of small proprietors having little or no capital amongst them, can
possibly prove anything but abortive.

Returning once more to our point at the summit of
the hill. The great *sertão* of forest stretching away to
our left, extended in this direction for hundreds of
miles down the lower valley of the Tibagy and across
the great basin of the Paraná to an unknown distance
beyond. For the most part this vast extent of forest
was still in a state of nature, unknown and untrodden
by civilised man. At a distance from us in a straight
line of about seventy miles, two remarkable peaks,
sharply pointed, and placed very close together, rose
high up above the general level of the *sertão*. So clear
was the atmosphere in this direction, that I almost
fancied that I could distinguish, with the aid of my
field-glasses, the individual trees upon their summits.

By name I was already familiar with these two great

landmarks of the country, which, two generations before, had served as beacon hills to the savage Coroados Indians, at that time waging unceasing warfare with the new Brazilian settlers over the whole of these regions. They were the two highest points of a mountain range, which was variously marked on the maps as the Serra dos Agudos and the Serra de Apucarana. In the map which accompanies this book I have followed the more popular division, and made the river separate the two Serras, notwithstanding the fact that geologically they form one and the same range.

No civilised man had ever yet explored the river that lay above and below these two peaks, between which it was supposed to pass over a great fall, variously given as from 100 to 500 feet. About 100 miles of this part of the river remained to be explored, besides a considerable length, never yet mapped down, which was known only to a few adventurous *Caboclos* who had from time to time braved its mysterious dangers in the search for gold and diamonds.

Beyond these two peaks, at a distance of another seventy miles in a straight line, lay the valley of the Paranapanéma, famous in Brazilian history as the scene of some of the boldest of the labours of the Jesuits in South America, as well as of their most brilliant successes and greatest disasters,* and, in our own time, as one of the cross country routes by which the Brazilian Government sent men and material to

* See Appendix, Note L. "The Jesuits on the Paranapanéma."

their army, during the great life and death struggle with Paraguay.

It was this valley that was to be the "ultima Thule" of my present expedition, an account of some of the chief incidents of which will form the substance of the few remaining chapters.

CHAPTER II.

The first diamond.—The effect of its discovery.—Some of the consequences of the Paraguayan War. —The mines.—Their history.—Brazilian ideas of "profit."—Anecdotes of early days.—The first "Incumbent."

ONE moonlight night, just forty-two years ago, when the spot on which the town of Tibagy now stands was still waste prairie, a certain Senhor Manoël das Dores Machado was riding slowly towards his home, picking his way amongst the numerous ant hillocks and armadillo holes —which to this day cause rapid riding on these prairies to be a doubtful amusement—with his eyes bent downwards, when he saw a bright object glittering on the surface of a little mound, that had been freshly bought from the depths by some laborious "tatu," or industrious burrowing owl. He dismounted, picked up the object, and found it was a *diamond*.

On the following day, his slaves were taken off the Roças, and set to work at diamond hunting. The news spread. People flocked in from all parts; and in the first blush of success, Sr. Manoël, who was at this

time the owner of all the land about, made a grant of
a certain portion, for the foundation of a town.   This
was the site, and such was the origin of the present
town of Tibagy; though it was not till the year 1873,
that it attained to the full municipal rights of a town-
ship (Villa).

The town and immediate district around it, in that
year, contained 4890 inhabitants, chiefly of the *Caboclo*
class—*Caboclo* being here understood to include all
persons of mixed blood who were neither *negociantes*
(merchants), nor *fazendeiros* (large farmers).

During the Paraguayan war, when the whole country
was being scoured by the recruiting agents of the
Government, it was a bad time for this, as well as for
all young settlements.   Many of the able-bodied men
were carried off to serve in the army, and great
numbers, in order to avoid a similar fate, fled to the
forest, and there lived in concealment the life of wild
Indians.   As a natural consequence most industries
were stopped or greatly crippled, the diamond workings
not being exempt from the general depression.

At the conclusion of the war the people returned,
though thinned in numbers, and once more the
district grew prosperous, its population increasing
year by year.

On the diamond workings becoming exhausted, or,
more correctly speaking, becoming less profitable, the
prosperity, originally started by them, did not at once
fall off, as has been the case with so many Brazilian
mining settlements.   The miners merely changed their

profession, becoming small farmers, whose degree of success is limited only by their own requirements, which, unfortunately for rapid progress in these parts, are few and simple, being easily satisfied by three months' labour out of the twelve.

The reasons of this exception to the almost universal rule, attending the decay of mining districts, are two ; one being the very advantageous position which the settlement holds for agricultural purposes, and the other being due to the fact that the diamond mines have never been worked by any great company, whose collapse—when a collapse does take place—is usually sudden and complete, carrying everything down with it within a radius of a score of leagues perhaps, but have, as it were, and as will be presently shown, merely been " scratched," no machinery having ever been employed and no capital having been sunk upon them.

The regular and systematic (if such an epithet can here be applied) working of the mines was discontinued in the year 1871, in which year it was calculated that only about £4000 worth of the precious stones had been exported from them. The collapse of so small an industry as this figure implies could not be attended with any very disastrous consequences, and, probably, not fifty men were directly affected by it.

Thus far my information has been derived chiefly from one man, the chief *negociante* of the town of Tibagy, by name José Manoël da Silva, an old-standing merchant of the place. This gentleman waxed indignant, whenever in his conversation he touched upon the subject of the abandonment of the workings; for, poor man, most of the diamonds found, had formerly passed through his hands, greatly no doubt to his contentment. According to him, one *feitor* with half a dozen slaves could have done the whole amount of work that was got through in the entire year of 1871, in six months; and yet, forsooth, they had found that a gross income of £4000 for that year had not been sufficient to render the working profitable!

It is very necessary in Brazil to take every thing *cum grano*, more especially when the subject is "mines;" and I do not suppose the reader will be willing to put implicit faith in the mere uncorroborated statements of Sr. José Manoël, any more than I was myself. Nevertheless there was sufficient *primâ facie* evidence of a heedless haste in the abandonment of the mines, to make it worth while to push one's inquiries somewhat farther into the matter. ·This I resolved to do in the few days that I had to spare while awaiting the completion of arrangements for continuing the exploration of the Tibagy valley. The following additional information will first be interesting, the anecdotes which follow not being without their hidden morals.

Since the year 1871 the workings, which were chiefly confined to one spot, have been thrown open to all comers, with a result that about £200 worth of diamonds, are now annually extracted by individual workers. The reason given for the abandonment of the mines was not that they were exhausted, but that the depth to which the diamond-bearing stratum had then reached below the surface of the ground had brought the expenses of working to a point beyond which it was considered no sufficient margin would be left for profit.

As the word " profit " in Brazil bears a popular signification, differing according to locality and according to the idiosyncrasy of the individual making use of it, I may as well at once explain that 24 per cent. per annum on capital laid out on the best security is considered, in the province of Paraná, a very moderate return, in fact, barely a " profit " at all. It may well be imagined, then, that in the case of so fluctuating and uncertain a property as a diamond mine, a Paraná capitalist may call even a cent. per cent. return not " profitable," and will even act up to his ideas of what constitutes profit by withdrawing from such a meagre enterprise !

Here, then, we get a clue to the apparent contradiction between the *fact* that the Tibagy diamond mines are now abandoned, and the *statement* of the indignant *negociante*, Sr. José Manoël da Silva, that so much labour had produced so much gross earnings during the last year of their having been regularly worked : naming amounts which were no doubt somewhat inaccurate, but still not so absurdly improbable as at first sight might appear.

Here is a story that eclipses the palmiest days of gold-digging in California. "'Donna' Maria Machado, the wife of the discoverer of the mines, set her heart upon possessing a certain slave, the property of another 'Donna.' For this slave, who was worth in the market about £100, 'Donna' Maria gave a cupful (*chicara cheia*) of picked diamonds." Again: "A *Caboclo*, working on his own account in some gravel in the river bank, found a diamond weighing an oitava and a half; with this he bought a house worth £40, the same diamond afterwards realising £1,400! The same individual sold two more fine stones, together weighing an oitava, for only £50!" So little then was the real value of the stones understood in this remote district.

No story in this part of the country is considered complete without the inevitable priest, especially when it savours at all of rascality. The following was strictly vouched for by the "oldest inhabitant."

"Frei Mattheo, one of the earliest of the 'incumbents' appointed to take charge of the souls of the miners, being a holy man, of tender sympathies withal for the little everyday troubles of his flock, nobly insisted upon relieving them from those carnal cares and worries which were inseparable from the possession of wealth of a certain kind, for which there was no near market, by buying their diamonds himself at the rate of £2 per quarter oitava* for all stones large and small!" Now, by the ordinary rules for valuing

* The oitava is equal to 17·44 carats.

diamonds, a stone of pure water, weighing a quarter oitava in the rough, could seldom be worth less than £50. " Thus the holy man speedily began to grow rich, and by the end of a few months had so lined his own pockets with *contos* that he was able to retire from the scene of his labours without lament, just about the time when a dim sense of their having been in some sort victimised began to dawn upon his flock, but *before* this new awakening had ripened into action, which might, had it taken place, have proved detrimental to his future enjoyment of life."

These, and many other traditional tales of the early days of the mines, though no doubt somewhat distorted and exaggerated by much telling, yet sufficiently show that, for the first few years of their existence, the mines obtained no great patronage, and that nothing like systematic working was then carried on. Later on, no doubt, some attempt at systematic working was made, and kept up with more or less success till the final abandonment in 1871.

Thus much for the documentary and hearsay evidence with relation to these mines. It now only remains to record the results of a careful personal inspection that I made of them, to ascertain how far the chief points of present interest can be borne out by facts.

CHAPTER III

The mines examined.—I find a runaway.—Description of presen
appearance of the workings. — Why abandoned. — Conclusion
arrived at.—"A missing mine."—Ignorance of the workers.—
Important indications.—A probable diamond-field.

AT a distance of somewhat less than three miles
from the town of Tibagy, situated on ground
which is now the common property of about 100
persons, are the main workings of the diamond
mines.

Early one morning, a day or two after our arrival
at Tibagy, I rode with Mercer to this spot with the
intention of giving the whole day to the business of
inspection and examination, not only of this particular
working, but also of the whole district around, in which
diamonds either had been, or had been reported to
have been, discovered.

Shortly before arriving at the main diggings, which
are situated within the forest borders, we passed
several little ranchos, inhabited by Caboclos and
their families. These men still occasionally dug in
the mine, whenever the spirit happened to move

them, which by all accounts was not more frequently than once or twice a month. For the remainder of the year they passed an existence of pure and unadulterated idleness, with the sole exception of the short period of labour required for cutting a *Roça* in the forest that came up to their very doors, planting it, and in due time gathering in the produce. These were the gamblers or fatalists—words almost synonymous—a type of *caboclo* the least attractive of any that I am acquainted with. We dismounted at and entered several of their abodes. Almost without exception, the men seemed nerveless, spiritless creatures, fitted only for the wretched existence that no doubt was theirs.

To my surprise, in one house or rather hut, I recognised an old *camarada* of ours; one of the very men who had stolen a canoe and fled one night from the Areranha in dire terror of the Indians who had not then appeared. " Well, Ignacio," I said, " got back with the whole skin? I hope you have not forgotten to tell your friends the tale of your bravery? " The man looked sheepish, and did not reply. I fancied he had some vague idea that I had come, armed with the authority of the *subdelegado*, for the especial purpose of dragging him back again to the forests of the Ivahy.

When I began to talk to him about the diamonds, he cheered up a little, and presently produced a tiny bamboo stem, the open end of which was stuffed with a twisted leaf of *milho*. Having extracted this, he tipped out of the hollow stem, into the palm of his hand, a number of small diamonds, the biggest of which weighed perhaps a little more than one carat. I asked him how much labour that number of stones represented. " Oh," he replied, "I found them all within the last eight or nine months, but I have not worked for more than twenty days in that time." These diamonds were perhaps worth £10 or £12 altogether. I offered him 70$000 for the lot, but he declined to take that amount.

Most of the *caboclos* we visited had a little store of diamonds of a similar kind, varying in value from £3 or £4 the lot to £12 or £14. The biggest and best I saw was a very perfect octahedron of about two carats. Its owner asked 80$000 (say £8) for it. It might or it might not have been worth it. I came to the conclusion, however, that the priest of forty years ago, would find his flock a good deal sharper now to deal with than they had appeared to be in his time.

My first impression of the mine was that it looked like a common gravel-pit, dug out of the side of a hill.

Presently, however, when the eye had had time to take in the details and the surroundings, one recognised that it had once been, if it was not still, something more than this.

Here and there were heaps of yellow, unwashed gravel, lying on the level bottom of the pit, whilst at a little distance outside were larger mounds of white, washed-out looking stuff, the refuse of the washings. On one side of the pit, a rough conduit, made out of split and hollowed palms, tapped the water from a little stream flowing about thirty paces off, bringing it down to the entrance of the pit, close to which appeared the dilapidated remains of an old trough, that had long since forgotten how to hold water. A lofty wooded hill rose at the back of the mine, and other hills flanked it on the right. In front, a deep narrow valley ran down, along whose bottom the little stream that fed the workings splashed and tumbled in eager haste to yield its tiny tribute to the larger and more sedate stream that flowed below at the distance of about a mile.

A glance sufficed to show the reason why the workings had been abandoned. It was in fact what I had already heard.

While the surface of the ground rose rapidly in the direction in which the mine was worked, the diamond bearing strata, namely, the various thin beds of gravel, ran nearly on a level. Consequently, every yard of additional progress increased the depth at which these strata lay below the surface, and added an ever-increasing ratio to the proportion of working expenses.

I will not weary the unprofessional reader with minute details of the examination which I now made, which would have but little interest for him; but will at once proceed to give the general conclusions at which I ultimately arrived. If these conclusions are, as I believe, in the main correct, wonderful fortune must some day be in store for the people of this now quiet little district.

(1). That the diamonds lie in certain thin, horizontal strata of gravel, several in number, and separated by other layers or strata of gravel, of slightly different composition.

(2). That these gravel deposits mark the site of an ancient river bed, which, after having received, in common with the whole surrounding country, the vast deposits of subsequent ages, which latter deposits now form the hills in the immediate neighbourhood, had once again been upheaved, and subjected to "denudation," whereby the chief features of the country, as they now existed,—the mountains and valleys, hills and ravines,—had been carved out.

(3). That this carving process had cut through the ancient river bed already mentioned, at the point where the present diamond mine now stood, and that, in all probability, another similar mine, as yet undiscovered, corresponding to the other exposed section of the old river bed, existed at no great distance, which intelligent research could at any time bring to light with little difficulty.

This much with reference to the diamond deposit itself. Next, as regards the working of the existing mine. It was not until some days later, after having, in addition to careful personal examination, made exhaustive enquiries amongst the old miners themselves, and amongst the older inhabitants of the town, that I felt enabled to come to a conclusion on this point, based on sufficiently substantial grounds to merit attention.

Briefly stated, the opinion I ultimately formed was this. That the existing workings, apart from any considerations of the more than probable existence of another mine in the immediate neighbourhood, are capable, with improved methods of washing and an average intelligent management, of yielding a further large profit. At present, the mine labours under the disadvantage of never having had a name, a natural consequence of its never having produced any very large stones. It is however a fact worth noticing, that in the river, all local tradition agrees in saying, not a few large and valuable stones have been washed. Why is it, then, the mine itself has been so disappointing in this respect; for I failed to obtain satisfactory evidence of more than one or two diamonds of value exceeding a *contò* of reis (£100) having been discovered in it?

A very possible reason is the following :—It was early observed that the finer gravel strata were far richer in the number of their diamonds than the coarser strata. In fact, the latter seemed to be altogether barren. Observing also that the coarser gravel was very deficient in the *formação*—a miner's name for a certain little black stone generally found accompanying the diamond—the miners altogether neglected to wash these coarser gravels, ignoring or ignorant of the fact, that, if any large diamonds existed at all, they would assuredly be found here, rather than amongst the finer deposits. No doubt, in any case, these larger stones would be comparatively few and far between; but, that the only likely formation in which they would be found should have been thrown aside as not worth the washing, without first being subjected to a long trial, seems assuredly the very height of folly.

On the whole, then, it was abundantly evident that the mine had never yet had a fair chance given it, notwithstanding that it was worked to a profit for as long as the regular working had continued; the reason of the abandonment having been, not that the mine had then reached a stage when it produced a loss, but that it was *possible* that a loss, or rather a smaller profit than a Paraná Brazilian deigns to accept, would in time have resulted therefrom.

On our way back from the mine where we had spent several hours, we visited two other small gravel deposits which cropped up in the open prairie. Neither of these, of course, was the *missing* mine. Small stones had however been extracted from both of them. We next went to look at another outcrop of gravel on the bank of the Tibagy itself, out of which a large diamond had been extracted only the year before, which had been sold to a merchant in the town for a *conto* (£100). I learnt also, that other small outcrops of gravel occurred a short distance higher up the river, from which small stones had been from time to time washed. I did not, however, visit these myself.

Indications were not wanting that the few gravel outcrops discovered up to the present time, were but part of a large system of ancient beds of streams, which the denudation of former ages had here and there laid bare. If such be the case, it may be confidently asserted that the town of Tibagy is situated on a diamond field of very considerable extent, wanting but the application of modern intelligence to bring it fully to light. I shall have done my modest part if I have succeeded in drawing to it the attention which it seems to deserve.

CHAPTER IV.

Change of plans.—Departure of Telemaco.—The "Sogro do Mercer."—
The great mule trade. —Reminiscences and anecdotes of the
"Sogro."—An awkward mistake.—A prairie garden.—Magnificent
lace.—Why cotton is not grown in Paraná.—A Brazilian rider.—
Taming a wild mule.

GREAT as are the resources of Tibagy in precious
stones and fertility of soil, for my more immediate
object it proved as useless as though it had been a
barren desert. No men could be got, at any price,
to engage themselves with me for the exploration of
their river. Unknown dangers have no charm to
the ordinary *Caboclo* mind, even when gilded with
the bait of a new diamond mine in prospective. As
for canoes, there was not a decent one belonging to
the town. Ultimately, I resolved to travel by land to
the colony of Jatahy, the native place of my companion Telemaco,* and from thence explore the river
downwards and upwards.

On the 3rd of June Telemaco started in advance

* Telemaco M. Borba, brother to the director of Colonia Thereza,
and my companion throughout the whole of this expedition. In every
respect a thoroughly "good fellow."

for that place, in order to prepare men and canoes
to put this plan into execution, while I remained
behind for a day or two longer, to complete my explorations of this part of the valley, and to collect
supplies with which to follow on to Jatahy.

After Telemaco had started on his journey, I went
one day to pay a visit to a large *fazendeiro*, whose house
was situated about two leagues outside the town.   He
was the father of the young lady to whom the English
colonist Mercer was shortly about to be married, and
was already spoken of to me as the "Sogro (father-
in-law) do Mercer," by which name alone I knew
him.*   He proved to be a most entertaining old
gentleman, overflowing with anecdotes of his early
experiences in the country.   In his more youthful
days he had been a large mule trader, and had, in
fact, only within the last year or two given up that
business.   Once a year he had been accustomed to
ride down to the great mule breeding plains of the
province of Rio Grande do Sul, buy a troop and
bring it up to sell in the province of São Paulo.
He and his *camaradas*, numbering perhaps six men
in all, would bring a troop of a thousand wild mules
right up from Rio Grande do Sul to the great mule

---

* Brazilian family nomenclature is often a puzzle to the foreigner.
This arises from the fact that the woman does not formally change her
family name on marriage. Consequently, the children have *two* family
names, the grandchildren *four*, and so on *ad infinitum*. Thus, a
Brazilian rarely asks another, "What is your name?" but, instead,
"How do you sign yourself?" Nicknames are also very generally
employed as adjuncts to the first name, instead of any family name.

mart at Sorocaba, a distance of nearly 2000 miles, without losing more than one per cent. of their animals from all causes.

To be a successful mule trader required a man of iron constitution, whom no fatigue and no hardships could conquer, a splendid rider and lasso thrower, and, lastly, a man with a thorough knowledge of mule nature in all its moral and physical characteristics. Without these especial qualities, which must be common also to the *camaradas* whom he takes with him, he will lose perhaps half his mules, from various causes, on the long weary journey northwards. In the early days of the mule trade, not only had the traders to encounter and overcome the ordinary difficulties inseparable from so long a journey through a wild country, but they were liable at any moment to be attacked by wandering parties of wild Indians, against whom they had to defend not only their property but their lives. The labour and the risk were thus very great, but the net profit was often more than cent per cent.

The old man told me that the palmy days of the trade were now gone by. The price of the mules in the South had risen, and the corresponding values at Sorocaba had fallen. Nevertheless, the trade was still carried on, though to a smaller extent than formerly.

The town of Tibagy lay right on the main mule track from the south to the north, and Mercer told me he had many a time seen troops of 500 and 1000 wild mules go by on their way to São Paulo. There

existed, too, a very large estate on the other side of the
town, of which I shall have an opportunity of speaking
presently, on which these great troops of wild mules,
lean and weary from long travel, often rested for
three weeks or a month, to recover flesh and strength
before being finally taken to the market, 200 miles
beyond.

We in England can scarcely picture to ourselves,
even dimly, the kind of life led by the men in charge
of one of these grand mule marches of 2000 miles
through an almost uninhabited country. The vivid
pictures which the old man drew in the course of his
stories, of what his life had at times been, I could
not reproduce, however I were to attempt it. Night
attacks by Indians, encounters with jaguars, wild
stampedes, in which, in one short hour, their whole
troop would be scattered to the four winds of heaven,
the patient, yet vigorous and untiring toil of once
more collecting it together—all this and much more
the old man painted graphically, till I began to think
that I was listening to some new and thrilling tale by
the talented Captain of the " Far West."

The " Sogro " had now sobered down to the milder
duties of a prairie *fazendeiro*, leaving to his son to
follow in the footsteps of his sire's ancient fame in the
wide prairies of the South.

Mercer had so far done his duty to the family of his
future wife, that he had taught them some of the more
ordinary ways and customs of civilised life. For
example, the wife and daughters sat down to table

with us at dinner, though it was sufficiently evident
that the new *régime* did not sit altogether comfortably
upon them.   The youngest girl whom I wrongly took
for Mercer's *fiancée* was remarkably pretty and even
distinguée looking—so much so, that, after dinner,
I warmly congratulated my " compatriota " on his
choice of a bride.   I felt rather uncomfortable when
I found that I had been admiring the wrong one.

The garden round the Sogro's house rivalled and
even excelled that of Sr. Garses' at the Freguezia da
Ribeirinho.   Oranges, plums, peaches, pine-apples,
ginger, potatoes, onions—all were cultivated with
evident care and intelligence ; and lastly, several fine
cotton trees adorned the garden, the produce of which
supplied the household with cloths, sheets, and also
with the material for lace manufacture.

The Senhora was very proud of her skill in the
manufacture of all these necessary household articles.
She took the trouble to show me the various processes
by which she and her daughters produced the finished
article, whether cloth or lace, from the raw material.
The implements were all of the rudest description, but
their clumsiness of design was almost neutralised by
the marvellous delicacy and skill with which they were
used.

The lace, which was shown to me as home pro-
duction, was simply magnificent.   Much of it was
nine and ten inches deep, of exquisite design and
perfect execution.   I offered to buy as much as they
could let me have, but they could only spare a few

yards of a comparatively narrow and coarse pattern, all the rest being required in making up the *trousseau* of their daughter. The old lady showed me a towel which she said she had made more than twenty years before from the cotton grown in their own garden, and which, notwithstanding that it had been in constant use for all those years, was still apparently as good as new.

The question may naturally be asked, " why is not cotton grown on a large scale in the province of Paraná ? " It is true that in isolated cases, and in small quantities it is found to grow, not perhaps luxuriantly, for prairie soil is seldom very fertile, but still well enough, to all appearance, to encourage a more extended trial. The only answer to this question, which was one that I myself have several times put to Brazilians without getting any satisfactory statement from them, seems to be, that, at or about the time when the crop should be gathered, rains come, thereby causing the cotton to rot on the trees. I never gave much inquiry to this subject, chiefly because I so seldom met with the cotton tree under cultivation in the province, and not one individual in a hundred of the average natives had ever bestowed a thought upon the matter.

If the daughters of this house excelled in the purely feminine accomplishment of lace-making, the son surpassed all other Brazilians that I have ever met in the more manly art of riding. Just before we were leaving to go back to the town, Mercer begged his brother-in-law-to-be, to give me a specimen of his skill in this line. The first performance consisted in galloping a tame horse full speed over the prairie, the rider standing upright on its bare back. This feat was many times more difficult than the common circus riding that we see at home; for, in the first place, the Brazilian disdained the use of the flat-board to stand upon, and in the next place, he neither rode in a circle nor chose out any beaten path for his career, but rode hither and thither on the rough prairie, amongst ant hillocks and armadillo holes, and stumbling traps of all kinds. He varied the performance by occasionally jumping on to the ground and then back again upon the horse's back, while the animal was still galloping.

The next exhibition of skill, that he gave us, was less showy but, doubtless, even more difficult than the first.

A wild mule was first selected from a number that were at the time in the *portral*, and neatly caught with the lasso. Some quarter of an hour then elapsed, while the young Brazilian with the assistance of a *camarada*, forced a powerful bit into the animal's mouth, and got the saddle equipments on its back, these operations being performed while the animal was blindfolded. The mule was then led out into the open, and the bandage removed from its eyes. Two *camaradas* now held its head firmly between them with lassoes while the rider mounted, this preliminary feat not being accomplished without a good deal of difficulty. The moment the brute felt the man upon its back, it became literally mad with terror, screaming as though in mortal agony; neither was it till the lassoes had been tightened to such an extent as almost to throttle it, that the *camaradas* could approach near enough to slip the nooses off. When this was at length accomplished, the animal was free, *except* for the rider upon his back, with whom now commenced a fierce fight for mastery.

Trembling in every limb from terror and excitement, the mule for a brief moment, stood stock still; then, either a prick of the sharp spurs, or a twitch from the powerful bit which could have broken the jaw of a tiger, set it off. Down went its head to the ground and up flew its heels, and from that moment for the next ten minutes the eye could scarcely follow its movements. One second it would be galloping madly over the prairie, rearing, kicking, and buck-jumping. An instant after, it would be down on its knees, preparing to roll, till a jerk of the bridle brought it up again with a bound, snorting with fright at the unaccustomed pain; then, away once more it would tear across the prairie, urged on by the shouts and sharp spurs of its fearless rider. In less than half an hour from the time the first lasso caught it, the animal was entirely subdued and broken, being brought back by its rider to where we stood, with its flanks heaving, and its whole body pouring down with sweat, and with an eye that told a tale of submission brought about by dire fear and intense physical exhaustion.

The rider himself took it all very calmly, and seemed to think very little of the feat he had just accomplished. After this exhibition, I was not surprised to learn that a mule was generally perfectly tamed to the saddle in three lessons, being then fit to be sold as a *mula mansa*.

Thus terminated a day which to me is still full of lively reminiscences. When I and my companion again reached the town it was already dark; the primitive inhabitants had retired to rest with the sun, and we rode through the streets as through a city of the dead, without meeting a living thing, till finally we reached Mercer's *chacara* half a mile beyond the outskirts on the other side.

CHAPTER V.

IT was late in the afternoon of the 5th June. Tibagy with its thriving *fazendas*, its diamonds, its *mineiros* and *fazendeiros* had been left fifteen miles behind, and I, with my little troop of five fat well-fed mules, was safely domiciled for the night within the thick mud walls of the once famous "Fortaleza," 1200 feet above the level of the river.

Though I was sufficiently provided with the means of camping out in comfort, I had had no scruples in soliciting the hospitality of the *feitor*, or overseer, in charge of the "fortress," *fazenda*, having long since learnt the lesson that a traveller in these primitive regions is always welcome, whenever and wherever he chooses to ask for bed and board. It is indeed looked upon almost as an insult for a traveller to pitch his tent outside the walls of a *fazenda* and not to enter and, at the very least, partake of coffee and smoke a cigarette. By the observance or non-observance of these simple acts of politeness, a foreigner, travelling in the country, gains or loses the good-will of the people. Yet I have come across "cockney" Britishers who, with the supreme contempt for good manners that characterises their class when let loose from the "four mile radius," have not been ashamed to pitch their tents in front of a Brazilian's very door, without considering it necessary either to ask the owner's permission, or to conform in the slightest degree to the recognised customs of the country in which they are travelling, but have puffed their cigar in the face of the *fazendeiro* when he has come to pay his complimentary visit, and calmly demanded his business.

Sr. Gregorio, the *feitor* of the Fortaleza, welcomed us heartily and, when he had learnt the object of my journey, pressed me to stay for the whole of the next day, when he himself would take me about the country to the best view points around, and give me all the information that might be in his power. I accepted this offer gladly, and now, while the slaves were laying out the repast in the broad verandah upon a table, which, from its massive structure and venerable aspect, might have been a relict of the old baronial days of England, Gregorio began to give me a sketch of the past and present history of the place, which, in its time, as already stated, had been famous.

First, however, I must briefly describe the "fortress" as it now appeared.

From the verandah in which we were standing, we looked out on a great square, bounded on two sides, partly by rows of low white-washed buildings—the quarters of the slaves—and partly by solid mud walls, tile covered and white-washed. The third side was bounded for its whole length of perhaps eighty or ninety yards by another mud wall, built to a height of about eight feet. Opposite the low buildings stood a row of posts, with corners well rounded and worn. These were the whipping-posts which in the old days had witnessed many a blood-curdling scene.

The "casa" itself was a large and massive-looking building, built of timber and mud, and covered by a huge gabled roof of very low pitch, tiled with the usual large and heavy pantiles common to all parts of Brazil. On the side facing the square, the eaves of this ponderous roof had been prolonged some twelve feet beyond the walls, being supported by a row of solid timber pillars, between which another thick mud wall had been built breast high. Though the walls generally are spoken of as being built of mud, it must not therefore be supposed that they were anything to be despised. On the contrary, these mud walls, if kept covered with tiles on the top, and occasionally patched up and whitewashed on the face, will last for centuries, and bid defiance not only to the attacks of Indians, against which in this instance they had again and again been proved, but also to all atmospheric influences.

The present owner of the Fortaleza, as I learnt from Sr. Gregorio, was a certain Manöel Ignacio Costa, the estate itself being of no less extent than twenty-one square leagues, chiefly consisting of campo or prairie land, but also including a considerable extent of *capões* and forest proper. It had been built by the grandfather of the present owner, the latter himself being now an old man, as a stronghold and a point of general rendezvous against the Indians, who at that time infested the whole country round, disputing possession with the new Brazilian settlers. Before the existence of the Fortaleza, these Indians therefore had been a constant thorn in the side of the *fazendeiros*, attacking their small numbers in detail both when out in the roça by day, or at night in their timber-built *ranchos*, and giving them no peace or security from year's end to year's end.

The Fortaleza was built, and became, as was intended, the rallying point, whether for offence or defence, of all the settlers round. At last the Indians had found their master. Carefully guarded by day and by night, this new stronghold resisted all their efforts to take or destroy it.

The story of their last attack was thus related to me by the *feitor* :—

One day, the father of the present owner—the grandfather being then dead—who had succeeded to the estate, was out working with his slaves in one of the roças, having his little son Manoël with him, suspecting no danger, when suddenly from the forest around the

Indians commenced the attack. To fly without fighting was impossible, for the Indians were surrounding them, and, under cover of the forest, were throwing in arrows on all sides. The little Manoël was playing on a heap of corn that had been cut that day, all innocent of the danger. At the first alarm the father hastily covered him up with fresh corn, and telling him that the *bugrés* had come, and that he must remain quite still and quiet, and not move, went to fight his way through with the half-dozen slaves who were with him. They succeeded in reaching the Fortaleza with the loss of one or two of their number. Reinforced by large numbers of " niggers " they returned with all speed to the Roça, the father hardly daring to hope to find his child again. The Indians did not appear, and the father, running to the spot where he had left his little son concealed, pulled off the covering of corn with nervous haste and there found his boy safe and unharmed, the Indians not having discovered him, and the child himself having obeyed his father's instructions to the letter, and neither moved nor made a sound to tell his presence.

That night the Indians attacked the Fortaleza in force. So fierce and sustained was the fight, that the defenders had no time to load from the usual slow-working belt. Every two men, therefore, had their powder poured out in a heap on the ground between them, and thus they loaded and fired with the utmost obtainable rapidity. All night long the battle continued—on the part of the Indians, with demon cries,

arrows, and firebrands, and on the part of the defenders, as men whose fate was in their own keeping.
At length the day dawned, and there, upon the top of
a hill overlooking the fort, stood out against the
brightening sky the form of the Indian "cacique," or
chief, waving his arms aloft to call away his beaten
warriors. The fight was over, and from that day to
the present no Indian had ever approached this stub-
born stronghold with hostile intent.

Notwithstanding the harassing presence of Indians in
the country round, those were the prosperous days of
the fazenda. A hundred slaves were kept to work the
estate, where now but eight remained. Military dis-
cipline was preserved within the walls of the Fortaleza,
and the whipping-posts were in constant requisition.
But nigger blood was human blood, and when they
were relieved from the ever-present fear of the Indians
by the last great fight, nigger nature began to speak
with no uncertain signs. Dark deeds were done, and
brutal overseers were murdered. The little boy
Manoël had grown up to man's estate, and had in his
turn succeeded his father. He dared not, however,
on account of his slaves, continue to reside at the
Fortaleza. The glory of the old place now departed
from it. The slaves were sold off, and the fazenda
ceased to be agricultural, becoming solely a vast cattle
and mule keeping wilderness.

On its vast prairies, as we know, the great troops of
wild mules, coming up from the south, rested and fattened. Thousands of cattle were also annually brought

upon it, to be fattened for market. It was calculated that there was sufficient good pasture to fatten 16,000 head of cattle in three months (meaning of course, the three summer months when the pasture is freshest and most abundant), and that it would keep cattle for breeding purposes to the amount of double that number throughout the year.

The chief profits of the estate, since the wholesale reduction of its labour establishment, are made by letting the pasturage, the price charged per head being 2$000 or say 4s. per annum. Practically, the only limit to the amount of money the fazenda could be brought to yield is the demand of the markets around, namely, the towns of Curitiba, Antonina, Ponta Grossa, Castro, and Sorocaba. As the exportation of cattle or their produce from the province is almost "nil," the demand of these markets must be regulated "cæteris paribus" by the growth of their populations. Judging in this manner, the value of the fazenda should be continually and rapidly increasing.

Though this enormous estate might be made to yield a revenue almost unlimited by a combined system of agriculture and cattle-breeding, as a matter of fact its nett income is but little over ten *contos* (say £1000) per annum, or an average yearly return of about one penny per acre !

This is one of the evils of large estates, when held, as is the case with nineteen out of twenty in this country, by men of limited intelligence and small money capital. A few more such fazendas as the Fortaleza, held by

such men as Sr. Manoël Ignacio Costa, would turn
the whole province of Paraná into a desert, as might
be proved by a simple calculation.

The whole estate occupies no less than 340 square
miles of the zone or belt of mixed forest and prairie,
the very belt from whence, as I have shown, all the
prosperity of which the province can boast has been
primarily derived. Yet its owner will neither use it
himself, except to an insignificant extent, nor will he
sell any portion of it to others. On both sides, *i.e.*,
towards and beyond the two towns of Tibagy and
Castro, it is flanked by the chief agricultural districts
of the province, supporting between them a large
population, while itself, it supports just a dozen
persons, eight of whom are slaves.*

Here is a tract of land, upon which, if English
colonization is ever to succeed at all in the province
on a large scale, the experiment might well be tried
with the best prospect of success. Until, however, the
revolving years shall have brought a new and more
intelligent owner to the fore, this magnificent estate
will doubtless continue to be lost to the province.

The programme for the next day sounded well.
We were to explore the country, to hunt a pet *capão*

---

* An obvious remedy to this evil, which is a crying one throughout
the province of Paraná, would be the imposition of an Imperial land-
tax, to be levied on all estates whose extents reach above a certain
minimum. Such a tax would at once break up all large, idle estates,
increase the productive power and consequently the prosperity of the
province, and lastly, add a good round sum to the annual revenues of
the empire. At present there is no land-tax in Brazil.

for deer, to visit various mule troops and cattle herds which were that day to receive their monthly dole of the much-prized salt, and lastly to witness the spectacle of marking wild cattle in one of the big yards or *por-trões* attached to the Fortaleza.

On turning out the following morning, I found the *feitor* already up and standing in the verandah, receiving the salutations of the slaves, who, with hats doffed, came up one by one and solicited the blessing of their lord and master in the abbreviated form, " '*su Christo*," the formal reply to which being, " God bless thee " (*Que Deos t'abençoa*).

Hot coffee, that most acceptable of morning beverages in this country, was now brought out to us. The horses and mules were already standing in the yard saddled. Two slaves, each armed with a long lasso, were to accompany us, for there was work to be done. Breakfast, consisting of beans, farinha, and xarqui, was already strapped on to one of the saddles. Two couples of hunting-dogs were ready, held in leashes by the slaves, and in another minute we were all in the saddle, passing out through the great gates of the court-yard : the *feitor's* son, a little boy of about eight or nine years, whose diminutive legs could scarcely span the top of the saddle upon which he was perched, royally leading the way.

For a wonder the morning was free from the usual dense fog, though down far below us to the south, in the valley of the Iapó, a river that we had crossed the previous day, thick white clouds were rolling slowly up under the stirring influence of the rising sun. Beyond this valley, which itself was full ten miles distant, the view extended for another ten or fifteen miles, up a long slope of yellow prairie, dotted with dark green *capões*.

There is something, either in the atmosphere or the scenery of these prairies, or in both combined, too subtle to be analysed or explained, which yet exerts a most powerful influence upon the spirits. I can indeed imagine no restorative more effectual for the cure of the complaints to which we of the present day are supposed to be especially subject, than a month or two of travel upon these breezy plains. Simplicity of living would not be a mere matter of choice but of necessity, and the complete change of life in every respect—a change from the unnatural to the natural in which a man eats only to satisfy hunger, sleeps only during the hours of darkness, and rises with the sun to a day, not of "ennui" and fretful boredom, but of vigorous enjoyment of every power and faculty both of mind and body—this is what does more to bring back perfect enjoyment of existence than all the tonics ever brewed from the pharmacopœia.

After a ride of some miles, during which we obtained magnificent glimpses of the country in different directions, we arrived at a large *capão* and, following a mule track leading into it, presently found ourselves in an open patch of prairie, entirely surrounded with pine forest. Here was to be our hunting ground, and no more likely-looking locality for sport could have been selected.

On three sides of the enclosed prairie the forest was but a narrow strip of wood, perhaps fifty yards in width. Through one corner, adjoining the *capão* itself, a broad ride had been cut, to allow the cattle to enter and feed in the enclosure. This was the point to make for, in case the deer was found in or driven into the outer circle of forest.

The dogs were now slipped and cheered on into the *capão*, and almost immediately began to give tongue; but, as we knew from the sound, they had not yet put up the game, but were merely working on a night scent. We stood all together, without dismounting, in the centre of the open space which was about a mile long and a quarter of a mile wide, ready to ride at a moment's notice to any point, should the game break cover in sight. For a long time we waited patiently, cheered, however, by an occasional " yap " from one or other of the dogs, showing that they were still working. Suddenly a chorus of quick eager cries announced that the deer was on foot. The excitement now commenced, and we eagerly followed with our ears the lively music of the dogs, as they hunted the game hither and thither in the great *capão;* their voices echoing beneath the broad canopy of pine trees, till the very birds were startled from their hidden recesses, multitudes of blue jays and gaudy-crested woodpeckers coming flying away past us, scared at the unwonted uproar going on beneath them. Every moment we expected that the deer might break cover and race across the open, and all eyes kept watch along the border of the wood to catch the first glimpse of the quarry.

At length the dogs passed out of the main *capão* into the narrow strip at one side.

"Off! off! to the other end," said Gregorio. "Dig your spurs in if you want to be there before the deer." Away I galloped as hard as I could split, regardless of armadillo holes or ant hills. Luck and a good horse favoured me, and I dismounted at one end of the broad "ride" before referred to, within two minutes of the time I had started, and before the dogs had yet come within hearing. The deer, however, I knew might already be close at hand, a quarter of a mile or more in advance of the dogs. With gun cocked I waited, almost with as much eagerness as though I had never shot a deer before. All at once, with a light graceful bound, the quarry leapt into the ride, and, catching sight of the horse, paused for a quarter of a second to gaze. Poor animal! at that moment its earthly anxieties ceased for ever, for a bullet pierced its shoulder, and with one more bound it fell dead in the open path. The dogs were nowhere, and did not appear upon the scene for at least two minutes after the shot was fired. Their mongrel breed evidently wanted more pace, their deficiency in this respect being a very general fault in all classes of Brazilian hunting dogs.

The others now coming up we sat down to a hasty

breakfast, it being past ten o'clock, and the best part of the day's programme being still before us.

Soon after getting into the saddle again, I witnessed an involuntary feat of horsemanship on the part of one of the slaves, which is worth mentioning. The "nigger" in question had been sent to make a short détour to the top of some rising-ground, to look for cattle. Going at a sharp gallop, his mule suddenly put its foot into a *tatu's* hole, and went down like a shot. The rider, instead of attempting to stick to the saddle, as we Englishmen instinctively do on all occasions, threw his body back, opened his legs, and alighted running on to the ground at some distance in front of his prostrate animal. In a few strides he stopped himself, and, quickly returning, caught his mule just as it had got upon its legs again, and, remounting, rode on as though nothing had happened.

Gregorio turned to me, and said, laughing, "That's a trick you English could never do with your 'monkey' style of riding." The remark was true enough, for while we English keep our seat by "grip," the Brazilian keeps his wholly by balance. The small size of a Brazilian stirrup-iron, which only admits of the insertion of the rider's big toe, is also of advantage, as offering no possibility of dangerous entanglement. There is no doubt but that the Brazilian style of riding is pre-eminently suited to the country, and their small stirrup-irons even more so. Indeed, these latter might with advantage be introduced by English riding-masters into their establishments at home, for such of their pupils whose object so often seems to be to try and get legs as well as feet through their stirrup-irons.

At length we reached the first "rendezvous," where about 300 wild mules were already assembled, preparatory to the much-prized salt being distributed. They were collected in groups of about ten or a dozen individuals, each group being presided over by a mare, who seemed to have trouble enough with her unruly followers. In order to keep up her dignity and a proper respect for her chieftainship, she allowed no mule to approach within the radius commanded by her teeth or heels, laying down her ears and lashing out all round, whenever they showed an inclination to press too closely upon her. It was curious to observe that the mules themselves never attempted to bite or kick their foster-mother, in return for her rough treatment of them. Amongst themselves individually, however, there was no such kindly feeling, but each one seemed to hate the other with mortal spite, and frequent and loud-sounding were the blows of jealous heels on unwary ribs.

In obedience to a sign from the *feitor* the salt bags were opened, and the contents distributed upon the ground in several little heaps at sufficient distances apart.

Now the battle commenced. All respect even towards their foster-parent was forgotten in the intense eagerness of each animal to reach the salt. The law of the strongest and most courageous was

SALTING WILD MULES ON THE FORTALEZA FAZENDA.

paramount in the wild medley that ensued. Now one mule, with ears well laid back and mouth wide open, would charge into the excited throng, and lash out with tremendous force, fury, and rapidity, clearing a complete ring round it for one brief minute, during which it would have the salt heap all to itself. Short was the time allowed it. Another mule, rendered frantic at the sight of the salt disappearing, would charge into the circle, and a savage duel would commence, during which other animals would slip in, and, meeting each other, all again would become an indescribable scene of dire fighting and tumult.

The blows given and taken were something frightful to witness, yet, as far as I could see, no animal exhibited any sign of pain, but again and again each would return to the charge furiously eager for the salt. I recalled my memorable mule ride from Antonina to Curitiba, and no longer wondered at the little impression my heavy hunting crop had made upon the mule I then bestrode. Compared to the punishment that these animals voluntarily endured for a single lick of salt, such blows had been but touches of a rat's tail.

It was remarkable that no mule would allow another mule to lick at a salt heap at the same time as himself. Fighting, therefore, could not have been avoided by any practicable multiplying of the number of heaps.

While the mules were thus amiably engaged, Gregorio and his slaves were not idle. Each animal in turn passed under the keen scrutiny of their sharp eyes, and here and there a wound or sore was

detected, which, if left unattended, would have bred
maggots and spread, till in a few months the animal
would have been eaten up alive. Lassos had been
already uncoiled, and one of the slaves, watching his
opportunity, now singled out his intended prisoner
and deftly dropped the strong plaited noose of raw
ox-hide upon the devoted neck, causing a frantic
stampede of all the mules far and near, to whom the
lasso is an instrument of the greatest dread. The
prisoner at first madly bolted with the rest, but presently another lasso was skilfully thrown to catch
his two hind legs, while the terror-stricken animal
was still at full gallop. Now came the punishment.
A sudden jerk of this lasso at the right moment
brought the mule down to the earth with a " bang."
In a second he was on his legs again, and, mad with
fear and not yet conquered, again started off at a
frantic gallop. Another sudden tightening of the
lasso, and another rib-breaking fall resulted. This
was sufficient. The men could now approach, and
while one sat on the head of the poor trembling
animal, keeping it down, the other rapidly put the
cleansing " mercurio " into the wounded part. The
lassos were then removed : a sharp cut on the flank
brought the animal on to its legs again, and away he
rushed to bury himself in the midst of his brethren,
who were standing at gaze a hundred paces off watching
the proceedings.

Towards the latter part of the time the scene was
very exciting, for the animals, growing wilder, had to

be driven and lassoed from horseback.   By the time
this work was done, I had obtained some little insight
into the nature of the duties required on a large
pasture *fazenda*.   The lasso is the great implement in
the whole work, and the terror which the very sight of
it inspires in a troop of wild mules or cattle is quite
pitiable to see.

In the latter part of the afternoon I witnessed the
operation of cattle-marking, in which again the lasso
was the implement employed for throwing the animals,
preparatory to the application of the branding-iron.

Such is a glimpse of one day's life of a *fazendeiro* in
these regions.   It is not surprising that they should
be, to use an expressive phrase, as " hard as nails."

CHAPTER VI.

I WILL pass over the details of the next three or four days' travelling, they being, for the most part, of a character already described. The two places marked on the map by the names "Monte Alegre" and "Alagoa," were smaller editions of the "Fortaleza," of which they were, in fact, off-shoots, having originally formed part of the great estate. They both belonged to female members of the family of Manöel Ignacio, and, as in the case of the Fortaleza, were barely kept going by a few slaves.

"Alambary," two days' march from Alagoa, is a small tobacco-growing settlement, numbering about forty inhabitants, all told. The tobacco, which is of very good quality, is manufactured in twists, and finds a ready market in the prairie towns.

Towards the evening of the fourth day after leaving the Fortaleza, while I was riding at some distance in front of the "troop," hoping to get a shot at pigs, of which we had already come across many herds, I was startled by the apparition of six nearly naked Indians, three men and three women, who suddenly stepped out of the forest on to the *picada*. My horse, which was a nervous animal, swerved right round in its tracks with fright at the wild appearance of these beings. To me also the apparition would have been alarming enough, appearing as it did in a very lonely part of the forest, had I not at once recognised the familiar cropped head, telling that the individuals were Coroados, and therefore *Indios mansos*.

One of the men was carrying a pig on his back, while the women each carried a long bamboo basket, suspended down the back by a band passing over the crown of the head, this being their usual mode of carrying burdens. The baskets were partly full of pine nuts, which were now in season, and on which I had myself feasted for the last two days. The Indians were returning from a hunting expedition in the forest, the women now carrying the bows and arrows of their lords and masters. They told me their camp was about half-a-league farther on, and I promised that I would camp with them for the night, and buy some of their nuts and pig-meat.

If I except the inhabitants of "Alambary," these were the first human beings that we had met with for four days; the meeting thus constituted quite an event. This was to be complemented on the same afternoon by another encounter of a very much more civilized character, being with no less a personage than the Postman!

This man I met travelling alone and on foot, carrying his provisions, cooking-pot, and sleeping-gear on his back, *en route* from Jatahy to Castro, a distance of about 145 miles, more than half of which being through the wild and uninhabited forest. I had a short conversation with him, for, on journeys such as these, travellers never think of passing each other on the road without exchanging at least a few words. He found time to tell me that he performed the double journey of 290 miles once a month, and that, though he might have a mule if he chose, he preferred travelling on foot, as he could thus save a little time. His pay was 24$000 (say £2 8s.) for the double journey, which usually occupied him about a fortnight.

This journey was remarkable, not so much for its length as for its intense loneliness, for along the whole route there were but three points where the man could sleep under shelter. Three nights at least had thus to be passed in the gloomy solitude of the forest, or upon the desolate prairie. Here is a life that would have suited equally the misanthropy of a Timon, and the adventurous courage of a knight-errant. Doubtless this Brazilian postman could have told many a tale of his musings over his many lonely watch-fires.

I arrived at the camp, of which the Indians had told me, in due time, and soon made myself at home with the *Bugrés*, while awaiting the arrival of the mule-troop.

The accompanying illustration is from a sketch taken on the spot, of one of the Indian women. The broad band shown across her head is of bark; and her offspring, in this case an infant of about ten months

COROADA WOMAN AND CHILD.

old, is comfortably seated in the lower loop of the band, the whole weight of the child being supported on the mother's head.

During the months of May, June, and July, it is the custom of the tame Coroados Indians of these parts to leave their *aldeamentos*, or villages, and roam about the great pine forests, living upon the products of their bows and arrows, and the fruit of the pine trees themselves. The pine-nut, which is an oblong fruit about an inch and a half in length and from a half to three quarters of an inch in diameter in the thickest part, has a leathery shell like that of a Spanish chesnut. In flavour it is, however, far superior to this latter, and, as an article of food, it will be sufficient to say that the Indians often live on it and nothing else for many weeks at a time. It can be eaten raw, but more usually the Indians roast it in the ashes of their fires till it "pops," when it is ready to be eaten. The flavour is even better brought out by boiling, this, however, being a mode of cooking that the Indians do not themselves practise.

The most delicious stage of the nut is when it has just begun to germinate, a tiny green shoot appearing at one extremity. Nothing can surpass the delicacy of the nut in this condition. Wild pigs go long distances after it, having frequently been known to travel in the fruit season ten or fifteen miles across the open prairie, to reach a favourite pine *Capão.* The Coroados are also accustomed to preserve the fruit for future consumption. This they do by packing several bushels of the nuts into a bamboo basket, and then placing the latter under running water for about forty-eight hours. At the end of that time the baskets are taken out, and the contents spread in the sun to dry. Thus preserved, the nuts are dry and tasteless, and have no

doubt also lost a great deal of their natural nutritive
proprieties. Could they be imported into England in
their fresh state, they would doubtless make the fortune of the gentlemen who, at certain seasons of the
year, greet us at every street corner with the insinuating
cry, " All 'ot, all 'ot."

Late in the afternoon of our seventh day from Tibagy
we sighted the little village of S. Jeronymo, standing
alone on a patch of open Campo or prairie, which
here, strangely enough, rises up bare and bleak from
the midst of a luxuriant surrounding forest.

Knowing nothing about the place or its inhabitants,
I had the tents pitched about a quarter of a mile outside the village, and sent one of my *camaradas* to buy
chickens and eggs for our mess. He presently returned, bringing with him the village priest and
director of an adjoining colony of tame Coroados, by
name *Frei* Louiz. The latter pressed me strenuously
to take up my quarters in his house, but I would not
accept his invitation for this night, as my camp was
already pitched, though I gladly promised to go to
him the next day.

Frei Louiz told me that there was a *compatriota* of
mine, by name Elliott, living in the village, who had
been a great explorer in his day, but who was now
old, worn out, and very poor; he brought me also a
message from him (Elliott) excusing himself, on account
of his age and weakness, for not coming to pay me a
visit, but begging that I would go up and see him.
Together we walked up to the village to the house of

my supposed fellow-countryman. He had just risen
from his chair to receive us when I, following close on
the heels of *Frei* Louiz, entered the room where he was.
As he stood for a moment before seeing me, I thought
I had never seen so splendid a wreck of a man. He
was above six feet in height, with a frame that must
have once been massive, but which was now shrunken
and gaunt, and with one of those countenances that
seem to have been moulded in iron, indicating a
vigour and energy of character such as Pallas offered
Paris, to push him "forward through a life of shocks,
dangers, and deeds," such indeed as for forty long
years his own life had actually been.

Elliott welcomed me in English, into which several
Portuguese words unconsciously found their way, as
though the mother-tongue had almost been forgotten
from long disuse. In spite, however, of this, and in
spite of the poor surroundings, which had nothing in
them to remind me of the old country, I was at once
struck with the accents and manner of his greeting.
They were those of a perfect English gentleman, such
as I least expected to meet with in these remote regions.
My heart grew soft at the sight of this poor old man,
thus apparently forsaken by the very country in whose
service he had spent his best days.

I remained with him till a late hour, and little by
little learnt the history of his life, which did not belie
his appearance. His Christian names were John Henry,
and he was an Englishman only on his mother's side,
his father having been an American. He was born in

the year 1809. When quite a boy he entered the American navy as a "middy," and a year or two later exchanged into the Brazilian service. In one of the almost perennial squabbles between Brazil and the Southern Spanish States, he was made prisoner and kept in confinement for two years. He then succeeded in escaping, and from this time his life as an explorer commenced.

In his own words, "You know, I had seen those big mountains" (referring to the lofty range of the "Serra do Mar") "so often now from on board ship, that I began to get curious to know what there was behind them, and I determined to go and have a look." Thus he left his sea life, and for forty years had been "having a look" behind the great seaboard mountains of Southern Brazil. Commencing under the auspices and patronage of Sr. Silva Machado, who afterwards became "Barão de Antonina," Elliott explored vast tracts of the remoter regions of the Provinces of S. Paulo (which then included what is now the Province of Paraná), Minaes Geraes, Matto Grosso, Santa Catherina, and Rio Grande do Sul, making rough maps of the course of various rivers, and laying down the approximate positions of mountain ranges, and the general divisions of forests and prairies.

During many years his life had been one of extreme peril and hardship, passed in the midst of the great *sertões*, cut off from the haunts of civilized man by immense distances of unknown country, and often surrounded by hostile Indians. He had, however, one companion, who seems to have equalled himself in hardihood and courage. This companion was a Brazilian named Lopez, who was still living and still even working.

Amongst the multitude of experiences which the old man related to me on this and other occasions, was one which illustrated very forcibly the difference of the state of the country now from what it had been only in the last generation. He said that in the Indian *reducção*, established not a league from S. Jeronymo itself, there were now peaceably living many individual Indians from whom, in the course of his earlier explorations, on more than one occasion, he had had to flee for his life. Through him chiefly, and through his companion Lopez, as the first explorers of the district, not only the immediate environs of S. Jeronymo, but the whole of the right bank of the Tibagy had been reclaimed from the hostile savages, who themselves had either been driven out or forced to submit and to live in peace with the new settlers.

So pleasant and entertaining did I find it, listening to the old man's experiences and adventures of a life that was one altogether after my own heart, that, when, two months or so later, I was once more at S. Jeronymo, I was accustomed to go every evening to his house, and sit with him, his wife (who, alas, was a mulatto and a shrew, the folly of his middle age), *Frei* Louiz, and other people of the village, round a great fire piled up on the floor of his kitchen, hearing neverending tales of his former life, sucking *mate* from a bomba, and smoking cigarettes. The pleasure of these evenings would have been perfect but for the shrew of a wife, who seemed to have the very poorest opinion of her husband, ordering the poor old man about like a dog.

One tale of animal life in the forest that Elliott related was so like what we might ourselves have seen, and is so true to nature, that I may be pardoned for reproducing it.

"One night," said the narrator, "Lopez and I, who were then alone together, were camped in the forest between the rivers Ivahy and Tibagy, squatting round our fire, bemoaning our lot at not having been able to get anything to eat all day but fruit and honey, and devoutly hoping for better luck on the morrow, when suddenly we heard, at a little distance from us, a tremendous uproar of grunting, squeaking, and clacking of tusks. 'Pigs,' said we both, 'now for a dinner at last.' It was bright moonlight, and the sound came from the direction of a little open patch in the forest, such as frequently occur where pine trees grow. Snatching up our guns from the ground beside us, we crept cautiously towards the sounds which still continued, though with less uproar than at first, and soon came to the edge of the little clearing. Standing upon the extreme summit of an ant-hillock about five feet from the ground was a Jaguar, surrounded by a large drove of pigs, perhaps fifty or sixty in number, all in a state of furious rage, and vainly endeavouring to get at their enemy perched on the ant-hill. We did not fire.

hoping to obtain our supper without having to waste a
shot, for ammunition was precious. Meantime the
Jaguar, with his tail stuck well up into the air, and
with all four legs close together, balancing himself on
the point of the ant hillock, kept facing round uneasily
first in one direction and then another, as the infu-
riated pigs threatened this side and that side. It was
clear that the game could not long be carried on in
this fashion; either the pigs would give up the siege
as hopeless, or the Jaguar would get tired of his
uncomfortable position and make a dash to escape.
The end however came in a manner we did not expect.
In a moment of forgetfulness, the tiger allowed his
tail, which he had hitherto been holding well up out of
reach of his besiegers, to droop slightly. In a second
the unlucky appendage was seized by the pigs, its
owner was pulled down from his perch into their
midst, and a terrible battle began. Every now and
then we could see the big yellow body of the Jaguar
surge up above the seething mass of pigs, and his
powerful forepaws striking out deadly blows to right
and left, only to sink down again the next instant into
the midst of his raging enemies. Presently the uproar
began to subside; but the Jaguar had not emerged
from the crowd, and we could see him nowhere.
After waiting some little time longer the herd of pigs
began to disperse, and, the tumult being now over, we
walked into the clearing where the fight had so lately
been raging. Still no Jaguar was to be seen, but no
less than fourteen pigs were lying dead or dying upon

the ground. Presently Lopez, stooping down, picked
up a fragment of something, and holding it up said,
' *Aqui o tigre,*' 'here's the tiger.'   It was a bit of the
Jaguar's skin.   He had been literally torn to pieces by
the pigs, and his body and flesh devoured or carried
away by them.   Only a few fragments of skin and hair
remained on the field of battle.   From his victims, the
dead pigs, we secured our supper and many more
meals besides, without having had to waste a shot."

This story was no doubt literally correct in every
particular, for our own experience had shown enough
of what pig nature is when thoroughly aroused.   Fear
is then unknown to them, and woe-betide the strongest
enemy that cannot get out of their way.   Such is one
of the typical scenes of forest savagery, which no doubt
has oftentimes been repeated with but slight variations
in these wild and lonely backwoods.

Perhaps even more interesting to me, under the
circumstances, than these sensational tales, were the
more sober narrations of the discoveries which these
two hardy explorers had made in the parts of the
Province through which I was now travelling.   As I
have already mentioned, S. Jeronymo was situated
on an open patch of prairie, standing in the midst of a
vast surrounding forest.   There were two of these
open patches of prairie, one called the " Campo de S.
Jeronymo," and the other the " Campo de Inhohõ,"
this latter being the name of a *Coroado* " Cacique,"
whose tribe held possession of these regions at the
time of their discovery.   Both of the " campos," were

situated high up on the range of the "Agudos," which, as before stated, runs almost at right angles across the valley of the Tibagy, being continued on the other side under the name of Šerra d'Apucarana.

From a point in the immediate neighbourhood of S. Jeronymo, and at a distance of about twenty-eight miles from it, a rugged peak, standing up from this great range, at once attracts attention, from the clear abruptness of its outline as compared with its brethren around. When all the country between Tibagy and Jatahy was as yet unknown and uninhabited except by the wandering Indian, Elliott and Lopez, while seeking to find their way across country from the Ivahy to the Tibagy, first ascended this peak and from its bare top discovered the two *campos* of S. Jeronymo, and Inhohŏ. This was about the year 1840, at which time the law of *posse*, "possession," regulated the rights of land ownership throughout the whole of the "backwoods" of Brazil.

This law, which was in fact no law, gave rise to terrible crimes and outrages of an agrarian character, whereby practically only those who were themselves powerful, or who had powerful friends at their back, could in safety settle down upon any of the more favoured backwood lands.* Lopez and Elliott had,

---

* The law of "Posse" was abolished in 1850, since when it has been illegal to acquire unappropriated lands except by purchase from the State. The only exceptions being in the case of lands situated within a zone of ten leagues from the boundaries of the Empire with foreign countries.

however, a sufficiently powerful patron at their back in the person of Sr. Silva Machado (Barão de Antonina), in whose name, therefore, they took possession of the newly discovered *Campos*, upon which, shortly afterwards, the present village of S. Jeronymo was founded.

As a reward for the discovery, the *Barão* made a present to Elliott of a house and a considerable tract of land in the new settlement, and here it now was that the latter, prematurely old and broken down by the severity and hardships of the past forty years, was lingering out the few remaining days of his long and most arduous life.

It was sorrowful to see a man who had done so much and suffered so much now dying in a foreign land, all uncared for; bullied, moreover, day after day by a vixen of a wife, whose vile temper and shrewish tongue not even the presence of a stranger could altogether keep within decent bounds. As the most valuable present I could make him, I gave the old man a bottle of "Grande Marque" Cognac, one of two that I had been hoarding up for the unknown contingencies of the future. I was obliged to smuggle the bottle into his house artfully, for had the wife known anything about it, but very little of its contents would have gone to cheer the heart of the old man.

There were many objects and subjects of interest in the neighbourhood of this little backwoods' settlement of S. Jeronymo, not the least of which was the curious occurrence of these two little patches of open *Campo* themselves, situated in the very heart of a forest district, at a distance of nearly fifty miles from the nearest border of the prairie proper. For the benefit of those whom such scraps of geological reasoning may interest, I have reproduced in the Appendix a portion of a paper read last year before the Royal Geographical Society, in which I showed how the phenomenon might be accounted for. It is worthy of remark to note with what eagerness this oasis in the forest desert was appropriated and colonised immediately upon its discovery, notwithstanding its remoteness from the more settled parts of the province. This is but one more proof of the value that is so justly set upon the combination of pastoral and arable land, such as is attained only on the borders of the prairie and in cases such as the present.

We left S. Jeronymo on the 16th, and on the same night, as we were camping in the forest, a somewhat alarming incident occurred, which might indeed have had serious consequences to one of our party.

Our camp, consisting of three small tents, was pitched in a little clearing on the banks of a small river called *Tres Barras*. It had happened that on this day's march I had killed a wild pig, whose carcase was now suspended from a branch of a tree overleaning the tents. All, with the exception of one man who was keeping solitary watch by the fire, had retired within the tents and were sleeping soundly, when the report of a pistol rudely broke our slumbers and brought every man rushing out, fearing none knew what. Revolver in hand I rushed out with the rest prepared to shoot beast or Indian. The fire was blazing brightly and illuminating the whole circle of the clearing. One of the tents had vanished from its place, and, at some little distance from where it had stood, a confused mass of canvas was undergoing fierce contortions upon the ground, as though some demon had taken possession of it. One of the *tropeiros* was seen to be missing. Suddenly the folds of the struggling mass of canvas were rent asunder, and from out of the gap a *jaguar* leapt quickly forth and disappeared with a bound into the forest. The act was so instantaneous and our astonishment so great that no one had the presence of mind to send a bullet after the animal, which for a second or two after its disappearance could be heard bounding through the jungle as though fleeing for its life. The contortions of the canvas upon the ground did not at once cease, but continued for a few moments longer, till presently the missing *tropeiro* emerged and stood up looking around with a bewildered and affrighted countenance.

Soon all was explained. It appeared that the man on watch had caught sight of the jaguar stealthily creeping into the clearing from the forest, attracted doubtless by the smell of the before-mentioned pig. He had at once saluted it with a shot from his pistol, whereupon the animal in its sudden fright and confusion had bounded blindly into the nearest tent, knocking it down and burying both itself and the unfortunate *tropeiro* in the folds. For some few seconds —sufficiently long to admit of our being witnesses of the *finale*—the man and the beast had rolled about on the ground together, each probably more terror-stricken than the other, till at length, as we had seen, the jaguar had succeeded in rending its way out and escaping into the forest. When the story was told, roars of laughter greeted the unfortunate victim of the tiger's practical joke, and for the whole remainder of the journey he was unmercifully chaffed by his comrades on the subject of his unbidden bedfellow.

Late on the evening of the 18th of June we arrived at Jatahy, and were comfortably domiciled for the night in the house of my old companion, Telemaco.

CHAPTER VII.

THE military colony of Jatahy,* at which I had
now arrived, merits a few words of description, both
on account of its past and possible future interest.
It is a comparatively young settlement, having been
established by the Government about thirty years
before, from the reports and recommendations of the
two explorers, Elliott and Lopez. Its topographical
position is such as to make it a place of no little
importance in certain eventualities, for it stands at the
terminal point of the road (at present, alas! but a
mule-track for the greater part of the distance) which
connects the nearest Atlantic sea-port, namely, Antonina, with a wide-spreading network of inland navigable

---

* So called after the tree of the same name. The *Jatahy* (Hymenæa
Courbaril) grows to a large size, and yields a fruit like a large bean-
pod, the pulpy contents of which, surrounding the seeds themselves,
is not unpleasant to the taste, being much appreciated by both Indians
and Brazilians, as well as by parrots and monkeys. The *Jatahy* is
very common in both the Ivahy and Tibagy valleys.

rivers, reaching northward, southward, and westward, whose total connected length, available for navigation partly by steamers of light draught and partly by large-sized canoes, amounts to no less than 1,290 miles.

This great inland water system, whose counterpart may be seen in the recent discoveries made in Central Africa,* is, at the present time, almost completely barred to commerce, by reason of the want of a good connection between it and the sea-coast. During the last great struggle with Paraguay, it was nevertheless utilized to a considerable extent by the Brazilians for the cross-country transport of munitions of war to the frontiers of Paraguay, which are in direct water communication with Jatahy by means of the rivers Paranapanéma and Paraná. Were a good road to be constructed down the valley of the Tibagy from the town of Palmeiras to Jatahy, or to the mouth of the river, the effect would be the opening up to civilisation and commerce of an area of rich and healthy country of at least 100,000 square miles in extent, which is now only occupied by half-a-dozen scattered colonies maintaining a bare existence amidst the great deserts of untrodden forests by which they are surrounded on every side.†

* If we call the prairies of the province of Paraná its *lake district* (though the lakes are here chiefly represented by swamps), then the basin of the Paraná, with its 1300 miles of inland navigable highway, will correspond to that of the African Congo, and the parallel is completed by the comparison of the cataracts of the lower Paraná with those of the lower Congo, which in both rivers alike debar direct communication with the sea.

† See Appendix, Note N.

Returning, however, to the colony of Jatahy.   This little backwoods settlement was a good specimen of its class, comparing favourably with most others in the province.   Its Brazilian inhabitants, who by courtesy must, I suppose, be called agriculturists, numbered somewhat less than 500.   The soil of the surrounding forest-land is extraordinarily fertile, being largely composed of *débris* of friable volcanic rocks.   Every other house in the village possessed a small coffee plantation attached to it, with perhaps half-a-dozen trees in each ; and, though the roots of these trees were never touched from one year's end to another, props had to be put beneath their branches every season to aid in supporting the weight of the berries upon them, so abundantly did they yield their fruit.   Notwithstanding bad roads and great distances, it was even found profitable to carry on a small trade with the prairie towns in *cachaça*, sugar, and coffee.   For home consumption everything that a Brazilian usually eats was grown; beans, corn, and rice being the three staple products, besides sugar and coffee before mentioned. Rich, however, as are its agricultural resources, the progress of the colony, since the temporary stimulus given to it during the war has been taken away, is almost *nil*.   Owing to the importance of its position as a military colony, it is, to a certain extent, bolstered up by Government.   It possesses, in conjunction with the little hamlet of S. Pedro d'Alcantara on the opposite side of the river, no fewer than three salaried Government officials, namely, a director, a *frade*, and

a schoolmaster, to the two former of which, sums of
money are from time to time remitted for what may be
termed the public works expenditure of the place.*

The *frade*, *Frei* Timotheo by name and an Italian by
birth, was lord over the little hamlet on the left bank
of the river, with its colony of semi-wild Coroados
Indians attached. He was supposed to inculcate
knowledge, art, and enlightened religion into the
minds of these beings, and transform them from
useless or dangerous lumber into profitable citizens of
the State. How this monk performed the high duties
connected with his important charge, I have elsewhere
shown.† The schoolmaster, Sr. Bitancourt, with
whom and with whose work I later on became well
acquainted, was a man of very different stamp, energetic and honest, and well earning his small stipend of
a *conto* a-year.‡

Telemaco had already prepared everything necessary
for an immediate start down the river. A big canoe,
forty-six feet in length and three feet wide, hollowed
out of a single *Piroba* trunk, was awaiting us. Pro-

---

* At the time of my visit the first-named official had just been
suspended from his functions, pending an inquiry into an alleged
extensive misappropriation of the moneys thus received by him.
Whether true or not in this particular instance, there can be no doubt
that the lax notions of what constitutes honesty, so universally pre-
valent amongst the minor officials, are a real drawback to the proper
development of the province of Paraná.

† Vide Appendix, Note G.

‡ In the province of Paraná an obligatory system of primary
education has been for some time in force, and promises to yield good
results.

visions had been purchased and men engaged for the
journey; and, on the second day after my arrival at
the colony, we were once more embarked on the river
en route for the Paranapanéma.

Our crew was composed of five pure-blooded Caioá
Indians, men who had been brought up amongst
Brazilians from their birth, who had married Brazilian
women, and to whom the name *Bugré* applied to them
would have been a mortal offence. My companion,
Telemaco, who had engaged these Indians for me,
strongly recommended them in preference to any
Brazilian whatever; and never was a recommendation
better justified by results.

The mode in which they worked the canoe was
altogether different from that to which we had been
accustomed on the Ivahy. A narrow footboard, five
inches in width, ran all round the gunwales of the
canoe, being firmly supported by brackets at intervals.
Upon this board, two on each side, the Indians worked,
while one stood up in the stern to steer. The four
men who worked in front were each armed with a
strong and heavy iron-shod *varejão* or, as it was here
called, *zinga*, twenty feet or more in length, made of
the young stem of the *Pindahyba*, which is stronger
and tougher than the finest ash. Each pair of men
starting from close to the bows simultaneously drop
the iron points of their long poles to the bottom of the
river, and, facing round to the stern, run along the
gunwale boards, pushing with their whole weight upon
the slanting poles. The heavy canoe is thus impelled

forward, and continues to progress by its own momentum even against a strong current, while the men, having got to the end of their "run," quickly gather up their poles and, balancing themselves with the skill engendered by long practice, run back along the narrow footboard to their original starting-point at the bows, from whence the same operation is again gone through. In ascending a powerful rapid two men "hold" the canoe while the other two are running back to the bows; these latter in their turn "holding" till the former have again joined them, when all four together impel the canoe forward for another length. In this manner very powerful rapids and even cataracts can be ascended, provided that they afford a good foothold for the poles, and that the waves are not high enough to swamp the canoe by breaking over her bows. The skill required of a man to be a good pole-worker is the work of a lifetime, and even then many men fail from want of the requisite nerve.

The part of the steersman is a still more important one, more especially while the canoe is being poled *up* a rapid; for, in this case, the slightest twist given to her head in a wrong direction may either wrench the poles out of the hands of the workers or jerk the men themselves overboard, whence instant shipwreck results.

At first starting the Caioás appeared to be a little out of form, and twice one of the pole-workers tumbled off the footboard into the water. By the second day, however, the men recovered their proper style, and mishaps of this nature no longer occurred. About noon on this day we reached the first serious impediment existing on the river below Jatahy. Before this, the obstructions met with, though numerous, had been merely of the nature of long, even inclines, with slopes only sufficient to produce mild *corredeiras*.

Now, however, the mighty roar of falling water, heard from afar, warned us that more serious business was at hand. Telemaco, who for the last hour or two had been lazily reclining beneath the palm-leaf *toldo*, or awning rigged up over the stern, smoking the never-ending cigarette, roused himself at the sound. The Indians, who before had been poling listlessly along, scarcely exchanging a word with each other, now began to discuss with eager voices the coming cataract, while at the same time they rapidly proceeded to divest themselves of all garments. I took the hint, and securely stowed away in a strong box, expressly prepared for these occasions, all instruments and note-books.

One of the Indians, named Joaquim, now mounted upon the raised point of the prow of the canoe, and, balancing himself there by means of his long *zinga*, scanned with careful eye the mass of troubled waters which had now come into sight and towards which we were being rapidly drifted by the current. The remaining three men stood upon the gunwale boards with poles uplifted, ready at the slightest sign from the bowman to drop them forward and arrest the canoe's course should it be necessary. Glancing

behind for a moment over the *toldo*, I saw that
Telemaco had taken possession of the great steering
paddle, and was likewise awaiting the *fiat* of the
bowman. Our speed was momentarily increasing as
we got more into the suck of the cataract. The
banks, distant as they were on both sides,—for the
river was here full 500 yards wide—already seemed to
be flying past us, and still Joaquim stood motionless
on the bows, steadily gazing before him.

"Will it do?" "Can we run it?" "Yes!"
"No!" are the various exclamations of the other
Indians, who are already becoming excited. In
another second it will be too late to stop the canoe,
even should we so wish.

"*Que vá!*" thunders out Joaquim from the prow.
"Let her go!" and now the men are transformed to other
beings. With a series of rapid and skilful movements
of their poles, and aided by the steersman behind, the
canoe is brought opposite and head on to a funnel-
shaped opening that marks the entrance to one of the
main channels of the cataract. A second later we
shoot down its slippery plane with flying speed, and
are straightway in the midst of the mighty rush of
boiling waters, which lead onward without a pause in
their wild career for two-thirds of a mile. Now commenced a scene of excitement, that surpassed even the
wildest tapir hunt. The men shouted and yelled, making
their voices heard above the roar of the waters. Their
long heavy poles were whirled round and round, now
on this side, now on that, like feather wands. Now we

dashed headlong into a big wave which burst upon their naked bodies, scattering its spray high above the *toldo*. Now we were racing past a long low island on our right, against which the waves were dashing up like sea breakers.   Once, twice we bump heavily on sunken rocks, and for the moment I draw my breath hard. But the danger passes, and the next instant we drop down a fall of some four feet, and are again drenched from stem to stern by the wave at the foot.   Two minutes have passed, and the din of waters in our ears seems growing less.   Behind, the scene is wild and chaotic enough, but in front the water, though here and there still throwing up ridges of white foam across its current, showing the presence of rocks beneath, has become suddenly smoother.   The huge Piroba, which, with her ton or more of live and dead cargo, was but a second before tossing about like a cockle-shell in the waves of the cataract, is now racing swiftly but steadily along through *agua lisa*, or "slippery water."   All at once an appalling shout from Joaquim made my hair stand on end with sudden fear : "*É Salto! É Salto! 'Stamos perdidos!*"   "A Fall! A Fall! We are lost!" I jumped up to stand for a moment on the top of the cargo.   Not three canoe lengths ahead I saw that the channel down which we were rushing at the rate of full fifteen miles an hour, came to an abrupt termination.   No rock or breaker stood in the way, but merely a *line*, beyond which *nothing*.   Joaquim had missed the proper channel, and brought us down a *false* one.

At the first shout of "*Salto!*" Telemaco from the
stern had perceived that our only chance was to keep
the canoe head on, and, if possible, still further increase
her speed that she might overleap the yawning abyss
at the immediate foot of the Fall, and drop her bows
on to the raised crest of the wave beyond.* He shouted
to the Indians in front to give way with all their
strength to accomplish this object. They compre-
hended, and responded vigorously to the call.

In less time than it takes to relate, the canoe had
reached and was overhanging the abyss, and the great
stationary wave at the bottom came into view. The
Indians had now dropped their *zingas* and leapt down
from the footboard on which they had been previously
working, and were leaning forward against the bows
with the object of forming a bulwark of their bodies
against the coming impact. For the hundredth part
of a second we poise on the top, and look down into
space; then the bows of the great dug-out tilt downwards with a jerk, a mighty roar and rush of water
comes into our ears, and the next moment we emerge
on the other side of the wave, with our gunwales down
to the water's edge, and the canoe apparently on the
verge of sinking from beneath it. Two of the Indians
were lying bruised and half-stunned against the cargo,
where they had been hurled by the force of the wave
against which we had struck; the other two were already

* At the bottom of every *salto* there is always first a chasm, then a
wave, the latter rising usually about six feet beyond the immediate foot
of the fall, the distance, however, varying according to circumstances.

engaged in baling out the water which had swept on board like an avalanche. I speedily joined them in their occupation, and in a few minutes we had baled out enough to insure the safety of the canoe. We then poled to the nearest bank in order to land and count the cost of our escape. Great were our rejoicings to find that nothing worse than a few bruises had been sustained by the two Indians, and that only a few pots and pans had been swept overboard, the rest of the cargo escaping with merely a good soaking. I do not think any one of us expected that we should have saved more than our own lives. Had but another inch of water come on board, the canoe could never have emerged from the great wave. The pluck and presence of mind of the Indians in turning off the great mass of the water with their bodies was no doubt the straw that saved us. The total fall of this cataract proved to be about twenty-nine feet in a distance of a little over a mile ; the *salto* at the bottom being an eight feet sheer drop. There was another channel by which this *salto* could have been avoided at the expense of a slight increase in the length of the run down. This channel the Indian Joaquim, who had had the direction of our course in charge, had somehow missed, and had not discovered his mistake till it was irremediable.

Shortly after this occurrence, after again resuming our course, we passed a small island, known as the *Ilha das Araras,* from which a flock of many hundreds of blue and scarlet macaws (*araras*) rose from the trees and from the ground where they had been lirt eating. On the bank we observed a *schosse* which had been built by the Coroados Indians for the purpose of capturing these magnificent birds, whose flesh they much enjoy, and whose feathers they use on the festive garments. A *schosse* of this kind is merely a tiny hut constructed of bamboo stems, and thinly roofed over with palm-leaves resting on a bamboo framing. It is made of the smallest possible size so as just to admit one man; the sides also are carefully draped with palm-leaves, so as perfectly to conceal the hunter inside from the birds. The macaws when first the *schosse* is built naturally fight shy of it, and the hunter keeps away. In a day or two, however, they become accustomed to the new erection, and begin to perch upon its roof as a convenient resting-place near to their favourite dirt. The hunter now comes at earliest dawn and conceals himself within the *schosse*. As soon as it is daylight the macaws come as usual in crowds from the forest, some perching, all ignorant of the lurking foe within, upon the covering of the *schosse*. A sudden jerk, a shriek abruptly stifled, and down one disappears, through the treacherous palm leaves, spreading a momentary alarm amongst the others which rise up for a moment, screaming like a flock of rooks, to look around them. Finding, as they think, all quiet, they again descend to their feeding-places. The operation is repeated—another bird disappears through the roof of the *schosse*—and again the flock takes alarm. This time it is rather slower in returning to the ground, and many of the older and warier birds steer away for the forest and return no more. The concealed hunter meanwhile watches quietly through the interstices of the leaves of his abode till once more an unwary bird alights upon the roof. Thus he goes on bagging the birds, till, after about the sixth or seventh alarm, the entire flock takes wing to the forest and returns no more that day. Now it is time to give the *schosse* a rest, or the macaws will forsake the spot for good and all; once a fortnight being generally as much as they will stand of this nervous kind of work.

On my return to Jatahy, ten days later, I engaged a Coroado Indian to capture one of these birds for me alive. He did so, and I gave him 3$000 (say 6s.) as payment. He was much astonished at the munificence of the sum, and offered to get me as many more as I liked for a milreis (2s.) apiece. Unfortunately, as it happened, I declined the offer. The individual I had thus obtained escaped about a month later, and when afterwards I tried to replace it from the live stock market in Rio de Janeiro, I found I could not buy one under £5.

On the evening of the 23rd of June, after a voyage on the whole pleasant and successful, we emerged from the mouth of the Tibagy into the broad waters of the Paranapanéma, and camped for the night upon an island in mid-stream. From this point westward the river flows with scarcely an obstruction upon its course for 140 miles, when in its turn its waters are lost in the great Paraná itself, whence ultimately, after being carried along another 1200 miles, they are merged in the mother Atlantic of the distant South. I, however, was destined to follow their downward course no farther, but to retrace our steps to Jatahy, and thence to make a final attempt to force a passage up the 200 miles of cataracts and waterfalls that separated that colony from the town of Tibagy, a feat that hitherto had never been accomplished.*

* Two attempts had previously been made to explore this portion of the Tibagy river : one by Elliott, in the year 1846, and the other in the year 1865, by the two Kellers, German engineers, both of which had resulted in failure.

CHAPTER VIII.

A struggle against the Rapids—A great flood.—The pass of the Agudos.
—The *Salto Grande.*—Wild Indians.—Arrival at Tibagy.

WE remained one day encamped upon the island of
the Paranapanéma, killing two tapirs and numerous
Jacus. On the 25th of June we commenced the
return journey, amidst a downpour of tropical rain.
For three days this rain continued, and our progress
against the many rapids became hourly more tedious
and laborious as the water in the river swelled higher
yard by yard. I feared to delay our journey on this
account, for fear we might be cut off from Jatahy for
an indefinite time by the floods rising still higher.
The Indians made no complaint, but for ten hours
each day stuck to their work manfully, with the rain
constantly streaming down upon their naked bodies.
On the 4th day after leaving the Paranapanéma we
took five hours in poling up one mile of rapid, so
enormously had the force of the river by that time
increased against us. On the morning of the 6th
day, we being still some twenty miles from Jatahy, I
told the Indians that I would not wear them out any

more in the tremendous struggle against the floods, but that we would remain in camp till the river should have become somewhat more navigable; but they laughed the idea to scorn, and begged that they might be allowed to work on. For two more days, therefore, the struggle was continued, by which time we had diminished our distance from Jatahy to seven miles. It seemed, however, impossible to get the canoe another hundred yards farther, for the river, swelled by the tribute waters of a thousand little *barras* that were pouring in their yellow floods from the surrounding hills, had now become a furious torrent. But three miles higher up, could we only get so far, there was a *picada* leading straight from the water's edge to Jatahy. As a last resource, we determined to lighten the canoe of all our baggage and stores, and, leaving them under cover, proceed by ourselves alone. For this purpose the Indians built a strong and watertight hut of bamboo and palm, into which the tents and all other heavy stores were safely stowed. Thus relieved of nearly all our dead weight, we again embarked, and after another eight hours' struggle against the torrent, which again and again in places would sweep us back over the ground that we had just before laboriously ascended, we reached the *picada*, and by nightfall were once more safely domiciled in the colony of Jatahy, little the worse for our week's toil, notwithstanding that we had not had a dry shred of clothing amongst us for the whole of that time.

We had returned none too soon, for in the next seven days the Tibagy rose another fifteen feet, and the biggest flood that had been known since the year 1859 swept over the tops of the banks, which were fully thirty-three feet above the ordinary level of the river, and stretched away far inland to right and left of the village in seas of turbid water. For a whole week this extraordinary flood continued, the roar of whose waters, laden with the great trees and masses of minor forest *débris* that had been torn from the banks above, combined with the incessant roll and din of the thunder overhead and amongst the hills around, transformed this usually still and peaceful tropical scene into a wild pandemonium.

For nearly one month I was kept a prisoner at Jatahy, waiting for the waters to return to their normal level so as to allow of our journey up the river being resumed. During this time I chiefly occupied myself in visiting the large Indian colony, consisting of 500 semi-wild Coroados, and studying the various modes and customs of life in use amongst them, of which however I have no space here to give any account. I made a collection of their several manufactures, which included a beautifully woven shirt and various fancy costumes and head-dresses of feathers. In the illustration I have shown one of these curious feather-dresses, which are manufactured entirely of bark-fibre and the feathers of toucans, macaws (*araras*) and other bright-plumaged birds.

At length the waters subsided, and on the 25th of

July we bid farewell to Jatahy, the inhabitants turning
out *en masse* on to the river bank to speed us on
our way, with shouts and firing of pistols. The ⸌big
canoe that had taken us down to the Paranapanéma

COROADO DRESSED IN FESTIVE COSTUME.

had been discarded, two smaller and less cumbrous
dug-outs having been especially made for this portion
of our journey. Besides Telemaco and myself, our
party now consisted of six Caoiá Indians and a
Brazilian *mineiro*, whom we took to aid us in the

exploration for gold and diamonds which undoubtedly existed in many sections of the river. Our difficulties early commenced, for on the 27th one of the canoes was swamped while ascending a cataract, and half our provisions lost. This necessitated the sending the Indians back by land to Jatahy for further supplies. For the next week we continued to make slow but steady progress up a never-ending series of rapids and cataracts. Everywhere the marks of the recent flood were visible; in some places the banks being swept clear of vegetation to a height of twenty feet, and in others the water-line being visible on the leaves of the trees full forty-five feet above the present level of the river. We passed one long, low island, in the middle of a rapid, which seemed to have been cut in two by the flood, and upon which the trees, to the number of several hundreds, some being of large dimensions, were lying flat in swaths, like mown corn. We saw footprints of wild Indians here and there upon the banks, and occasionally observed the smoke of their fires rising above the trees of the inner forest. Whenever it was possible, we pitched our camps upon islands in mid-stream, so as to be safe from any risk of being attacked. On the 1st of August a canoe was again swamped, and one of the Indians was severely crushed against a rock in the rapid where the occurrence took place. We, however, on this occasion lost no stores, for they had previously been carried up by the bank. On the 3rd our labours were rewarded by the sight of a little colony of tame Indians, which once

more brought us into connection with civilization; for
from this point there was a mule-track leading to S.
Jeronymo.   Here we were detained a week, having to
send a special messenger by land to Jatahy to obtain a
substitute for our disabled man.

On the 10th we renewed the start, and now we had
fairly entered the lower outlet of the wild and unknown
pass by which the Tibagy forces a tumultuous passage
through the great range of the Agudos mountains.
To recount the details of the next ten days' journeying
would be but a weary repetition of similar incidents.
A sufficient idea of the kind of labour which we went
through each day may be gathered from the simple
statement, that we had to entirely unload the canoes
no less than thirty-two times and carry their contents
toilsomely on our backs for long distances over slippery
rocks and thorny forest *picadas*, to overcome so many
obstacles on the river.   Three times the canoes themselves, which each weighed three-quarters of a ton, had
to be taken out of the water, and dragged through the
forest by roads which we had to make for the purpose,
in order to get round each impassable cataract.
During the many weeks of inaction at Jatahy, I had
had time to cogitate fully upon the general plan of
action by which we might overcome these 200 miles of
cataracts with the least chance of failure, and as the
result of these cogitations I had determined to eschew
every kind of rashness, and undertake any amount of
the tedious labour of carrying stores and dragging
canoes by land, rather than risk the loss of a canoe or

of a life. The one or two little accidents that had already occurred served only to strengthen me in this resolution. My companion Telemaco, though naturally of a daring disposition, faithfully seconded this policy, and the Indians proved the most obedient and patient, as well as the most courageous and hard-working of men.

By the 20th we had well emerged from the pass of the Agudos, and were beginning to congratulate ourselves upon the happy accomplishment of the most difficult part of our labours, when we suddenly came in sight of an obstruction to which all that we had previously encountered and overcome were but as pigmies. A combined salto and cataract, whose total fall proved to be no less than 114 feet, stood before us—a giant and impassable barrier of rock and foam and falling water. The right flank of this obstruction was guarded by a perpendicular wall of basalt rising to a height of perhaps 200 feet, with a steeply sloping mountain above. On that side, therefore, no road could be made over which the canoes could be hauled. On the opposite side the ground seemed to be less impracticable, and here ultimately I laid out a line through the forest for a road of about a mile and a half long, no shorter route being possible. The *picada* having been cut, we were forced to construct along it a timber causeway for two-thirds of the distance to counteract the sidelong slope of the ground towards the river. For five days we worked hard at the making of this road, and when completed another four days were spent in laboriously dragging the canoes over it.

Before commencing this work we had had a hair-breadth's escape from a serious disaster. Telemaco, myself, and two of the Indians, had gone in an empty canoe to endeavour to get as close to the foot of the great fall as possible, the better to examine it. At the foot of this fall was a long rapid, which with some difficulty we succeeded in getting up. In the middle of the river was an island, or rather several islands, which divided the channel longitudinally into two parts, the one side showing a great vertical fall with a long rapid at the foot of it, while on the other side the water descended in a cataract over a steep, broken incline, which terminated at the foot in a vertical fall, below which powerful whirlpools were continually forming and reforming, churning up mud and stones in their vortices. After completing the examination of the great fall, we re-embarked, and the canoe being empty of baggage we decided to "run" the rapid up which we had previously come. Owing to a momentary misunderstanding between the bowmen and steersman, instead of the canoe going head on down the first little fall, she struck it obliquely, shipping a quantity of water and carrying away a paddle. At the foot of the rapid, which was run in about one minute, we touched the back water of the great cataract close on our left. The canoe being about one-third full of water, and having but one paddle in the bows, became unmanageable, and, to our dismay, we found ourselves being rapidly drifted, broadside on, towards the foot of the cataract, where our fate would not have been doubtful. Just as we were preparing to jump overboard and leave the canoe to its fate, another eddy caught her, and we were suddenly shot off in an opposite direction round the outer circumference of a whirlpool. By a tremendous spurt of paddling with the two remaining paddles, we succeeded in extricating the canoe from this new danger and ultimately in getting safely to the bank. This was the only occasion on which I ever saw my companion Telemaco, who was steersman, exhibit fear. When the danger was over, I turned round to make some observation to him. His face was as white as death, and he could only say, "Don't speak, Doctor, don't speak." I believe his emotion was far more on my account than on his own, for he knew how intensely anxious I had always shown myself that no disaster should occur to mar the successful issue of the exploration.

While we were engaged at this salto in making the road and dragging the canoes over it, we discovered that there were wild Indians around us, their tracks being visible in several places. Two of the Caioás at different times declared that they had seen Indians watching us. One night we thought we were attacked by them, for a terrific howl broke our slumbers, and we presently found that the solitary hunting-dog which we had all this time kept with us, had been carried off—without doubt by a jaguar, for in the morning we found tracks of this animal close outside the tents.

On the 29th we were enabled to say farewell to this great salto, and on the following day our *mineiro* found the first gold in the river that we had yet discovered. On the 1st of September our eyes were gladdened by the sight of prairie, and on the same evening we were met on the bank by my mule troop which I had sent on three weeks before from S. Jeronymo, with instructions to get fresh supplies and to force its way down the banks of the river as far as the open country would permit. We had been living on nothing but pig-meat and rice for several days, our other provisions having become exhausted. We now took the first day's rest that we had had for nearly a month, and ate and drank of the best things that the province could yield. From this point upwards the river was more or less known. On the 8th of September we landed at the town of Tibagy—just six weeks having elapsed from the day of our departure from the colony of Jatahy, during the whole of which period the roar of falls and of cataracts had scarcely once, day or night, been absent from our ears, and a journey had been accomplished that is scarcely likely to be repeated for many long years to come.

CHAPTER IX.

CONCLUSION.

My travels in Brazil have come nearly to an end.
On the 25th of September I reached Colonia Thereza,
to leave it again for the last time on the 6th of the
following month, *en route* for Rio de Janeiro. At
the colony I changed my travelling companion—
Telemaco going down the Ivahy river to join the staff
that was still working there, and Vander Meulen, who
had previously been my most intimate companion for
four months on the same exploration, now returning
with me on his way to England, his health having been
severely tried by the many hardships of the past twelve
months.

On the 17th of October, we arrived both together at
Antonina, in time to just miss the mail steamer, which
had left Paranaguá that very morning, two days before
its calculated time. After a wearisome delay of nearly
three weeks at Antonina and Paranaguá, we got off by
the next steamer, which happened to be our old friend
the *Camöens*. On the 10th of November, I landed once
more at the capital of the empire, after an absence of

more than two years, and took up my solitary abode
at the Hotel Carson; Vander Meulen soon after
sailing for England. Of the whole original staff of
seventeen members, with which the expedition had
started, but two besides myself were now in Rio. Of
Staff No. 2, I was the sole remaining member.
Captain Palm, the originator of the expedition, was
dead; Veal, the chief of the 4th Staff, was dead; four
members had been invalided; three others had left
from various causes; while the remainder were still
buried in the forests of the Ivahy, their labours not
yet concluded.

The next five months I heartily wish I could blot
out of my memory as though they had never been.
Let the reader imagine himself bound down by hard
fate, to remain week after week, and month after
month, in close confinement in one of the most deadly
cities that the world contains—in the very height of
the fever season, when pestilence, under the dreadful
form of *Febre Amarella*, stalked about the hot and
reeking streets by day and by night, and at all times
hovered like a black pall above the unclean city,
crushing out all healthy spirit and enjoyment of
existence from those who dwelt in it.

I might draw many a dreadful picture of the horrors
of these five months—of the morbid interest we took
day by day in conning over the ever increasing list of
deaths, as the season advanced, and the fever grew in
intensity,—of the daily spectacle of uncovered and
unsightly coffins, galloped through the streets of the

city in grim haste to the cemeteries—and lastly, of the slow sapping of the powers of both body and mind brought about in each one of us.*   One by one, the few remaining members of the expedition, as they came in from the interior, were struck down and obliged to flee for their lives up to the hills. Again and again, in my case, this process was repeated, till at length we were able—though not till the month of April of the following year (1875)—to shake off from our feet for the last time the dust of this pestilent city, and embark for England.

Apart from the last days that have been thus briefly alluded to, I ever recall the times spent in the Empire of the Southern Cross with an inward hope that I may some day revisit its great prairies and grand, silent forests, and perhaps smoke another *cigarro de milho* with a Brazilian *camarada* beside a lonely camp fire.

---

* In Rio, during the fever season, a man may be apparently in perfect health one day, and twenty-four hours after he may be not only dead, but already buried. It would be well for the inhabitants if they would devote a little of this same alacrity which they bestow on burying their dead, to the cleansing of the thousand foul fever-dens which are a standing disgrace to their city, and to themselves, as a civilised community.

APPENDIX.

APPENDIX

APPENDIX.

Note A.

" Abolition of Slavery in Brazil."

By the law of the 28th September, 1871, it was declared that from that date every new-born of a slave within the limits of the empire should be free. All government slaves and slaves of the Imperial household were also declared free. With the object of gradually freeing the slaves of private individuals, the same law established an emancipation fund, the proceeds of which are now annually applied for this purpose.

The total extinction of slavery, without danger to public safety and without detriment to the established rights of private property, is thus assured at no distant date.

(*The Empire of Brazil at the Vienna Exhibition*, 1873.)

Note B.

Given a staff of four engineers and surveyors A., B., C., and D. Given also a large tract of mountainous country, covered with forest so dense that, without the aid of the axe and the knife, the visible horizon of any person stationed in it may in most cases be touched by the hand, it is required to find, survey, and map down the best obtainable line along which to carry a railway to connect two known points, distant from each other from 200 to 300 miles.

This was the problem with which the 2nd Staff started ; —shorn of all details of supplies and such like, which in reality, however, formed by far the most difficult part of it, notwithstanding that their consideration is here purposely omitted.

A. is given a day's start. His work is to decide approximately the course which the line of exploration to be surveyed and mapped down by B., C. and D. shall take. He starts off early in the morning, accompanied by one or two men armed with knives, bill-hooks, and axes for cutting paths (*picadas*), and, occasionally, view points where such can be obtained. He takes with him two small pocket instruments—a magnetic compass and an aneroid barometer. With these two instruments and a note-book, he can, in the course of the day, make a very fairly accurate map of say two or three square miles of country, not a fiftieth part of which, however, he has been able to see ; his great natural aid, in default of extended vision, being the *flow of water*.

In the highlands of Brazil generally, and more especially in the upper valleys of such rivers as the Ivahy, the whole surface of the country is intersected by a perfect network of small gullies and streams. In the forest through which our work at this time lay, it was scarcely possible to cut a path for a hundred paces in any direction without having to cross one or more such water courses. The amplest scope for the exercise of intelligent observation, therefore, existed in the making of these preliminary explorations. It was the only one of the four divisions into which I am here supposing the work of the staff to be divided, that was never felt to be a drudgery.

B. now takes possession of A.'s sketch map thus formed, and by its guidance lays out and measures with accurate instruments (theodolite and chain) a series of lines upon the ground, following as nearly as possible the direction and course that the proposed railway is intended to take. In order to lay down these "trial" lines, straight paths or *picadas* have to be cut through the dense forest undergrowth, which *picadas* afterwards serve also to facilitate the instrumental observations of C. and D., who now follow on the same lines. C., with other instruments (the "level" and clinometer), takes the levels of the various points along the lines cut by B., and also of other points to some distance on each side to right and left of the same lines. D. comes last of all. He is already in possession of the combined observations of B. and C., by which alone, without himself having to go upon the ground, it is possible for him to make a complete map or *plan* of the line surveyed. In order, however, to make assurance doubly sure, and to fill up any slight omissions made by B. or C., he also walks the ground with other instruments (plane table and chain). The *final* line, that is, the line representing the exact course that the railway will take when laid out for construction, is then laid down upon the plan and in some cases upon the ground also, and thus the survey is completed.

This description will give a good enough idea of the *modus operandi* as attempted to be approached by us in carrying on the surveys. Practically, owing to the many disturbing influences, this perfect simplicity of operations was never attained, and, as time went on, we drifted still farther and farther away from it. Frequently A. or B. would have to do the work of two or four. Yet in every event the same "field" work as above described had to be done, whether by one alone or divided between two, three, or four.

The nearest approach to this theoretical design of work was attained by the 1st Staff, the number of whose members remained intact throughout the whole period of its labours, and which besides was not troubled with weighty commissariat arrangements, all necessary supplies being continually within easy reach.

Note C.

"*Brazilian Wild Pig.*"

On the occasion of one of our many pig-hunts, which took place in the orange-groves of the lower Ivahy valley, a "squeaker," about three weeks old, was captured alive. When first caught, the little animal used every effort to make its escape, struggling and squealing as though in mortal terror. The Brazilian who had seized it carried it for a few minutes in his arms till it became quite quiet. He now put it down upon the ground, and I expected to see it at once rush away. But no; far from attempting to escape, the little "porco" would not now leave its capturer, but stuck close to his heels and followed him like a dog for the next quarter of an hour, till we all reached the camp. The dogs were then each and all brought up and introduced to the young stranger, and strict injunctions laid upon them not to hurt it. Our little yellow-bristled guest was then allowed to run about the camp as it liked, being petted by everybody. Even the dogs inspired it with no terror or animosity, for every night regularly it would go and cuddle itself up close to any one of them that would permit of the liberty, for the sake of warmth. At the end of the fourth day the poor little creature died, sorrowed for by all.

The Brazilians say that, though the *porco do mato* may be thus readily tamed when young, its savage nature still remains, and grows with its growth. When captured young and successfully reared, it will attach itself to one person and one only—its master or keeper; but to all others it will be as savage as a tiger, attacking them with the utmost fury on every possible occasion.

Note D.

The Staff at this time consisted of about sixty men of various nationalities, for the most part Brazilians, but including also Indians, Swedes, Danes, Germans, and Frenchmen; a fleet of about twenty canoes, large and small, and a pack of hunting dogs, upon which latter we were now beginning to depend not a little for our daily supplies. For the purposes of the exploration, this miscellaneous assemblage of men and material was divided into three chief sections; namely, that of the *supply service*, chiefly carried on by means of the river; the *forest service*, including all exploration and survey work, and the moving and building of camps; and lastly the *scout service*, in which was included the hunting for meat and the scouting for Indians. The forest service, which absorbed rather more than one half of the total strength of the staff, I now still further subdivided into gangs of eight men, and, seeing that it was impossible for me to be constantly with any one party, I caused each gang to elect its own foreman from amongst its own members, whom the remaining seven then willingly obeyed.

The normal work of these gangs was the cutting *picadas* for the exploration, a line being given to each once or twice daily according as required. Every two gangs had a small camp between them, situated on the bank of the river close to the *picadas* upon which they were daily at work. One canoe was continually employed in keeping these several little camps fully supplied with all necessaries from the nearest depôt camp. At any time any one or more of these gangs could be taken off for other work without prejudice to the efficiency of those that remained. By this system of multiplying the number of gangs, and rendering each independent of the working of the others, I was enabled, single-handed, to carry on the whole work of exploration with considerable speed as well as economy of men and material, while at the same time the chief source of danger, namely, that always to be feared from the combination of the *camaradas* against the *patrão*, became more under control.

Note E.

Tables A. and B. are from observations taken by Mr. W. Braund, a settler in the province ; the thermometer being suspended in a log hut, sheltered from the sun, but with a free circulation of air around it. Tables C. 1, and C. 2, which are both deduced from one and the same series of observations, are from a very complete record of observations taken by the author, and by others under his direction, during the year 1873. The observations were taken three times a day, and for a great part of the year, four times a day ; namely, at 4 A.M. (when the cold is usually greatest), 7 A.M., noon, and, lastly, at 3 P.M. in the summer, or 2 P.M. in the winter, at about which hours the temperature usually reached its highest point for the day. The thermometer was suspended

TABLES OF TEMPERATURES (1) ON THE PRAIRIES, AND (2) IN THE FORESTS OF PARANÁ.

TABLE A.
On Prairie; height 2925 ft. above sea; near town of Curitiba. Lat. 25° 25'.
1871.

	Maximum.	Minimum.	Mean.	Extreme Monthly range of Temperature.
	F.	F.	F.	F.
January	100°	56°.5	78°	44°
February	87°	51°	69°	36°
March	94°	56°	75°	38°
April	91°	38°	64°.5	53°
May	86°	31°	58°.5	55°
June	90°	28°	59°	62°
July	80°	24°	52°	56°
August	81°	28°	54°.5	53°
September	89°	41°	65°	48°
October	92°	41°	66°.5	51°
November	84°	45°	64°.5	39°
December	88°	54°	71°	34°
Mean	88°.5	41°	64°.78	47°.42

TABLE B.
On Prairie; height 2925 ft. above sea; Lat. 25° 25'; near town of Curitiba.
1872.

	Maximum.	Minimum.	Mean.	Extreme Monthly range of Temperature.
	F.	F.	F.	F.
January	90°	58°	74°	32°
February	88°	57°	72°.5	31°
March	91°	52°	71°.5	39°
April	59°?	35°	47°.5?	24°??
May	84°	26°	55°	58°
June	70°	31°	50°.5	39°
July	78°	24°	51°	54°
August	85°	36°	60°.5	49°
September	91°	41°	66°	50°
October	84°	48°	66°	36°
November	90°	54°	72°	36°
December	98°	53°	75°.5	45°
Mean	·58°4?	43°?	63°.46?	41°.08?

1873.
In forest on banks of the river Ivahy; height above sea from 1500—1600 ft.; Lat. from 24°35'—25°00'; between Colonia Thereza and Salto d'Areranha.

TABLE C.—I.

	Maximum.	Minimum.	Mean.	Extreme Monthly range of Temperature.
			F.	F.
January	98°	64°	81°	34°
February	92°	60°	76°	32°
March	88°	57°	72°.5	31°
April	86°	53°	69°.5	33°
May	77°	42°	59°.5	35°
June	77°	38°	57°.5	39°
July	80°	40°	60°	40°
August	79°	38°	58°.5	41°
September	84°	41°	62°.5	43°
October	89°	48°	68°.5	41°
November	93°	53°	73°	40°
December	96°	58°	77°	38°
Mean	86°.58	49°.33	67°.87	37°.25

TABLE C.—II.

	Mean Maximum.	Mean Minimum.	Mean Monthly Temperature.	Mean Diurnal range of Temperature.	No. of days on which rain fell.	
	F.		F.	F.		
	84°	69°	76°.5	15°	21	January.
	86°	67°	76°.5	19°	21	February.
	81°	65°	73°	16°	12	March.
	77°	59°	68°	18°	11	April.
	70°	57°	63°.5	13°	13	May.
	67°	50°	58°.5	17°	3	June.
	70°	54°	62°	16°	11	July.
	72°	50°	61°	22°	5	August.
	76°	55°	65°.5	21°	8	September.
	80°	58°	69°	22°	9	October.
	87°	60°	73°.5	27°	4	November.
	82°	65°	73°.5	17°	19	December.
	77°.67	59°.08	68°.37	18°.6	137 total	Mean.

NOTE.—Probable extreme range of temperature occurring in any 24 hours on these prairies, 50° Fahr.

NOTE.—Greatest range of temperature observed in the forest in any 24 hours was 42° Fahr.

in a bamboo or palm-built *rancho* with a free circulation of air around it, the *rancho* itself also being generally more or less sheltered from the direct rays of the sun.

The records of the *daily* observations which were doubtless taken by Mr. Braund, are not in the author's possession. For the sake of comparison, Table C. 1, of the forest observations, has been drawn up in the same form as those of A. and B., containing the prairie observations.

Table B. is vitiated by an obvious error in the maximum temperature recorded for the month of April. Comparing, however, the results of Tables A. and C. 1, one fact stands prominently out, namely, that the extremes of temperature experienced on the lofty, open prairie are far greater than those occurring in equal periods of time in the forest region, the proportion being as 47·42 to 37·25.

By Table C. 2, column 4, it will be seen that the mean diurnal range of temperature for the year in the forest was no less than 18°·6 Fahr.; which, in one particularly dry month (November), actually amounted to 27° Fahr.; on one occasion a fall of no less than 42° Fahr. occurring within twenty-four hours. These wide ranges of temperature are the more remarkable from the fact that they are usually unaccompanied by even the slightest atmospheric disturbance. They are almost solely due to radiation alone, the ranges being greatest with a clear sky, and a still, dry atmosphere. The *causes* of these wide diurnal ranges of temperature are sufficiently intelligible, and are principally due to the latitude ; altitude, however, and the general features and configuration of the country, not being without considerable influence also. The *effects*, except upon the personal comfort of the traveller who chances to be benighted without shelter or covering, are altogether beneficial. Owing to the length of the nights even in the summer months, the radiation of heat goes on uncompensated for a much longer period of time than is the case in the summer months of more temperate latitudes. The air being usually still at night, dense, dripping fogs are formed towards morning, when the reduction of temperature has proceeded far enough. These fogs tend marvellously towards keeping up the level of water of the rivers and streams in the dry season, so important to settlers upon their banks, and are more especially useful in preserving the pasturage of the great prairies, which would otherwise be utterly scorched up in the dry months, to the destruction of tens of thousands of head of cattle, horses, and mules, which now form the chief wealth of the settlers in these districts.

The mean annual temperature on the prairie in the vicinity of Curitiba, is seen to be about 64° Fahr., and that of the upper valley of the Ivahy, about 68°, the difference thus corresponding within 1° of what it should be theoretically, according to the difference of altitude and latitude of the two districts. Thus, then, it appears, from the above tables, that the influence of forest is practically *nil* in determining the mean *annual temperature* of a district, but that it is very potent in limiting the extent of the mean *diurnal ranges of temperature.*

Note F 1.

"*State Colonies and Private Colonies.*"

There are, in Brazil, two classes of colonies, namely, State Colonies, such as that of Assungui, and Private Colonies— colonies, that is, promoted by private individuals or companies, generally as speculations.

I have before me, as I write, the "prospectus" of one of these latter, headed, "The Colonization of Kittolands." Being fairly well acquainted with the country in which "Kittolands" lies, which, indeed, forms a portion of the prairie lands of the province of Paraná, I will take this as a sample of a private colony, or rather as a sample of the means by which it is sought to establish such a colony.

The "Kittolands" prospectus is accompanied by an explanatory (?) map of the province, purporting to show the roads, tramways, railways and projected railways, besides the chief rivers and towns both upon and surrounding the district ceded for colonization.

This map is calculated seriously to deceive the intending emigrant.

(1). Upon it no distinction is made between the grand carriage road which runs up the Serra do Mar from Antonina to Curitiba, and the vile and often impassable mule-tracks, which are almost the sole means of communication existing in all other parts of the province. Both are represented alike upon the map by a broad red line, which, on being referred to under the heading "Explanations," is found to mean "Road"! A certain portion of the province is thus made to appear to possess a network of highways of a total extent of more than a thousand miles, the fact being that the only road, properly so called, in existence in the entire province has a length of somewhat less than one tenth of this amount.

(2). A railway is represented as already connecting Paranaguá and Curitiba. No such railway is in existence.

(3). Again, on the same map a full green line is shown running from Curitiba to the centre of the proposed settlement, a distance of about sixty miles by scale. A reference to the heading "Explanations," informs the confiding emigrant that this line represents a "steam-tramway." No such tramway is in existence.

(4). Finally, the names of insignificant villages are printed in the same type as those of large towns.

Emigrant! Go out to this province if you will, for

undoubtedly there is a fine country before you there ; but, be not deceived. You will find no railways, no steam-tramways, no "water-highways" to Curitiba (*vide* "prospectus "), and scarcely even a piece of road on all the 2,000 square miles of country Mr. Kitto has provided for you.

The prospectus, you will say, tells a flattering tale of "noble rivers," "broad expanse of green waving grass," and "belts of well-grown timber that recall to mind the more favoured parts of England." Yes, it is true ; you may see all these things, and more besides. You may even have a share in them, under certain conditions, should you be so disposed. But what will you do with them when you have got them? You cannot put them into your pocket and take them home to England. You cannot sell them, because they are nothing more than a drug in the market. You cannot utilise them on the spot, till you have first spent an enormous amount of time and labour upon them (see Vol. I., Part I., Chapter 9). In the meantime you *starve*.

But, you will say, a "*steady inflow of population is guaranteed;* " * my property will be "doubled in value in four years." Tom Hodge, your ploughman's wit is not sufficient to tell you that where 25 per cent. per annum is "guaranteed," and where the "guarantee" is real, even such rare benefactors to humanity as speculative emigration pro_ moters would not offer it first to *you*. Not even the attrac_ tion of "having the option" of selling your produce (when at length your "waving grass" is transformed to waving corn) at "Rio de Janeiro, where the demand is large," or in England, which is but a trifle over 5,000 miles distant, or "in any other part" of the world that you "may deem best," (not excluding, may we hope, the regions of Central Africa or the North Pole) should persuade you *lightly* to give up

---

* The italics are in the original.

your straw-thatched cottage at home, and your humble but safe ten or twelve shillings a-week.

The misrepresentation as to the navigability of the rivers Iguassú and Barrigui occurring in the same prospectus, has already been pointed out (*vide* Chapter 1, Part III.).

To all promoters of new companies a certain limited margin for exaggeration is indeed usually allowed; but not so for deliberate misrepresentations and misstatements. To induce persons by such means as these to become emigrants, is to traffic in human flesh, and the individuals doing so should be justly held responsible for the worst consequences that may ensue. It is in this way also that the good name of Brazil as a fit and proper immigration country is unfairly dragged in the dirt.

There is one obvious and very simple condition which, could it be enforced upon emigration promoters, would do more to strike at the root of the present evil than volumes of correspondence. No emigration promoter should be permitted to lure ignorant labourers away from their own country to foreign settlements, without giving a substantial guarantee, in some form or other, to find each person so taken away suitable work at fair wages for a period of *at least* one year, counting from the time of his arrival at the Colony. No longer then would it be worth the while of promoters to import worthless men whom they would themselves be bound to employ, for the sake of the capitation or other grant. No longer would good men be first discouraged, then demoralised, and finally ruined by being set adrift on their resources at the moment of landing. The scandal under which Brazil now labours in respect of English colonization would be, if not altogether removed, at least considerably lessened, and in time we should learn to estimate the country at neither more nor less than its real value. For the present I would merely remind the intending emigrant, that philanthropy and speculation cannot in the nature of things co-exist in one and the same scheme governed by one and the same mind.

Note F 2.

Colonization of Kittolands.

Extract from Prospectus.

"The river Baraguy (Barrigui), which almost skirts the macadamised road at Curitíba, flows through valleys till it reaches this river (Iguassú), thus presenting *a through communication and cheap water highway* between the Settlement and the Provincial Capital (Curitiba); *the immense advantage of which will be readily apparent for the purpose of transporting general merchandise, as also the Pine Timber, Wheat, Indian corn, Potatoes, Dairy and other bulky or surplus produce, to the most remunerative markets.*"

Either the exact surveys of a body of competent and responsible English Engineers are wholly worthless, or the above statement and deduction therefrom are the most remarkable examples of the elasticity of conscience indulged in by speculative génius that could easily be met with in the course of a good long day's reading. As a matter of fact the statement above quoted is pure fiction, as explained in the text.

Note G.

" *Observations upon the present system of reclaiming the wild Indian of Brazil, and upon its working, as exemplified in two of the colonies of the province of Paraná.*"

The number of Indians who are still living in a wild state in Brazil, has been variously estimated at from half a million

to a million and a half. The latest estimates generally agree
in putting the number at about one million ; forming therefore nearly one tenth of the total number of the population
of the Empire. These Indians, as long as they thus continue
unreclaimed, are entirely lost to the service of the State—
and more : they are a positive nuisance, hindering the exploration and colonization of the parts which they chiefly
inhabit. On the other hand Brazil is crying out for an
increase of population, and is spending large sums annually
in importing foreign labour, which when it arrives is too
frequently found to be altogether unsuited to the country.

Fully appreciating the wealth that exists in the Indian
population of the interior, the value of which, when it can
be got at, was fully proved by the Jesuits in the earlier
days of colonization (see Note L), the State, following in
this respect the old system of the Jesuits, has from time
to time, as opportunity offered, established *reducções*, or
colonies of Indians, at various convenient points throughout the interior of the country.

At the present time there exist nearly seventy of these
Indian colonies scattered about in the different provinces,
each being under the directorship of a monk or *Frade*, who
is generally of the "Capuchin" order. In the province of
Paraná there are two of these colonies thus nominally ruled
by *Frades*—one at S. Jeronymo composed of about 150
Coroados Indians, and the other at Jatahy with about 500
of the same Indians. Besides these, there are the two
colonies at Colonia Thereza, and at S. Ignacio on the
Paranapanéma, numbering each about forty souls. Let us
take the larger colony at Jatahy for consideration.

This colony was formed spontaneously in the year 1859
by the Indians themselves, who, tired of being at war with
the whites on the one side and the Caioá Indians on the
other, voluntarily appeared one day on the banks of the

river, opposite the Brazilian village of Jatahy, and proclaimed, by means of an interpreter, their desire and intention to settle peaceably down in the neighbourhood of the whites. Here, then, was a splendid opportunity given for bringing every Indian in the whole wide district around into the first phase of civilization, and then of gradually working them up, as the Jesuits did of old, into becoming useful members of society. Seizing the opportunity, the government sends a special man to take charge of the new Indian settlement, to teach the people the commoner arts of civilization, such as agriculture and building, and generally to endeavour to fill up the gulf which must necessarily at first separate them from their fellow subjects, the Brazilians. But what kind of man does the government entrust with this important work? At the very least, one would imagine that the selection would fall upon a person having some *one* especial qualification for so high a task—either the intense earnestness of the Jesuit, without his selfishness; or the experience and broad-mindedness of an educated man of the world. But no, the choice falls upon an untried, inexperienced Italian monk! A man whose ignorance of the language of the country, of the country itself, of the people with whom he has to deal, both Indian and Brazilian, whose whole education, in fact, has been such as to render him the very last person in the world fit for such a post. Possibly some vague idea exists in the mind of the Brazilian government that the fact of being a *Frade* of the established religion is an all-sufficient proof of fitness in these cases. If so, it is grievously mistaken, as is abundantly proved by the present state of the two colonies of Jatahy and S. Jeronymo.

In the case of Jatahy, what has the *Frade* director done in the dozen years or so during which the Indian colony has been under his direction? I can speak, not from a hasty visit of an hour or so to the colony, but from the knowledge gained by a residence of a whole month on the spot, during which time I was in daily, indeed almost hourly, intercourse with the Indians themselves, besides having many opportunities of conversing with the more intelligent Brazilian colonists on the subject.

Taking first the adult Indians. Of the women there was absolutely not one who understood a dozen words of Portuguese, and of the men a few, a very few, understood a little of what you said to them, but none were capable of replying in Portuguese, except by monosyllables. Next as regards the children, all of whom may be supposed to have been born in the light of civilization. These, I found, knew even less of the language of the country than did their fathers. Not one that I saw could speak a word of Portuguese, or understand it when it was spoken to him. Now what did this fact signify? Why, simply that the prime object of the government had been defeated. The impassable barrier of ignorance of each other's language still remained in full force, and hence, as was to be expected, not the smallest sign or symptom of a future amalgamation of the two peoples was to be detected. The Indians were still as distinct and separate a people as on the day when they first settled down at the colony, fifteen years before. Their Brazilian neighbours merely suffered their presence in the neighbourhood, but neither dreamt of associating with them, nor even of employing them as hired labourers for any kind of work. Thus the very A B C of Indian catechising had been shamefully neglected; for all history and all experience proves that when a civilized race comes into contact with a savage race, the latter must either learn the language of the former or die the inevitable death.

As regards the arts of civilization and enlightened religion, these Indians, notwithstanding their fifteen years' supposed tuition under the *Frade,* and the not inconsiderable sums of money devoted to their improvement by the government, had in no degree got beyond the knowledge and practice of their wild brethren whom we had previously met with on the lower Ivahy. They built and inhabited the exact same type of *rancho*. They repudiated all clothing, except when walking abroad in the Brazilian parts of the settlement, when they wore some sort of garment, as it were under protest. Polygamy still remained a permitted custom, and the doctrines of Christianity generally were evidently utterly unknown to them. In brief, they still remained in all points utterly useless as members of the State to which they had voluntarily offered themselves. Compare this with the advanced stage of civilization to which the same Indians were brought under the energetic and conscientious rule of the Jesuits! Who will then doubt where the fault lies?

It is difficult under all the circumstances to doubt that common report speaks truth, when it accuses the director of one at least of the Paraná Colonies, not only of indolence and entire incompetence, but also of turning the government subsidies intended for the advancement and improvement of these poor Indians to his own use.

The Colony of S. Jeronymo is in no higher state of culture than that of Jatahy. Both are directed by Capuchin monks! Let us hope that these two colonies and their rulers are not fair samples of the remaining sixty odd *reducções* established in the other parts of the interior of the Empire.

Note H.

Luco the Caioá.

In June 1873, shortly after the Areranha camp had been built, we were astonished one day by the unexpected apparition of six half-starved and semi-naked people—three men and three women—in our midst. The men were evidently Indians, though of some tribe not familiar to most of us. They proved to be Caioás, many families of which tribe we knew to be settled on the Tibagy river. Of the women, one alone seemed to be a pure bred Indian, while the others were scarcely different from the ordinary Brazilian Cabocla type; and were in fact Paraguayan Caboclas, understanding only Spanish and the Caioá language. The men all three understood Portuguese. Being questioned, they said that they were natives of Jatahy (a colony on the lower Tibagy); and that, having heard of our Expedition, and that we were in want of men, and above all that we paid them well, they had taken a canoe and embarked themselves and their wives to come and meet us on the Ivahy. The journey from Jatahy had taken them four months, owing chiefly to the tremendous series of cataracts which they said they had encountered on the Ivahy. They had lost their dog, which had been killed by a jaguar two months before ; their supplies of food and powder had been exhausted for a long time, and for weeks they had subsisted entirely upon fruits, and upon what fish and birds they had shot with the bows and arrows that they had themselves made. On arriving at the Salto de Areranha, they had been at first appalled at the magnitude of the obstruction that now opposed them ; but, speedily catching sight of some canoes of ours that were moored just below the Falls, they had cautiously approached to reconnoitre, fearing lest they might fall into a trap of Coroados Indians, and had then discovered on the ground the impressions of hob-nailed boots, and thus knew that at length they had found the Expedition. Leaving their canoe, which was enormously big and heavy, below the Falls, they had followed our *picada* till they found themselves in our camp.

Such was their story; and at the time, and for several months after, we had no reason to suspect that there was anything more behind it. We engaged the men then and there, and found them very steady hard-working fellows. The head man of the three, by name Luco, proved himself a most accomplished forester and hunter, so much so that I usually took him with me on all my forest excursions, whether for hunting or merely for exploration, in preference to all others. Several months later some other men from Jatahy joined the Expedition. They at once recognised Luco as a man that had, just before his disappearance, committed a horrible murder upon a fellow Indian, under circumstances of the greatest brutality which they related in detail. Chief amongst Luco's accusers was a Brazilian, by name Moneca 'Capanga,' who swore he would himself kill Luco in return. The men were separated and kept apart by being placed on different sections of the river service. We should have had enough to do if we had constituted our-selves judges of the antecedents of each one of our *cama radas*; we therefore thought no more of the matter. Shortly afterwards, Luco suddenly disappeared ; and for a time it was thought that he in his turn had met with foul play. It was found, however, that his wife almost simultaneously disappeared from Colonia Theréza. The two had gone off together, and we heard no more of them from that day forth. Thus Luço the Caioá, the hero of these chapters, vanished from the scene as suddenly and as unexpectedly as he had appeared.

" On the theory of the formation of Campos *in the midst of forest."*

Extract from paper read before the Royal Geographical Society, June 12th, 1876.

" At a short distance from the little settlement of Alambary the base of the Apucarana and Agudos range is reached; and, about half way between Alambary and St. Jeronymo, the road crosses the ridge at an elevation of 3,400 feet above sea level, and shortly afterwards emerges into an open patch of prairie or *campo* which here rises up bare and bleak out of the midst of the luxuriant surrounding forest. A similar patch, called the Campo de Inhohô, appears a little nearer to the river.

" These little bare patches or *campos* seem altogether out of harmony with the surroundings, not only in their comparative sterility, but also in the configuration of the ground. For whereas, in the forest land surrounding them, it would be difficult to find a level spot of five square yards together, here you have many square miles of an almost perfect plain; and so flat is it indeed on these *campos* that a large proportion of their extent is permanently covered by swamps.

" The following facts observed, appear to afford some key to their origin.

" The range of the Agudos and Apucarana is due to volcanic agency. Great masses of 'trap,' chiefly consisting of porphyries, have been upheaved and erupted through the overlying strata of sandstone and other formations, and have caused a vitrification of the latter at all the surfaces of contact.

" Subsequent to this eruptive upheaval (which must have

acted with nearly equal forces over large areas) denudation came into play, carving out the steep slopes and deep valleys and ravines over which the forest has now taken possession, and leaving exposed in such places to the disintegrating action of atmospheric influences the highly fertilising volcanic rocks; but, on the other hand, wherever the hardness of the stratum, aided by an absence of declivity or "dip" in its bed, over any considerable area, resisted these forces of denudation, there level tracts have been left remaining, covered only by their hard protecting shell.

"As a matter of fact, these 'campos' show (beneath a small depth of supersoil) a surface, more or less smooth, of hard, vitrified sandstone; and in one or two cases where, near their boundaries, small streams have, in the course of ages, cut their way through this upper shell, it is seen that the igneous rock lies immediately beneath, as must necessarily be the case if the above explanation be correct. The appearance of the tough prairie grass in the place of the luxuriant forest is also a necessary consequence of this theory of their formation, and thus the whole phenomenon is explained without difficulty."

NOTE L.

" The Jesuits on the Paranapanéma." Their rise and fall.

The history of the fortunes of this energetic class of "religioso" on the river Paranapanéma is powerfully dramatic. The period over which this history extends is very brief, being wholly comprised between the years 1609 and 1631. Yet in these twenty-two years they had established and had lost a little empire.

In 1609 they founded here their first Indian settlement, or *reducção*, at the mouth of the river Pirapó, a tributary of the Paranapanéma (see map). Other *reducções* soon followed, until in less than a score of years the great majority of the Wild Indians who had before roamed the vast forests on either bank of the Paranapanéma, with no fixed habitations, had been collected, and to a great extent civilised under the régime of the Jesuit. At two of the principal *reducções*, named Loretto and S. Ignacio, their success had been so great that large towns had been built, having streets regularly laid out, substantial "adobe" houses, schools, and churches. The doctrines of Christianity were sedulously inculcated into the Indians, while at the same time the arts of civilisation were taught with equal assiduity. Agriculture and farming were carried on to a sufficient extent to render each settlement entirely self-supporting, and, in short, the problem of civilising and utilising the savage was completely solved.

From afar jealous and greedy eyes were watching the rise and rapid progress of the good work. At this time there existed on the prairie district surrounding the present town of São Paulo a race of sturdy half-breds—*Mamelucos*—sprung up from the union of the original Portuguese settlers with Indian women. *Physically*, these *Mamelucos*, or "Paulistas," were a splendid race of men, combining in their persons the strongest points of both races; *morally*, the mixture of the two bloods had produced a nature savage and bloodthirsty as a tiger's, and more cruel than a cannibal's.

As the mule hates and despises its father the jackass, so did the Paulista hate and despise his mother's lower race. Hand in hand with his greed for the possession of

slaves, went his unquenchable and unnatural hatred of his
Bugré relatives; hence the hunting of these latter for
slaves was in all points dear to his heart; and hence also
it was that the Jesuits, who had ever fought with all their
power and great influence against the prevailing practice
of enslaving the Indians, likewise incurred his bitter
hatred.

The newly arisen *reducções*, populated wholly by peace-
loving Indians under their Jesuit directors, offered a
tempting bait to the Paulista to gratify his greed and
spite. It proved irresistible to him; and in the year 1629
he made his first onslaught upon them, destroying many
of the lesser *reducções* and putting to the sword or carrying
off into life-long slavery their inhabitants. Twice again in
the following year did the Paulistas, rendered still more
bold by impunity, and stimulated by success, make other
raids upon the unhappy *reducções*, which the Jesuits had
established with so much conscientious toil and labour.
On the last of these occasions the two largest of the
reducções, Loretto and S. Ignacio, already mentioned, were
attacked and utterly destroyed. This proved the death
blow to the Jesuit régime in this part of the country.

How great was the destruction wrought by the Paulistas
in these two years may be gathered from the fact, that out
of a total population of 100,000 Indians collected in these
reducções but 12,000 remained (Charlevoix).

How unworthy are the successors of the Jesuits in the
work of reclaiming the Indians is sufficiently shown in
another note.

Note M.

(1.)

Monetary System of Brazil.

Unit of value = *real* (plural *reis*), written : 0$001.

(1). The *vintem*	(copper coin) =	20 *reis*	written	0$020
(2.) „ "dump"	(ditto) =	40 *reis*	„	0$040
(3.) „ *testão*	(nickel coin) =	100 *reis*	„	0$100
(4.) „ *dois testões*	(ditto) =	200 *reis*	„	0$200
(5.) „ *patáca*	(non-existant) =	320 *reis*	„	0$320
(6.) „ *crusádo*	(ditto) =	400 *reis*	„	0$400
(7.)	(paper note) =	500 *reis*	„	0$500
(8.) „ *patacão*	(non-existant) =	960 *reis*	„	0$960
(9.) „ *milreis*	(paper note) =	1000 *reis*	„	1$000

Beyond the *milreis*, which at "par" is equal to 27 pence, there are other notes of various amounts, 2, 5, 10, 20, 25, &c., up to the maximum of 500$000. The *conto* (imaginary) is a thousand *milreis*, written 1:000$000, or thus : 1:000$.

The above table is sufficiently complete for all the ordinary purposes of the traveller.

(2.)

Common measures of length, with their equivalents in English measure.

		ft.	in.
Palmo	=	0	8·66
Vara = 5 *Palmos*	=	3	7·3
Braça = 2 *Varas*	=	7	2·6

		miles	yds.
Legua (usual) = 3000 *Braças*	=	4	178

(3.)

Common land measures, with their equivalents in English measures.

		A.	R.	P.
Geira = 400 square *braças*	=	0	1	36·5
Alqueire = 25 *geiras*	=	11	3	25·6
Legua quadrada = 900 alqueires	=	10,764	2	8

NOTE N.

"*The great inland navigable water-system of South Brazil.*"

The inland water system referred to in the text embraces portions of the following rivers, viz., the Tibagy, Paranapanéma, Tieté, Paraná, Ivahy, Ivinheima, and Brilliante. Of the 1290 miles spoken of as navigable, 510 miles could be at once utilized for continuous navigation by steamers of light draught (say 3 feet), and by a comparatively slight cost the remaining 780 miles could be brought under the same conditions of navigability, and a connected highway of 1290 miles thus established. Even with the present obstructions that exist on these latter 780 miles, canoes of one and two tons capacity can readily be worked over them at most seasons of the year.

At the present time, while no less than five schemes are before the Brazilian government for a trans-Brazilian railway, it is as well that the existence of this great system of ready-made highways in the interior of the country should be remembered, and the fact duly taken into consideration in weighing the relative merits of these various rival schemes.

As I think this question of the choice of a route for a trans-Brazilian railway may be of interest to many of the readers of this book, I give here a synoptic table, showing at a glance the most salient points of merit or demerit of each scheme when severally and collectively compared.

Nos. 4 and 5 are the only two of these which open up and utilize the great inland water system of the Paraná and its tributaries. No. 4 is, however, merely an expensive modification of No. 5, and need not be seriously considered. No. 1 possesses the great advantage of offering no break of gauge throughout its whole long course of 1851 kilometres between Miranda and the capital. Apart from questions of expense or of commercial gain, this undoubtedly would be the best trans-Brazilian line that could be built. On the whole, however, I think but few impartial persons, capable of forming an opinion on the subject, would doubt that the balance of advantages lies strongly in favour of route No. 5, unless indeed the line be required purely for strategical purposes, without reference to its value as a great factor of commercial gain and internal prosperity of the country.

Numbers.	Designations.	Railway already open, in kilometres.	Railway proposed in kilometres.	Estimated cost of construction of additional Railway.	River-road proposed, in kilometres.	Estimated cost of Works on River-road.	Total time of transit in hours.	Total length of line in kilometres.	Number of breaks of gauge.	Estimated total cost of construction exclusive of that of Railway already open.	Comparative costs of maintenance, exclusive of lengths already working.	Remarks.
1.	Miranda to Rio de Janeiro *via* Rio Grande.	226	1,625	£ 18,044,016	—	—	hrs. m. 61 42	1,851	—	£ 18,044,016	1·000	
2.	Miranda to Rio de Janeiro *via* Rio Claro and S. Paulo.	355	1,452	£ 16,123,023	—	—	hrs. m. 75 15	1,807	3	£ 16,123,023	·894	
3.	Miranda to Santos *via* Rio Claro and S. Paulo.	191	1,200	£ 13,324,812	—	—	hrs. m. 51 22	1,391	1	£ 13,324,812	·738	
4.	Miranda to Rio de Janeiro *via* S. Paulo and Curitiba.	356	1,405	£ 15,601,134	733	£ 455,913	hrs. m. 122 34	2,494	3	£ 16,057,046	·890	By either of these two routes the great inland navigable water system of the Paraná and its tributaries would be brought into direct communication with the sea coast.
5.	Miranda to Antonina *via* Rio Ivahy and Curitiba.		932	£ 10,351,480	733	£ 455,913	hrs. m. 89 56	1,665	2	£ 10,807,393	·599	

* The above table was compiled by the author in the year 1875, from *data* as then existing. Additions have since been made to the lengths of lines open, as given in the first column, which will *slightly* affect the other proportions.

EXPLANATORY NOTES TO THE FOREGOING TABLE.

(1.) The time column is calculated at the rate of thirty kilometres per hour for *railway*, and fifteen kilometres per hour for *river* transport, five hours being also added for each break of gauge.

(2.) The estimates of cost of construction are based upon the same scale as those which have been already submitted to the Brazilian government by the concessionaires of scheme No. 5 on table, being at the rate of 111:040$100 per kilometre of railway, and 6:218$384 per kilometre of river section, the value of the *milreis*, for the sake of simplicity, having been taken at two shillings, or threepence below par.

(3.) The proportions in the last column have been deduced by assuming the cost of maintenance to be in direct proportion to the cost of construction in every case.

THE END.